<u>**Songs fc**</u>

Text: Psalm 1:1-6, [1] How happy is the one who does not
walk in the advice of the wicked or stand in the pathway with sinners
or sit in the company of mockers!
[2] Instead, his delight is in the Lord's instruction,
and he meditates on it day and night.
[3] He is like a tree planted beside flowing streams
that bears its fruit in its season and whose leaf does not wither.
Whatever he does prospers.
[4] The wicked are not like this;
instead, they are like chaff that the wind blows away.
[5] Therefore the wicked will not stand up in the judgment,
nor sinners in the assembly of the righteous.
[6] For the Lord watches over the way of the righteous,
but the way of the wicked leads to ruin.

Truth: The text paints a picture of a man who is delighted, happy, joyful.
He is full of delight due to finding his way through the Word of God. Using
verse 2 as the focal point, you can see that part of the man's happiness is
being rid of the influence of those who are not God-followers because of
his focus on the Word. With the word as his root, he is able to bear fruit
and weather the challenges that different seasons bring.

Thought: The world provides seemingly endless opportunities for
negative thoughts, selfish actions, and un-Godly influence. The only true
antidote for this is Truth, God's Word. Ask God to give you a thirst for His
Word. This will result in delight, being rooted rightly, and righteousness.

Tune: Word of God speak, Would You pour down like rain
Washing my eyes to see Your majesty
To be still and know, that You're in this place
Please let me stay and rest in Your holiness, Word of God speak

Dear God, I ask you to give me a thirst for, a desire for, and an
understanding of Your Word. As we begin a new year, I pray that you
would increase my desire so that I could grow more in Your Word this
year than ever before.

Text: Psalm 2:1-6

[1] Why do the nations rage and the peoples plot in vain?

[2] The kings of the earth take their stand, and the rulers conspire together against the Lord and his Anointed One:

[3] "Let's tear off their chains and throw their ropes off of us."

[4] The one enthroned in heaven laughs; the Lord ridicules them.

[5] Then he speaks to them in his anger and terrifies them in his wrath:

[6] "I have installed my king on Zion, my holy mountain."

Truth: Standards are being compromised, un-biblical practices are being legitimized, and it seems nothing is forbidden. None of this catches God by surprise, nor should it be a source of fear for the Child of God. In fact, Scripture anticipates rebellion of the people and gives us a glimpse of God's reaction to it.

How does God respond? He laughs! He laughs with the confidence that only God can. In verse 5 we see that he "will speak to them in his wrath". We can rest assured that God will not be mocked and He will speak His wrath upon those who seek to compromise truth.

Thought: The key for the child of God comes in the phrase "in vain". Whoever plots against God or against His children plots in vain. God is more than capable of defending His honor, His children and His glory. Trust God today! Stand strong! Don't compromise on Biblical truth! Ask that God grant you the eyes to see things as He sees them.

Tune: Oh no You never let go, through the calm and through the storm
Oh no You never let go, in ev'ry high and ev'ry low
Oh no You never let go, Lord You never let go of me

Dear God, I am thankful to know that You are my Protector. I realize that Scripture is clear that in the last days people will be lovers of self and will turn to other gods, but I acknowledge You as God. My faith is not in vain and I cling to you as if my life depends on it, because it does.

<u>Songs for Life—Day 3—January 3</u>

Text: Psalm 2:7-12

7 I will declare the Lord's decree.

He said to me, "You are my Son; today I have become your Father.

8 Ask of me, and I will make the nations your inheritance

and the ends of the earth your possession.

9 You will break them with an iron scepter;

you will shatter them like pottery."

10 So now, kings, be wise;

receive instruction, you judges of the earth.

11 Serve the Lord with reverential awe and rejoice with trembling.

12 Pay homage to the Son or he will be angry

and you will perish in your rebellion,

for his anger may ignite at any moment.

All who take refuge in him are happy.

Truth: This passage is unique in that it is an OT passage with reference to the Father/Son relationship of God to Jesus. God has not only brought forth His Son as child, but as Authority over the church. Failing to honor the Son will subject us to wrath. There are five commands given to avoid wrath: 1) be wise, 2) be warned, 3) serve the Lord with fear, 4) rejoice with trembling and 5) Kiss the Son (honor).

Thought: A loving Father will look at things different for his child than he will for anyone else in the world. Part of the favor of being the child of a loving father is also being held accountable. Christ is the Lord of the church. He should be honored, worshipped, adored, and served, both enthusiastically as well as selflessly.

Tune: He loves us, Oh how He loves us
Oh how He loves us, Oh how He loves

Dear God, thank you for loving me as Your child. Everything I have is from You and you have provided for me as my loving and adoring Father. Teach me to love you back in a way befitting You as Lord. Teach me to serve you, to honor you, to glorify you with my life today.

Songs for Life—Day 4—January 4

Text: Psalm 3

[1] Lord, how my foes increase! There are many who attack me.
[2] Many say about me, "There is no help for him in God." *Selah*
[3] But you, Lord, are a shield around me,
my glory, and the one who lifts up my head.
[4] I cry aloud to the Lord,
and he answers me from his holy mountain. *Selah*
[5] I lie down and sleep; I wake again because the Lord sustains me.
[6] I will not be afraid of thousands of people
who have taken their stand against me on every side.
[7] Rise up, Lord! Save me, my God!
You strike all my enemies on the cheek; you break the teeth of the wicked.
[8] Salvation belongs to the Lord;
may your blessing be on your people. *Selah*

Truth: David felt completely surrounded by his enemies and even felt that there was no salvation for his soul. So he cries out to God! Only then was he able to find rest and let God shield him from his enemies.

Thought: We all have many enemies, physical and spiritual. The world may tell you that your sins are so bad that they can't be forgiven and you easily get discouraged. But God is there! He is! We don't have to wait for the bad times... we can call on God anytime! Good or Bad! He will be there for us and sustain us, give us rest and hope.

Tune: But Thou Oh LORD are a shield for me
My Glory and the lifter of my head
Thou, Oh LORD are a shield for me
My Glory and the lifter of my head.

Dear God, I know that there will be times that I will fail you, and feel that my enemies are completely surrounding me. It's then, Father, that I will call to you and you will answer and give me the strength and courage to make it another day. Thank you, Father, that I can take rest in You.

Text: Psalm 4:1-8

[1] Answer me when I call, God, who vindicates me.
You freed me from affliction; be gracious to me and hear my prayer.
[2] How long, exalted ones, will my honor be insulted?
How long will you love what is worthless and pursue a lie? *Selah*
[3] Know that the Lord has set apart the faithful for himself;
the Lord will hear when I call to him.
[4] Be angry and do not sin;
on your bed, reflect in your heart and be still. *Selah*
[5] Offer sacrifices in righteousness and trust in the Lord.
[6] Many are asking, "Who can show us anything good?"
Let the light of your face shine on us, Lord.
[7] You have put more joy in my heart
than they have when their grain and new wine abound.
[8] I will both lie down and sleep in peace,
for you alone, Lord, make me live in safety.

Truth: Apart from God we have no righteousness. Righteousness isn't just about doing right things but about being righteous. Because of our fallen nature we are unable to be righteous. As the light of Christ shines in us, He transforms us and "imputes" His righteousness on us, and we reflect His righteousness.

Thought: The sacrifice (V5) for the believer today is not a calf or a lamb, but a heart penetrated by God's love and poured out at His feet, worshipping the King of Kings and Lord of Lords. God desires that our actions would be a reflection of what is going on in our hearts.

Tune: Bless the Lord O my soul, O my soul, Worship His holy name
Sing like never before, O my soul, I'll worship Your holy name

Dear God, I realize that today you are not calling me or expecting me to sacrifice an animal on an altar. Instead, it is my heart that is on that altar. Today I ask you to burn away the impurities and fill it with your Spirit and Truth. Father, You are my righteousness. I trust you with my life today.

Songs for Life—Day 6—January 6

Text: Psalm 5:1-6

[1] Listen to my words, Lord; consider my sighing.
[2] Pay attention to the sound of my cry, my King and my God,
for I pray to you.
[3] In the morning, Lord, you hear my voice;
in the morning I plead my case to you and watch expectantly.
[4] For you are not a God who delights in wickedness;
evil cannot dwell with you.
[5] The boastful cannot stand in your sight; you hate all evildoers.
[6] You destroy those who tell lies;
the Lord abhors violent and treacherous people.

Truth: The Psalmist is expressing thanks to the Lord for His holiness, for loving what is right, and for His protection of the same. God and evil cannot dwell together, and to that end, the words hate, destroy, and abhors are used here to depict what God does to those who oppose Him. Yet, the cry is also personal, as the Psalmist seeks God's ear to his cry.

Thought: Sometimes it seems that the world has everything, and those who do evil prosper the most. We have an expectation that those who God will punish should receive that punishment on our timetable. This Psalm gives us encouragement in knowing that God does protect His righteousness as well as His children. I can cry to the Lord "in the morning" in confidence and watch His glory unfold before my eyes.

Tune: Lord, listen to Your children praying
Lord, send Your Spirit in this place
Lord, listen to Your children praying
Send us love send us pow'r send us grace

Dear God, Your Word says that you hear my voice in the morning. Today I cry out to you in the morning, in the afternoon, in the evening. I acknowledge that my need for Your presence is great. I'm so thankful that you will not stand for wickedness and that I can trust you for truth. Lord, I cry to you and ask you to help me to see, with my eyes, your work today.

Songs for Life—Day 7—January 7

Text: Psalm 5:7-12

[7] But I enter your house by the abundance of your faithful love;
I bow down toward your holy temple in reverential awe of you.
[8] Lord, lead me in your righteousness because of my adversaries;
make your way straight before me.
[9] For there is nothing reliable in what they say; destruction is within them;
their throat is an open grave; they flatter with their tongues.
[10] Punish them, God; let them fall by their own schemes.
Drive them out because of their many crimes, for they rebel against you.
[11] But let all who take refuge in you rejoice; let them shout for joy forever.
May you shelter them,
and may those who love your name boast about you.
[12] For you, Lord, bless the righteous one;
you surround him with favor like a shield.

Truth: The Psalmist realizes his unworthiness to enter into the presence of Almighty God, yet Holy God allows us to wear His righteousness and approach the throne, take refuge, rejoice, and sing for joy.

Thought: I can remember as a child going to the homes of my grandparents. I would look forward with great anticipation to walking in the front door and seeing the smiles on their faces and hear the excitement in their voices as I would walk in. It never dawned on me that they were excited to see my parents too. God's revelation to us is personal. As verse 12 says, He is ready to surround His children with His favor like a shield. It is the abundance of His love that invites us into His presence.

Tune: How deep the Father's love for us, How vast beyond all measure That He should give His only Son, To make a wretch His treasure

Dear God, It is only because of your abundant and steadfast love that I can even approach your throne of grace. I'm so thankful to have the privilege to come to you with my baggage, with my sorrows, with my challenges, and find that your love always greets me lovingly.

Songs for Life—Day 8—January 8

Text: Psalm 6: 1-5

[1] Lord, do not rebuke me in your anger; do not discipline me in your wrath.
[2] Be gracious to me, Lord, for I am weak;
heal me, Lord, for my bones are shaking;
[3] my whole being is shaken with terror. And you, Lord—how long?
[4] Turn, Lord! Rescue me; save me because of your faithful love.
[5] For there is no remembrance of you in death;
who can thank you in Sheol?

Truth: The Psalmist is greatly troubled and is asking for God's mercy over his sins. He felt that if he didn't receive forgiveness that he would be separated from God, even in death, in Sheol. Sheol is a Hebrew proper name and it's referring to the grave or a place that the evil people go who are not faithful believers. They are seeking God for salvation.

Thought: In today's world, there are so many distractions to us and we can easily stray away from God, His Word, or fellowship with other believers. At times, we feel our sins are too great and we have a deep unrest in our innermost thoughts. We even feel at times that we have become backsliders and there is no hope for us. But we CAN directly call on God, just as this Psalmist did, and ask for forgiveness and be saved from our sins or be restored to fellowship after a time of rebellion and not ever be separated from God and his love.

Tune: I am thine O Lord I have heard thy voice,
and it told thy love to me;
but I long to rise in the arms of faith
and be closer drawn to thee.

Dear Heavenly Father, I know that I am a sinner, and I need to ask for your forgiveness. I also know that you are a God of second chances and full of Mercy and Grace. The most awful thing would be to be separated from you and your love forever. Today, I seek your face and guidance for my life, and the peace that only YOU can give.

Text: Psalm 6: 6-10

[6] I am weary from my groaning; with my tears I dampen my bed
and drench my couch every night.
[7] My eyes are swollen from grief;
they grow old because of all my enemies.
[8] Depart from me, all evildoers,
for the Lord has heard the sound of my weeping.
[9] The Lord has heard my plea for help; the Lord accepts my prayer.
[10] All my enemies will be ashamed and shake with terror;
they will turn back and suddenly be disgraced.

Truth: The Psalmist is in great sorrow and suffering because of his sin. He is spending each night weeping and his enemies try to take advantage of him in this state of distress. Finally, out of severe desperation, he boldly seeks God for help. The Lord hears his repentant heart and forgives him and will not let the enemies overtake him.

Thought: When we are suffering because of our sin or wrong doing we can slip into a depression of sorts. Eventually we feel that we have reached rock bottom. It is then that we realize we can't do it alone, we call out to God for help and mercy. God will hear our repentant cries and forgive us and fight our enemies. If this is you, what are you waiting for? You have nothing to lose and everything to gain in surrender. Confession frees us, empowers us, and endears us to Almighty God.

Tune: Now let us have a little talk with Jesus,
Let us tell Him all about our troubles,
He will hear our faintest cry,
He will answer by and by.....

Dear Heavenly Father: Please help me to learn when I'm on the path of destruction and being coerced by my enemies and feel that I can't go on another day. I know that I can boldly come to you and ask for forgiveness and seek your mercy and grace with a repentant heart. Thank you, Father for hearing my cries deep in the night, and being there for me.

Songs for Life—Day 10—January 10

Text: Psalm 7:1-9

[1] Lord my God, I seek refuge in you;
save me from all my pursuers and rescue me
[2] or they will tear me like a lion, ripping me apart with no one to rescue me.
[3] Lord my God, if I have done this, if there is injustice on my hands,
[4] if I have done harm to one at peace with me
or have plundered my adversary without cause,
[5] may an enemy pursue and overtake me;
may he trample me to the ground and leave my honor in the dust. *Selah*
[6] Rise up, Lord, in your anger;
lift yourself up against the fury of my adversaries;
awake for me; you have ordained a judgment.
[7] Let the assembly of peoples gather around you;
take your seat on high over it.
[8] The Lord judges the peoples; vindicate me, Lord,
according to my righteousness and my integrity.
[9] Let the evil of the wicked come to an end, but establish the righteous.
The one who examines the thoughts and emotions is a righteous God.

Truth: The Psalmist is opening up his heart before God and throwing himself on the mercy of the court. The true believer wants to be right before God. Confession is a short-term pain for a long-term gain.

Thought: Have you ever had a situation where you knew you needed to "get something right" with someone, to confess a wrong, to own up to something you said that was hurtful? Often the anticipation is much worse than the result. Sometimes short-term pain leads to long term gain.

Tune: My Jesus I love Thee I know Thou art mine
For Thee all the follies of sin I resign
My gracious Redeemer my Savior art Thou
If ever I loved Thee my Jesus 'tis now

Lord, look within my heart and see if there be any wrong, any attitude, any bitterness, any offense in me. Be my righteous Judge in love today.

<u>Songs for Life—Day 11—January 11</u>

Text: Psalm 7:10-17

[10] My shield is with God, who saves the upright in heart.

[11] God is a righteous judge and a God who shows his wrath every day.

[12] If anyone does not repent, he will sharpen his sword;
he has strung his bow and made it ready.

[13] He has prepared his deadly weapons; he tips his arrows with fire.

[14] See, the wicked one is pregnant with evil,
conceives trouble, and gives birth to deceit.

[15] He dug a pit and hollowed it out but fell into the hole he had made.

[16] His trouble comes back on his own head;
his own violence comes down on top of his head.

[17] I will thank the Lord for his righteousness;
I will sing about the name of the Lord Most High.

Truth: If we fail to repent when we knowingly have sin in our heart, we become no greater than the wicked man. When the believer fails to look at his life honestly, in asking God to reveal the truth of his unrighteousness, he places himself in the position of judge of his own life.

Thought: Repentance means never having to say you are sorry for that offense again, because your heart turns from it, never to return. Repentance begins with looking at our lives through the lens of God's Word, then turns to confession before the gracious Father.

Tune: Just as I am without one plea,
But that Thy Blood was shed for me
And that Thou bidd'st me come to Thee,
O Lamb of God I come I come

Dear God, as the psalmist says in today's passage, "I will thank the Lord for his righteousness". I do not always understand Your ways or Your purposes, but I trust that they are always true and right. Even when I have to walk through the times of unsettledness in my heart due to my own sinful actions, I know that you are using them for my good. Use my life for Your good today, God!

Text: Psalm 8:1-9

[1] Lord, our Lord, how magnificent is your name throughout the earth!
You have covered the heavens with your majesty.
[2] From the mouths of infants and nursing babies,
you have established a stronghold on account of your adversaries
in order to silence the enemy and the avenger.
[3] When I observe your heavens, the work of your fingers,
the moon and the stars, which you set in place,
[4] what is a human being that you remember him,
a son of man that you look after him?
[5] You made him little less than God
and crowned him with glory and honor.
[6] You made him ruler over the works of your hands;
you put everything under his feet:
[7] all the sheep and oxen, as well as the animals in the wild,
[8] the birds of the sky, and the fish of the sea
that pass through the currents of the seas.
[9] Lord, our Lord, how magnificent is your name throughout the earth!

Truth: Magnificent, majesty – these are two words which paint a picture of who God is and how we can view Him in our mind's eye. He is majestic, amazing, radiant... and so much more! As magnificent as He is, He has us on His mind constantly.

Thought: There is nothing better to fill our minds with than praise to the King of Kings. As high and lifted up as His name is, and as lowly as we are in comparison, His love reaches us and surrounds us.

Tune: Oh Lord our Lord how majestic is Your name in all the earth
Oh Lord our Lord how majestic is Your name in all the earth

Dear God, how excellent, how majestic, how exalted, and how radiant is Your name. It is the name above all names. You are high and lifted up. Your name brings comfort, it brings peace, it brings love, it brings restoration. How awesome it is to know that you have ME on your mind!

Text: Psalm 9: 1-8

[1] I will thank the Lord with all my heart;
I will declare all your wondrous works.
[2] I will rejoice and boast about you;
I will sing about your name, Most High.
[3] When my enemies retreat,
they stumble and perish before you.
[4] For you have upheld my just cause;
you are seated on your throne as a righteous judge.
[5] You have rebuked the nations:
You have destroyed the wicked;
you have erased their name forever and ever.
[6] The enemy has come to eternal ruin.
You have uprooted the cities,
and the very memory of them has perished.
[7] But the Lord sits enthroned forever;
he has established his throne for judgment.
[8] And he judges the world with righteousness;
he executes judgment on the nations with fairness.

Truth: The phrase "I will" is repeated 4 times. This is showing us David's dedication to praise and thanking God for the wonderful things He had done for his people. Time and again, God has been there for his people.

Thought: There is no substitute for telling God how good He is. David begins to recount the things God has done, and you can almost sense his spirit pouring out to holy God. Our path to obedience is paved with our praise and thanksgiving to God for all He is and all He has done.

Tune: I sing praises to your name, O Lord, praises to your name, O Lord, For your Name is great and greatly to be praised.

Dear God, I praise your name for all you are, and all you have done and will continue to do throughout my life. Your blessings are too many to count, but I will continue to count them as long as I have breath.

Songs for Life—Day 14—January 14

Text: Psalm 9: 9-14

9 The Lord is a refuge for the persecuted, a refuge in times of trouble.

10 Those who know your name trust in you
because you have not abandoned those who seek you, Lord.

11 Sing to the Lord, who dwells in Zion;
proclaim his deeds among the nations.

12 For the one who seeks an accounting for bloodshed remembers them;
he does not forget the cry of the oppressed.

13 Be gracious to me, Lord;
consider my affliction at the hands of those who hate me.
Lift me up from the gates of death,

14 so that I may declare all your praises. I will rejoice in your salvation
within the gates of Daughter Zion.

Truth: The people who had put their trust in God were no longer oppressed. They were praying for deliverance and were vindicated because God avenged his people. Prayer is very prominent in these verses and it shows their dependence on God. God is our defender.

Thought: For you today, the Lord is a strong tower for you to seek refuge from in your times of trouble. There WILL be times of trouble. God will hear the cries of those in need and will not forget us or leave us. To know God is to trust God. To not trust God is not to really know Him. Trust the Refuge today for whatever situation you are going through.

Tune: The name of the Lord is, a strong tower,
the righteous run into it and they are saved.
The name of the Lord is, a strong tower,
the righteous run into it and they are saved.

Dear Heavenly Father: Today, may I seek you in my time of need, for safety and protection from my trials and enemies. I need your saving grace and salvation. Please give me the courage and strength to share what you have done for me with those around me, that they too may see, hear and believe in your goodness and mercies.

Songs for Life—Day 15—January 15

Text: Psalm 9: 15-20

[15] The nations have fallen into the pit they made;
their foot is caught in the net they have concealed.
[16] The Lord has made himself known; he has executed justice,
snaring the wicked by the work of their hands. *Higgaion. Selah*
[17] The wicked will return to Sheol—all the nations that forget God.
[18] For the needy will not always be forgotten;
the hope of the oppressed will not perish forever.
[19] Rise up, Lord! Do not let mere humans prevail;
let the nations be judged in your presence.
[20] Put terror in them, Lord;
let the nations know they are only humans. *Selah*

Truth: This psalmist here is describing the wicked people who are bringing about destruction on themselves. Those that continue to do evil will be separated from God. But those who are under threat, such as the Israelites who are needy and poor, will not be forgotten by God. It is time for them to all join together in prayer and ask that God would judge the nations and remember those who are totally dependent on God.

Thought: Many times, we see people participating in bad behavior choices and eventually they will be the cause of their own demise. Sometimes, we are our own worst enemy, whether that is in our own behavior, or making ourselves feel better by pointing out the questionable choices by others. It's then that we must be careful to guard our own behavior and spend time in prayer and the Word to help us make wise choices with our minds, hearts and actions. May we let others see Christ dwelling in us.

Tune: Holy is the Lord God Almighty, the earth is filled with His glory
Holy is the Lord God Almighty
The earth is filled with His glory, the earth is filled with His glory

Dear God, I come before you to humbly ask that You would guide my path, and help me to live each day for you. Father, please forgive my wicked thoughts and ways and let me seek You in my everyday life through prayer and songs of praise. God, You are worthy to be praised.

Songs for Life—Day 16—January 16

Text: Psalm 10:1-11

¹ Lord, why do you stand so far away? Why do you hide in times of trouble?
² In arrogance the wicked relentlessly pursue their victims;
let them be caught in the schemes they have devised.
³ For the wicked one boasts about his own cravings;
the one who is greedy curses and despises the Lord.
⁴ In all his scheming, the wicked person arrogantly thinks,
"There's no accountability, since there's no God."
⁵ His ways are always secure; your lofty judgments have no effect on him;
he scoffs at all his adversaries.
⁶ He says to himself, "I will never be moved—
from generation to generation without calamity."
⁷ Cursing, deceit, and violence fill his mouth;
trouble and malice are under his tongue.
⁸ He waits in ambush near settlements; he kills the innocent in secret places.
His eyes are on the lookout for the helpless;
⁹ he lurks in secret like a lion in a thicket. He lurks in order to seize a victim;
he seizes a victim and drags him in his net.
¹⁰ So he is oppressed and beaten down;
helpless people fall because of the wicked one's strength.
¹¹ He says to himself, "God has forgotten; he hides his face and will never see."

Truth: The psalmist is calling out to God with the desire that the wicked would receive "what they deserve", as well as expressing the honesty from his heart that he feels God has failed to act on his behalf.

Thought: We have to be careful about expecting those who do not know God to act as though they do. If you have Christ, rejoice! Let Him shine!

Tune: When peace like a river attendeth my way
When sorrows like sea billows roll
Whatever my lot, Thou hast taught me to say,
It is well, It is well with my soul

Dear Jesus, I confess that it is so easy to focus on my own circumstances and wonder why I'm not getting the blessings that others seem to receive. Forgive me, Jesus. You alone get the glory in my life and I need you to remind me that you have everything in my life under your control.

Text: Psalm 10:12-18

[12] Rise up, Lord God! Lift up your hand. Do not forget the oppressed.

[13] Why has the wicked person despised God?

He says to himself, "You will not demand an account."

[14] But you yourself have seen trouble and grief,

observing it in order to take the matter into your hands.

The helpless one entrusts himself to you;

you are a helper of the fatherless.

[15] Break the arm of the wicked, evil person,

until you look for his wickedness, but it can't be found.

[16] The Lord is King forever and ever;

the nations will perish from his land.

[17] Lord, you have heard the desire of the humble;

you will strengthen their hearts. You will listen carefully,

[18] doing justice for the fatherless and the oppressed

so that mere humans from the earth may terrify them no more.

Truth: The psalmist turns from his anxiety to intercession. It is as if the Holy Spirit changed his heart and opened his spiritual eyes during the midst of the prayer. In vs. 12-15 he prays for God's protection on the helpless – which really describes us all. In vs. 16-18, he ends this psalm by exalting God and trusting in his justice and power.

Thought: The tendency sometimes, when we feel alone or abandoned by the Lord, is to retreat, for our prayers to be no more than silent rituals. It is in those moments when our prayers should increase in intensity. In his honesty, the psalmist's heart was changed by the power of the Holy Spirit.

Tune: Holy holy holy, Lord God Almighty
Early in the morning our song shall rise to Thee
Holy holy holy, merciful and mighty, God in three persons, Blessed Trinity

Holy Father, let me not be so blind in my spiritual life that I only look at how situations affect me. Let me be one who exalts you with my whole heart. Father, put your hand on those who are helpless, struck down, in need. Today, I start by praising and worshipping you, Holy Father.

Text: Psalm 11:1-7

[1] I have taken refuge in the Lord.
How can you say to me, "Escape to the mountains like a bird!
[2] For look, the wicked string bows; they put their arrows on bowstrings
to shoot from the shadows at the upright in heart.
[3] When the foundations are destroyed, what can the righteous do?"
[4] The Lord is in his holy temple; the Lord—his throne is in heaven.
His eyes watch; his gaze examines everyone.
[5] The Lord examines the righteous, but he hates the wicked
and those who love violence.
[6] Let him rain burning coals and sulfur on the wicked;
let a scorching wind be the portion in their cup.
[7] For the Lord is righteous; he loves righteous deeds.
The upright will see his face.

Truth: The psalmist is feeling the effects of a world of believers that seems to be shrinking, as well as a continued opposition from the non-believers. At times, he may feel like he's the only one committed to the cause of serving God. However, he gets one thing absolutely right. "the Lord is righteous". God IS righteous. Man can only "put on" righteousness.

Thought: As the world seems to be more comfortable with those who fail to acknowledge Almighty God in their lives, we must understand something . . . the only way to true obedience is not righteous deeds for righteous deeds' sake, it is about embracing the character, the integrity, the person of God. Our deeds flow out of that growth in righteousness.

Tune: I worship You Almighty God, there is none like You
I worship You O Prince of Peace, that is what I want to do
I give You praise, for You are my righteousness
I worship You Almighty God, there is none like You

Almighty God, you are righteous, you are MY righteousness. The only way that I'm going to be found faithful is to allow your righteousness to change me, to transform me, from the inside out.

Text: Psalm 12

¹ Help, Lord, for no faithful one remains;
the loyal have disappeared from the human race.
² They lie to one another;
they speak with flattering lips and deceptive hearts.
³ May the Lord cut off all flattering lips
and the tongue that speaks boastfully.
⁴ They say, "Through our tongues we have power;
our lips are our own—who can be our master?"
⁵ "Because of the devastation of the needy and the groaning of the poor,
I will now rise up," says the Lord.
"I will provide safety for the one who longs for it."
⁶ The words of the Lord are pure words,
like silver refined in an earthen furnace, purified seven times.
⁷ You, Lord, will guard us; you will protect us from this generation forever.
⁸ The wicked prowl all around,
and what is worthless is exalted by the human race.

Truth: The tongue can be a sharp two-edged sword and can be abusive and lying. Here, the Psalmist feels that that liars are in control and dominating over those faithful followers. But God gives us His reassuring words that are pure, true and comforting.

Thought: God's Word is completely pure, refined like silver. We can always rely on the fact that God's faithful followers will always be protected if we place our total dependence on God and God alone.

Tune: The words of the Lord are like silver
Refined seven times in a furnace of clay
The Lord keeps us safe and protects us
His Word remains perfect now and always

Dear Heavenly Father: Today, I ask that you help me to guard my tongue and to know that you are my protector and that Your words are pure and I can rest in them.

Songs for Life—Day 20—January 20

Text: Psalm 13

¹ How long, Lord? Will you forget me forever?
How long will you hide your face from me?
² How long will I store up anxious concerns within me,
agony in my mind every day?
How long will my enemy dominate me?
³ Consider me and answer, Lord my God.
Restore brightness to my eyes; otherwise, I will sleep in death.
⁴ My enemy will say, "I have triumphed over him,"
and my foes will rejoice because I am shaken.
⁵ But I have trusted in your faithful love;
my heart will rejoice in your deliverance.
⁶ I will sing to the Lord because he has treated me generously.

Truth: How long? The psalmist asks this question four times. He asks for God to consider his request and remove his enemy. Even in his struggle, the psalmist realizes he has much to rejoice over. He can rejoice in his salvation and in the fact that God has dealt with him bountifully.

Thought: When you are struggling… rejoice. When you are victorious… rejoice. How can we rejoice in both of those circumstances? For the child of God, the grace of God is always sufficient. When I'm on the mountain, I rejoice in the blessings of God. When I'm in the valley, I rejoice in the grace and presence of God to be with me and carry me through.

Tune: I will enter His gates
With thanksgiving in my heart
I will enter His courts with praise
I will say this is the day that the Lord has made
I will rejoice for He has made me glad

Dear God, help me to realize how much you have blessed me with. Your grace is the only thing that allows me to take another step. Your breath is the only thing that allows me to breathe. Your love is the only thing that allows me to have peace. I rejoice for you have made me glad today, God!

Text: Psalm 14

¹ The fool says in his heart, "There's no God."
They are corrupt; they do vile deeds. There is no one who does good.
² The Lord looks down from heaven on the human race
to see if there is one who is wise, one who seeks God.
³ All have turned away; all alike have become corrupt.
There is no one who does good, not even one.
⁴ Will evildoers never understand?
They consume my people as they consume bread;
they do not call on the Lord.
⁵ Then they will be filled with dread,
for God is with those who are righteous.
⁶ You sinners frustrate the plans of the oppressed,
but the Lord is his refuge.
⁷ Oh, that Israel's deliverance would come from Zion!
When the Lord restores the fortunes of his people,
let Jacob rejoice, let Israel be glad.

Truth: Fool is a strong word in Scripture, and not used lightly. A fool rejects the wisdom of God. The psalmist here is referring to the Gentiles, the "children of man", as opposed to "my people".

Thought: The questions that come from verse 2 include "are there any who are wise?" and "Are there any who seek God?" To make this personal, consider for yourself this: are you embracing the wisdom of God? Are you looking at everything in life through the lens of how God's Word would look at it?

Tune: Be Thou my vision, O Lord of my heart
Naught be all else to me, save that Thou art
Thou my best thought, by day or by night
Waking or sleeping Thy presence my light

Dear God, Your wisdom is the source of every answer that I need in life. Your truth is the foundation to living within your will.

Text: Psalm 15

¹ Lord, who can dwell in your tent?
Who can live on your holy mountain?
² The one who lives blamelessly, practices righteousness,
and acknowledges the truth in his heart—
³ who does not slander with his tongue,
who does not harm his friend
or discredit his neighbor,
⁴ who despises the one rejected by the Lord
but honors those who fear the Lord,
who keeps his word whatever the cost,
⁵ who does not lend his silver at interest
or take a bribe against the innocent—
the one who does these things will never be shaken.

Truth: This Psalm asks a two-part question of who will go and dwell with God in his house. Then, he answers the question with a 12-part response of how we are to treat others with integrity and be mindful of our own actions and tongue. We are to not be greedy or harm our fellow friends. It ends with a promise of assurance for the ones who embrace these commands.

Thought: As a believer, we are to hold ourselves and our actions to higher standards that are full of integrity and self-accountability. We must strive to love one another, as Jesus tells us in John 13:34, and to always honor God with our actions and our words. It won't always be easy, but it is always worth it.

Tune: In my life Lord, Be glorified be glorified
In my life Lord, Be glorified today

Dear God, thank you for your words that so clearly define how we are to conduct ourselves in this earthly world. Please give us the strength and courage to always try and do the right things, even when they are not the easiest. Allow others to see you, God, through me and my words and actions and know that you are God of my life.

Text: Psalm 16:1-6

[1] Protect me, God, for I take refuge in you.

[2] I said to the Lord, "You are my Lord; I have nothing good besides you."

[3] As for the holy people who are in the land, they are the noble ones.
All my delight is in them.

[4] The sorrows of those who take another god for themselves will multiply;
I will not pour out their drink offerings of blood,
and I will not speak their names with my lips.

[5] Lord, you are my portion and my cup of blessing; you hold my future.

[6] The boundary lines have fallen for me in pleasant places;
indeed, I have a beautiful inheritance.

Truth: We see the request to "protect me", or something similar, repeatedly throughout the Psalms. Never do we get to a place where we do not need His protection, nor should we ever stop eagerly pursuing it. This dependence is underscored by the phrase "I have no good apart from you."

Thought: Anytime we seek fulfillment in anything besides the fullness of God, of Christ, in our lives, we run the risk of following in the footsteps of those described in verse 4. We can take that as a promise – that our sorrows will multiply. We cannot evaluate our lives based on our perceptions of God's dealings with others. God has brought us, through grace, to the place where we realize from His Word that we are to be totally dependent on Him. For those of us who trust God, we indeed have the promises of a "beautiful inheritance"

Tune: Hosanna, Hosanna, You are the God who saves us
Worthy of all our praises
Hosanna hosanna, come have Your way among us
We welcome You here Lord Jesus

Dear God, Hosanna to You in the highest! God, you are worthy of all of the praise, all of the glory, and all of the adoration I can ever give, and much, much more. You are my refuge and strength. You are the One who holds my present and my future in Your hands.

Songs for Life—Day 24—January 24

Text: Psalm 16:7-11

[7] I will bless the Lord who counsels me—
even at night when my thoughts trouble me.
[8] I always let the Lord guide me.
Because he is at my right hand,
I will not be shaken.
[9] Therefore my heart is glad
and my whole being rejoices;
my body also rests securely.
[10] For you will not abandon me to Sheol;
you will not allow your faithful one to see decay.
[11] You reveal the path of life to me;
in your presence is abundant joy;
at your right hand are eternal pleasures.

Truth: Some of the promises of God are prominent in this passage. He is the One who counsels, or guides, us. He is our Guide. He is always at our right hand. His revelation is personal and true, and His presence is absolute joy.

Thought: Sometimes we just need the reminder that Scripture gives us that God is . . . That's it, right there. . . God IS. He is what? He IS! He is whatever you need. He IS! What do you NEED today? He IS!

Tune: Give thanks to the Lord, our God and King,
His love endures forever
For He is Good He is above all things, His love endures forever
Sing praise, sing praise, sing praise, sing praise
Forever God is faithful
Forever God is strong
Forever God is with us, Forever forever

Holy Father, forgive me for the times when I fail to acknowledge Your presence, ignore Your instruction, or fail to seek Your face. You ARE. . . all I need. You ARE . . . Help me to practice that today.

Text: Psalm 17: 1-7

[1] Lord, hear a just cause; pay attention to my cry;
listen to my prayer— from lips free of deceit.
[2] Let my vindication come from you, for you see what is right.
[3] You have tested my heart; you have examined me at night.
You have tried me and found nothing evil;
I have determined that my mouth will not sin.
[4] Concerning what people do: by the words from your lips
I have avoided the ways of the violent.
[5] My steps are on your paths; my feet have not slipped.
[6] I call on you, God, because you will answer me;
listen closely to me; hear what I say.
[7] Display the wonders of your faithful love, Savior of all who seek refuge
from those who rebel against your right hand.

Truth: David is crying out a prayer to God for protection. He had been under attack for things he did not commit. He even asked to God to search out his heart and that he wouldn't find any wrong doing that he was being accused of doing. David was showing lots of effort to stay pure and he was continually seeking God for direction.

Thought: Have you ever been accused of wrong doing that simply was not true? Sometimes it's harder to prove your innocence than admit guilt. Even if you do not receive vindication from those accusers, you can rest assured that God knows the truth. He can and will search your heart. You are only responsible for your own actions, not those of others. Keep your heart pure before Him and ask God to take care of the rest.

Tune: I will call upon the Lord, who is worthy to be saved
             So shall I be saved from enemies, I will call upon the Lord

Dear Lord: I bow before you, humbly seeking your face and ask that you help me to stay true to your word and your ways. I ask for your protection to surround me. I praise YOU, Father, and your Holiness and I seek refuge in you.

Text: Psalm 17: 8-17

⁸ Protect me as the pupil of your eye; hide me in the shadow of your wings
⁹ from the wicked who treat me violently,
my deadly enemies who surround me.
¹⁰ They are uncaring; their mouths speak arrogantly.
¹¹ They advance against me; now they surround me.
They are determined to throw me to the ground.
¹² They are like a lion eager to tear, like a young lion lurking in ambush.
¹³ Rise up, Lord! Confront him; bring him down.
With your sword, save me from the wicked.
¹⁴ With your hand, Lord, save me from men, from men of the world
whose portion is in this life:
You fill their bellies with what you have in store; their sons are satisfied,
and they leave their surplus to their children.
¹⁵ But I will see your face in righteousness;
when I awake, I will be satisfied with your presence.

Truth: This is asking for God's protection from those attackers who show no remorse or pity for their evil deeds. They are those who just lay in wait to attack the righteous or the innocent and destroy them. These attackers should ask for repentance, but they won't. They are satisfied with the temporary things of this world such as possessions and children. As believers, we look forward to waking up with eternal fellowship with God.

Thought: Matthew 6:20, "but lay up for yourselves treasures in heaven, where neither moth nor rust destroys and where thieves do not break in and steal." Everytime we respond to negativity, to attacks, as Christ would, we are laying up treasures in Heaven. We do not want to compromise our witness with ungodly behavior.

Tune: In the shadow of Your wings,
Where I trust You Lord with everything
Take me in Your arms, surround me with Your love
In the shadow of Your wings

Dear Lord: Today, will you help me to keep my eyes on you, and not the things of this earthly world. I pray for protection that only you can give me.

Text: Psalm 18:1-6

¹ I love you, Lord, my strength.

² The Lord is my rock, my fortress, and my deliverer,
my God, my rock where I seek refuge,
my shield and the horn of my salvation, my stronghold.

³ I called to the Lord, who is worthy of praise,
and I was saved from my enemies.

⁴ The ropes of death were wrapped around me;
the torrents of destruction terrified me.

⁵ The ropes of Sheol entangled me; the snares of death confronted me.

⁶ I called to the Lord in my distress, and I cried to my God for help.
From his temple he heard my voice, and my cry to him reached his ears.

Truth: David was an unlikely King, one who was anointed from an early age, had great success, and was described as a "man after God's own heart". All of these traits in David, to a certain degree, put a target on his back. Here we see another instance of David asking for protection.

Thought: David uses reassuring descriptors for God like "my strength", "my fortress, "my deliverer", "my God", "my rock", "my shield", "the horn of my salvation", "my stronghold" and the "Lord, who is worthy to be praised". Sometimes verbalizing those traits revealing who God really is can help us get re-focused on WHO is really important.

Tune: When the oceans rise and thunders roar
I will soar with You above the storm
Father You are King, over the flood
I will be still and know, You are God

Dear Lord, today I am reminded that you are my strength, fortress, and deliverer. You are my God, my rock and my shield. You will not let be overwhelmed by the struggles of life if I will trust and obey. Lord, as the oceans of life rise around me, I will trust you. As the flood waters roll, I will be still and know You are God!

Text: Psalm 18:7-12

[7] Then the earth shook and quaked;
the foundations of the mountains trembled;
they shook because he burned with anger.
[8] Smoke rose from his nostrils,
and consuming fire came from his mouth;
coals were set ablaze by it.
[9] He bent the heavens and came down,
total darkness beneath his feet.
[10] He rode on a cherub and flew,
soaring on the wings of the wind.
[11] He made darkness his hiding place,
dark storm clouds his canopy around him.
[12] From the radiance of his presence,
his clouds swept onward with hail and blazing coals.

Truth: When God responds, there is no doubt He is responding. In this case, the response to David's call from the point of distress, God responded in a mighty way. He responds like an angry dragon. It is not only a reminder of God's response to the cries of His children, but His power and promise to destroy anything that would harm His children.

Thought: Do you ever wish you could see a mighty move of God like this in your life, where the earth "reeled and rocked"? God's glory is revealed in our lives every day, which is certainly a supernatural expression of His presence. Sometimes God's glory is revealed in the still small voice.

Tune: Indescribable uncontainable
You placed the stars in the sky and You know them by name
You are amazing God
All powerful untamable, awestruck we fall to our knees
As we humbly proclaim - You are amazing God

Jesus, I confess that there are times that I wonder if you are really there, if you are really listening. I'll admit I would sometimes like to experience an obvious move of your presence like David did in this Psalm. But Jesus, You protect me, You provide for me, and best of all, You love me.

Text: Psalm 18:13-19

[13] The Lord thundered from heaven; the Most High made his voice heard.
[14] He shot his arrows and scattered them;
he hurled lightning bolts and routed them.
[15] The depths of the sea became visible,
the foundations of the world were exposed, at your rebuke, Lord,
at the blast of the breath of your nostrils.
[16] He reached down from on high and took hold of me;
he pulled me out of deep water.
[17] He rescued me from my powerful enemy and from those who hated me,
for they were too strong for me.
[18] They confronted me in the day of my calamity,
but the Lord was my support.
[19] He brought me out to a spacious place;
he rescued me because he delighted in me.

Truth: God's movement is not only powerful, but it is also personal. David uses the words me or my ten times in the last four verses of this passage. The rescue was sure, and it was personal. The confrontation from the enemies was real, but God's presence was personal and complete.

Thought: Look at the personal touch from God that David describes in the latter verses. "He rescued me"… "he pulled me out of deep water…", "They comforted me…", "the Lord was my support"… God's involvement in our lives and in our situations is both real and personal.

Tune: The love of God is greater far, than tongue or pen can ever tell
It goes beyond the highest star, and reaches to the lowest hell
The guilty pair bowed down with care, God gave His Son to win
His erring child He reconciled, and pardoned from His sin

Father, I need to be reminded sometimes that you love me, that every interaction you have with me is personal to me. I don't always understand the trials and tribulations that you allow me to go through, but I am thankful that you have reminded me today that you pursue ME!

Songs for Life—Day 30—January 30

Text: Psalm 18:20-24

20 The Lord rewarded me according to my righteousness;
he repaid me according to the cleanness of my hands.
21 For I have kept the ways of the Lord
and have not turned from my God to wickedness.
22 Indeed, I let all his ordinances guide me
and have not disregarded his statutes.
23 I was blameless toward him and kept myself from my iniquity.
24 So the Lord repaid me according to my righteousness,
according to the cleanness of my hands in his sight.

Truth: It would be easy to read these verses and glean from them that David was bragging on himself about how righteous he was, how clean his hands were, or how blameless he was. However, we must look at the passage through the lens of where this righteousness, cleanliness and blamelessness came from. David is quick to say that these are the results of keeping the ways of the Lord, of placing His life in God's hand.

Thought: Any goodness that comes from us is God through us. Any keeping of God's laws or commandments is a result of us following His direction within us. There is no good in us apart from God though us. None. . . Our lives should be a daily dying to self and a surrender to His direction.

Tune: There's not a friend like the lowly Jesus
No not one no not one
No one else could heal all our souls' diseases
No not one no not one

Father, I need to be reminded sometimes that you love me, that every interaction you have with me is personal to me, and it is designed to help me to follow the perfect plan you have for my life. I don't always understand the trials and tribulations that you allow me to go through, but I am thankful that you have reminded me today that you pursue ME!

Songs for Life—Day 31—January 31

Text: Psalm 18:25-30

25 With the faithful you prove yourself faithful,
with the blameless you prove yourself blameless,
26 with the pure you prove yourself pure;
but with the crooked you prove yourself shrewd.
27 For you rescue an oppressed people,
but you humble those with haughty eyes.
28 Lord, you light my lamp;
my God illuminates my darkness.
29 With you I can attack a barricade,
and with my God I can leap over a wall.
30 God—his way is perfect; the word of the Lord is pure.
He is a shield to all who take refuge in him.

Truth: God is the Father of mercy, totally blameless and pure, the Lamp who lights our lives. God's ways are perfect and His Word is totally true and trustworthy. It is His light that brings hope in the darkness . . . comfort in the storm . . . The needs of man are only sufficiently met by the sufficiency of God.

Thought: "For by you I can attack a barricade, and with my God I can leap over a wall". This is reminiscent of "If God brings you to it, He will bring you through it", or "The Will of God will never lead you where the Grace of God cannot keep you."

Tune: But when I call on Jesus, all things are possible
I can mount on wings like eagles and soar
When I call on Jesus, mountains are gonna fall
'Cause He'll move heaven and earth to, come rescue me when I call

Father, Your Word clearly states that whatever You desire for my life, you will equip me and empower me to accomplish it. Sometimes I limit what I believe You would have me do based on what You've allowed me to do in the past, but I don't want to limit You. You are limitless! God, open my eyes to see what You have for me, even if it doesn't make sense now.

Songs for Life – Day 32 – February 1

Text: Psalm 18:31-36

For who is God, but the Lord?
  And who is a rock, except our God?—
^{32} the God who equipped me with strength
  and made my way blameless.
^{33} He made my feet like the feet of a deer
  and set me secure on the heights.
^{34} He trains my hands for war,
  so that my arms can bend a bow of bronze.
^{35} You have given me the shield of your salvation,
  and your right hand supported me,
  and your gentleness made me great.
^{36} You gave a wide place for my steps under me, and my feet did not slip.

Truth: The Psalmist refers to God as a rock. In Deuteronomy 32, Moses referred to God as "The Rock". God is indeed a massive, unshakable foundation and a source of protection. In the New Testament we see that the early church was built upon the Rock, the Rock that is Christ.

Thought: Our confession of Christ places our feet on this Rock. Upon this Rock, the Psalmist tells us we have been equipped with strength, we've been made blameless, our feet are like that of a deer, we are secure and trained for war. We have the shield of salvation, upheld by His righteous right hand, comforted by His gentleness. Our steps are sure upon the Rock. Taking steps without the sure foundation of the Rock is futile.

Tune: On Christ the solid Rock I stand
All other ground is sinking sand
All other ground is sinking sand

Father, I know that anywhere I stand is sinking sand unless I stand on You, Your Word, which is Truth. Help me today to turn from the temptations that would lead me to sinking sand, even when I can't see it myself. I trust you, my Solid Rock!

Songs for Life – Day 33 – February 2

Text: Psalm 18:37-45

[37] I pursued my enemies and overtook them,
and did not turn back till they were consumed.
[38] I thrust them through, so that they were not able to rise;
they fell under my feet.
[39] For you equipped me with strength for the battle;
you made those who rise against me sink under me.
[40] You made my enemies turn their backs to me,
and those who hated me I destroyed.
[41] They cried for help, but there was none to save;
they cried to the Lord, but he did not answer them.
[42] I beat them fine as dust before the wind;
I cast them out like the mire of the streets.
[43] You delivered me from strife with the people;
you made me the head of the nations;
people whom I had not known served me.
[44] As soon as they heard of me they obeyed me;
foreigners came cringing to me.
[45] Foreigners lost heart and came trembling out of their fortresses.

Truth: We can read this passage and get the idea that somehow the Psalmist, in his own strength, pursued and overtook his enemies. However, if we read verse 39, the truth is clearly there "you equipped me with strength". It reminds us of the spiritual armor in Ephesians 6:10-18

Thought: The man who goes into battle unequipped is prepared for only one thing . . . failure. As Ephesians 6 tells us, we are in a battle in this life, but not against flesh in blood. We must intentionally put on our battle armor daily – truth, righteousness, peace, faith, salvation, Word, & prayer.

Tune: Faith is the victory, faith is the victory
Oh glorious victory, that overcomes the world

Oh God . . . equip me for the battles of the day ahead. I cannot fight alone. You alone are my Equipper, my Shield, and my Protector.

Songs for Life – Day 34 – February 3

Text: Psalm 18:46-50

[46] The Lord lives, and blessed be my rock,
   and exalted be the God of my salvation—
[47] the God who gave me vengeance
   and subdued peoples under me,
[48] who rescued me from my enemies;
   yes, you exalted me above those who rose against me;
   you delivered me from the man of violence.
[49] For this I will praise you, O Lord, among the nations,
   and sing to your name.
[50] Great salvation he brings to his king,
   and shows steadfast love to his anointed,
   to David and his offspring forever.

Truth: Throughout the Old Testament, we see the promise of redemption to come. It is very clear in these verses. Phrases like "The Lord lives", "God of my salvation", "the God who…rescued me from my enemies", "Great salvation he brings to his king", and more, all point to the coming Messiah who is sure to bring salvation to His people.

Thought: The Gospel can be understood simply by focusing on verse 46. The Lord LIVES! He is the God of our SALVATION! Meditate on verse 46.

Tune: I will call upon the Lord
Who is worthy to be praised
So shall I be saved from my enemies
I will call upon The Lord
The Lord liveth, and blessed be The Rock
And let the God of my salvation be exalted
The Lord liveth, and blessed be The Rock
And let the God of my salvation be exalted

Lord, today I call upon You. You are the God of my salvation – in fact You ARE my salvation. I thank You for forgiving me and saving me.

Text: Psalm 19:1-6

The heavens declare the glory of God,
   and the sky above proclaims his handiwork.
[2] Day to day pours out speech,
   and night to night reveals knowledge.
[3] There is no speech, nor are there words, whose voice is not heard.
[4] Their voice goes out through all the earth,
   and their words to the end of the world.
In them he has set a tent for the sun,
[5]   which comes out like a bridegroom leaving his chamber,
   and, like a strong man, runs its course with joy.
[6] Its rising is from the end of the heavens,
   and its circuit to the end of them,
   and there is nothing hidden from its heat.

Truth: God reveals Himself in two basic ways. "General Revelation" comes as those things that are revealed to everyone. "Special Revelation" are those things that are specific to the individual, such as the call to salvation. Seeing the glory of God in nature is "General Revelation" - it can be seen by everyone, though not everyone acknowledges it.

Thought: The beauty of the sky, the sunrise and sunset, the waters on a lake, the beauty of trees . . . these all declare the glory of God. God has given us those things to enjoy, but most of all, to dwell in the glory of God. Revelation of God through nature really gives us no excuse not to acknowledge Him. The revelation of God reveals the glory of God.

Tune: For the beauty of the earth, for the glory of the skies
For the love which from our birth, over and around us lies
Lord of all to Thee we raise, this our hymn of grateful praise

God, your glory is evident in Your creation. From sunrise to sunset, to the beauty of the moon's glow in between, I can see your handiwork. Thank you for reminding me of your glory in nature. Let me never take it for granted.

Songs for Life – Day 36 – February 5

Text: Psalm 19:7-14

[7] The law of the Lord is perfect, reviving the soul;
the testimony of the Lord is sure, making wise the simple;
[8] the precepts of the Lord are right, rejoicing the heart;
the commandment of the Lord is pure, enlightening the eyes;
[9] the fear of the Lord is clean, enduring forever;
the rules of the Lord are true, and righteous altogether.
[10] More to be desired are they than gold, even much fine gold;
sweeter also than honey and drippings of the honeycomb.
[11] Moreover, by them is your servant warned;
   in keeping them there is great reward.
[12] Who can discern his errors?
   Declare me innocent from hidden faults.
[13] Keep back your servant also from presumptuous sins;
   let them not have dominion over me!
Then I shall be blameless, and innocent of great transgression.
[14] Let the words of my mouth and the meditation of my heart
   be acceptable in your sight, O Lord, my rock and my redeemer.

Truth: The law of the Lord, the Word of God, is perfect. It is the only source of Truth – it IS Truth. It lacks nothing for equipping us to love and serve God fully and wholly if we will ingest and digest it.

Thought: The Word of God revives, brings wisdom, rejoices the heart, enlightens the eyes, endures, is pure, righteous, and is sweeter than honey. It teaches servants about sin. It is the only document that leads to the regeneration of the soul and the revival of the spirit in man.

Tune: Words of life words of hope, give us strength help us cope
In this world where'er we roam, Ancient words will guide us home
Ancient words ever true, changing me changing you
We have come with open hearts, O let the ancient words impart

Let the words of my mouth and the meditation of my heart be acceptable in your sight, O LORD, my rock and my redeemer. Today and every day.

Text: Psalm 20:1-9

May the Lord answer you in the day of trouble!
   May the name of the God of Jacob protect you!
[2] May he send you help from the sanctuary
   and give you support from Zion!
[3] May he remember all your offerings
   and regard with favor your burnt sacrifices! *Selah*
[4] May he grant you your heart's desire and fulfill all your plans!
[5] May we shout for joy over your salvation,
   and in the name of our God set up our banners!
May the Lord fulfill all your petitions!
[6] Now I know that the Lord saves his anointed;
   he will answer him from his holy heaven
   with the saving might of his right hand.
[7] Some trust in chariots and some in horses,
   but we trust in the name of the Lord our God.
[8] They collapse and fall, but we rise and stand upright.
[9] O Lord, save the king! May he answer us when we call.

Truth: This is the prayer of God's people for their king, their general, "His anointed". No warrior would go to battle without preparation, and no God-fearing warrior would want to go into battle without the protection of God. Our salvation and our redemption, depend upon God's salvation, of and through the Anointed King.

Thought: Some trust in their chariots, horses, money or power, but nothing prepares and protects us like trusting in the name of the Lord our God! Jesus - Emmanuel - Son of God - Redeemer - Savior… that is where we place our trust.

Tune: Some trust in chariots, we trust in the name of the Lord our God
Some trust in horses, we trust in the name of the Lord our God

Some trust in chariots and some in horses, but I trust in the name of the LORD my God. Father, whatever comes today, I trust you!

Text: Psalm 21:1-7

O Lord, in your strength the king rejoices,
  and in your salvation how greatly he exults!
2 You have given him his heart's desire
  and have not withheld the request of his lips. *Selah*
3 For you meet him with rich blessings;
  you set a crown of fine gold upon his head.
4 He asked life of you; you gave it to him,
  length of days forever and ever.
5 His glory is great through your salvation;
  splendor and majesty you bestow on him.
6 For you make him most blessed forever;
  you make him glad with the joy of your presence.
7 For the king trusts in the Lord,
  and through the steadfast love of the Most High he shall not be moved.

Truth: This Psalm is talking mostly about thanking God for present and past victories that were only accomplished through the Lord. They are celebrating the Lords' many favors to the righteous and faithful king. Here, the king is trading his warrior helmet for a crown of fine gold and for having his life spared and receiving the blessings that can only come from our gracious Father. His blessings are personal and powerful.

Thought: Think about the blessings you have received in your life and how they came to be. Think of our daily battles that that we fight and one day, at the proper time, we too, can trade in our battle helmet for our own crown in glory. But first, we must have accepted the Lord as our personal Lord and Savior. If you have not done so, then what are you waiting for?

Tune: How great is our God, sing with me, how great is our God
        And all will see how great, how great is our God

Dear Lord: Thank you for the blessings you have so graciously given me. Thank you for being MY God, MY Creator, MY Savior. It's only through the sovereign grace of You, Lord, that I am saved

Songs for Life – Day 39 – February 8

Text: Psalm 21:8-13

[8] Your hand will find out all your enemies;
   your right hand will find out those who hate you.
[9] You will make them as a blazing oven
   when you appear.
The Lord will swallow them up in his wrath,
   and fire will consume them.
[10] You will destroy their descendants from the earth,
   and their offspring from among the children of man.
[11] Though they plan evil against you,
   though they devise mischief, they will not succeed.
[12] For you will put them to flight;
   you will aim at their faces with your bows.
[13] Be exalted, O Lord, in your strength!
   We will sing and praise your power.

Truth: This Psalm is speaking out about our future victories and how we can look forward and anticipate what God will do. We can rest assured and have confidence in our future that God will reign. God will be exalted. Those that may fight against the Lord, or even carry on any hostility passed to them from their parents, will not be successful.

Thought: Do you ever feel that the evil we are facing in our world today is overwhelming? Instead of passing on our Love for God and our fellow man, children today are being surrounded by hate and malice towards others. Rest easy, church, God is still on the throne. Instead, you be the one who exalts God and let your praise have a ripple effect to those around you.

Tune: He is exalted the King is exalted on high, I will praise Him
         He is exalted forever exalted, and I will praise His name

Dear Father: We are so relieved that you have our hope and our future in the palm of your hand. Lord, help me to put my hope and trust in you and have a heart full of praise that will help draw all those I encounter to You.

<u>Songs for Life – Day 40 – February 9</u>

Text: Psalm 22:1-8

My God, my God, why have you forsaken me?
  Why are you so far from saving me, from the words of my groaning?
[2] O my God, I cry by day, but you do not answer,
  and by night, but I find no rest.
[3] Yet you are holy, enthroned on the praises of Israel.
[4] In you our fathers trusted; they trusted, and you delivered them.
[5] To you they cried and were rescued;
  in you they trusted and were not put to shame.
[6] But I am a worm and not a man,
  scorned by mankind and despised by the people.
[7] All who see me mock me;
  they make mouths at me; they wag their heads;
[8] "He trusts in the Lord; let him deliver him;
  let him rescue him, for he delights in him!"

Truth: Though this is written quite some time before Christ comes in bodily form on earth, one cannot help but see the crucifixion story in this text. From the first phrase in verse 1, which Jesus quoted on the cross, to the vision of mocking in verse 7, the Psalmist is laying some groundwork for the coming of the Redeemer.

Thought: Throughout the Old Testament, we see Christ: the prophecy that He is to come, visions of His work, and the clear evidence of the need for Christ. From the beginning, God knew you would be born, knew you would need a Savior, and had the plan for your redemption. Awesome!

Tune: To God be the glory great things He has done
So loved He the world that He gave us His Son
Who yielded His life an atonement for sin
And opened the life gate that all may go in

God, I'm humbled to know that you had my plan of redemption planned out long before I was born. To God be the glory, great things You have done and continue to do!

Text: Psalm 22:9-15

9 Yet you are he who took me from the womb;
   you made me trust you at my mother's breasts.
10 On you was I cast from my birth,
   and from my mother's womb you have been my God.
11 Be not far from me, for trouble is near, and there is none to help.
12 Many bulls encompass me;
   strong bulls of Bashan surround me;
13 they open wide their mouths at me,
   like a ravening and roaring lion.
14 I am poured out like water, and all my bones are out of joint;
my heart is like wax; it is melted within my breast;
15 my strength is dried up like a potsherd,
   and my tongue sticks to my jaws; you lay me in the dust of death.

Truth: This passage reinforces for us the reality that nothing in our spiritual life is initiated by us. Everything is a response to something God has done in our lives, or an invitation He gives. It is He who took us from the womb and gave us the invitation to trust Him. Our responsibility is to respond in obedience and worship.

Thought: The Psalmist gives a vivid picture in verses 14-15 of one who is weak and dry, whose strength is gone. The only antidote for that is to seek the face of God. Confess your sin, seek His face, and wait. God will lead you through those dry times and pour water on your soul and spirit.

Tune: All who are thirsty, all who are weak
Come to the fountain, dip your heart in the stream of life
Let the pain and the sorrow, be washed away
In the waves of His mercy, as deep cries out to deep
(We sing) Come Lord Jesus come, come Lord Jesus come

Father, at times, I confess my spirit feels like the psalmist describes at the end of this passage. I feel dry, even distant from you. I don't like that feeling, Father. I need you to pour water on my dry and thirsty soul.

Songs for Life – Day 42– February 11

Text: Psalm 22:16-21

[16] For dogs encompass me; a company of evildoers encircles me;
they have pierced my hands and feet—
[17] I can count all my bones—they stare and gloat over me;
[18] they divide my garments among them,
   and for my clothing they cast lots.
[19] But you, O Lord, do not be far off!
   O you my help, come quickly to my aid!
[20] Deliver my soul from the sword,
   my precious life from the power of the dog!
[21]   Save me from the mouth of the lion!
You have rescued me from the horns of the wild oxen!

Truth: The psalmist feels that his pursuit of God is opposed on every side, that he has mockers and evildoers ready to cause him harm, like dogs, lions, and wild oxen. Yet, again we see a reference to the crucifixion in verses 16-18. A company of evildoers encircling Him, piercing His hands and feet, dividing His garments through the casting of lots . . .How amazing it is to see these details recorded by God through the author of the Psalm, hundreds of years before they occur. God has had a plan!

Thought: When we make the decision to deepen our walk with Christ, we can be sure of one thing . . . Satan is fully aware. He is prepared to bring opposition. Hold your ground, child of God. Satan can send the dogs, lions and oxen to oppose you, but he CANNOT remove God's hand from your life, nor can he do anything to you that God does not permit.

Tune: A mighty fortress is our God, a bulwark never failing
Our helper He amid the flood, of mortal ills prevailing
For still our ancient foe, doth seek to work us woe
His craft and pow'r are great, and armed with cruel hate
On earth is not his equal

Oh God . . . You are my mighty fortress. I want to walk confidently under the shelter of your fortress. Surround me with your hand of protection.

Text: Psalm 22:22-26

[22] I will tell of your name to my brothers;
   in the midst of the congregation I will praise you:
[23] You who fear the Lord, praise him!
   All you offspring of Jacob, glorify him,
   and stand in awe of him, all you offspring of Israel!
[24] For he has not despised or abhorred the affliction of the afflicted,
and he has not hidden his face from him,
   but has heard, when he cried to him.
[25] From you comes my praise in the great congregation;
   my vows I will perform before those who fear him.
[26] The afflicted shall eat and be satisfied;
   those who seek him shall praise the Lord! May your hearts live forever!

Truth: The psalmist is giving a "prefigure" of Christ in praising God for salvation. This is coming on the heels of passages where the psalmist was feeling Satan's attacks. Once the psalmist has expressed his fears, God has brought him joy and peace, as well as the confidence to say, "my vows I will perform before those who fear him". He is glad to give testimony of God's work in his life.

Thought: The spiritual life is a process and has processes within that process. We trust Christ and repent of our sins, yet we have to choose to deny self and follow Christ daily. When we have those times we feel stressed, depressed and oppressed. We can pour our hearts out to God and He gives us the peace that passes understanding. Stay until he does.

Tune: Thank You Lord for saving my soul
Thank You Lord for making me whole
Thank You Lord for giving to me
Thy great salvation so rich and free

Father, today I pour out my heart to you. You know all of my hurts and hesitations. I want to stay in Your presence and am counting on you to bring me peace and joy in the midst of my challenges.

Songs for Life – Day 44 – February 13

Text: Psalm 22:27-31

²⁷ All the ends of the earth shall remember and turn to the Lord,
and all the families of the nations shall worship before you.
²⁸ For kingship belongs to the Lord,
  and he rules over the nations.
²⁹ All the prosperous of the earth eat and worship;
  before him shall bow all who go down to the dust,
  even the one who could not keep himself alive.
³⁰ Posterity shall serve him;
  it shall be told of the Lord to the coming generation;
³¹ they shall come and proclaim his righteousness to a people yet unborn,
  that he has done it.

Truth: The promise that God gave to Abraham in Genesis 12:3 will be fulfilled as the message of Christ's resurrection spreads. We see this reflected in phrases like "all the ends of the earth shall remember", "all the families of the nations", and how he "rules over the nations".

Thought: Romans 14:11, "As I live, says the Lord, every knee shall bow to me, and every tongue shall confess to God", which this passage brings to mind, is actually a quote from the Old Testament, from the prophet Isaiah (45:23). The prime subject of Scripture is Jesus, from beginning to end - though He has no beginning or end. Let our knees bow in worship and our tongues confess today that Jesus is LORD!

Tune: He is Lord He is Lord
He is risen from the dead and He is Lord
Ev'ry knee shall bow, ev'ry tongue confess
That Jesus Christ is Lord

Father, today I will not wait until the end of this age to praise you and worship you. I look forward to the time that "every knee shall bow" and "every tongue shall confess" that You are Lord, but my journey has already begun, and I worship you today with all of my being. You are worthy!

Text: Psalm 23:1-6

The Lord is my shepherd; I shall not want.
2   He makes me lie down in green pastures.
He leads me beside still waters.
3   He restores my soul.
He leads me in paths of righteousness for his name's sake.
4 Even though I walk through the valley of the shadow of death,
   I will fear no evil,
for you are with me; your rod and your staff, they comfort me.
5 You prepare a table before me in the presence of my enemies;
you anoint my head with oil; my cup overflows.
6 Surely goodness and mercy shall follow me all the days of my life,
and I shall dwell in the house of the Lord forever.

Truth: This passage, often quoted at funerals, is very much appropriate for everyday life. It is a testimony by David to the Lord's faithfulness throughout his life. It pictures the Lord as David's, or any disciple's, Shepherd, his King and his Guide.

Thought: Whether we are really walking through the valley of the shadow of death, mourning the loss a loved one and living in the shadow of that loss, or whether we are in need of the Shepherd's work in our lives, this passage speaks of peace. It is surrender to God's leading to righteousness, which brings goodness and mercy. Do not fear, church.

Tune: Savior like a shepherd lead us, much we need thy tender care
In thy pleasant pastures feed us, for our use thy folds prepare
Blessed Jesus blessed Jesus
Thou hast bought us thine we are
Blessed Jesus blessed Jesus
Thou hast bought us thine we are

God, even though I walk through the valley of the shadow of death, I will fear no evil, for you are with me. I need to feel Your presence in my life today, God.

Songs for Life – Day 46 – February 15

Text: Psalm 24:1-6

The earth is the Lord's and the fullness thereof,
 the world and those who dwell therein,
[2] for he has founded it upon the seas
 and established it upon the rivers.
[3] Who shall ascend the hill of the Lord?
 And who shall stand in his holy place?
[4] He who has clean hands and a pure heart,
 who does not lift up his soul to what is false
 and does not swear deceitfully.
[5] He will receive blessing from the Lord
 and righteousness from the God of his salvation.
[6] Such is the generation of those who seek him,
 who seek the face of the God of Jacob. *Selah*

Truth: The focus here is that God IS the creator and owner of everything. We are not even our own. The priests are asking the questions of "who shall ascend the hill of the Lord"? The answer is, only those cleansed or made "clean" by the blood of Jesus. This Psalm speaks of those who have salvation, how they can be brought safely into Heaven, enabling them to see the ultimate, the face of God.

Thought: It's not hard to establish that God is the creator of the universe and all that is in it. God created the earth for us to live on, until the return of Christ. But to receive salvation, we must accept Christ as LORD to be cleansed by the blood of the Lamb. Just attending church worship services is not enough. Just doing good works will not be enough – it is about repenting from our sins and receiving Christ, period. Many who attend church will find themselves separated if they do not receive Christ.

Tune: I have decided, to follow Jesus, I have decided, to follow Jesus,
 I have decided, to follow Jesus, No turning back, no turning back.

Dear Father: Today, I make the decision to follow Jesus, and asking to be cleansed from sinful ways, so I can have intimate fellowship with you.

Text: Psalm 24:7-10

[7] Lift up your heads, O gates!
  And be lifted up, O ancient doors, that the King of glory may come in.
[8] Who is this King of glory?
  The Lord, strong and mighty,
  the Lord, mighty in battle!
[9] Lift up your heads, O gates!
  And lift them up, O ancient doors,
  that the King of glory may come in.
[10] Who is this King of glory?
  The Lord of hosts, he is the King of glory! *Selah*

Truth: The Ark of the Covenant was being brought into the gates of Jerusalem. In verse 7 the procession bearing the ark announces God's presence in the ark, seeking entry into his sanctuary. "Who is this King of glory?" is the reply, asking for further identification. The procession then says who the Lord is (The Lord, strong and mighty, the Lord mighty in battle!), and then repeats the request for entry. Again, the doorkeepers reply, asking for identification, and again the procession identifies the Lord.

Thought: In our lives today, you could easily make a parallel of the "gates" to the "door" of your heart. Revelation 3:20 says "Here I am! I stand at the door and knock. If anyone hears my voice and opens the door, I will come in and eat with him, and he with me." God is calling out to you, are you going to let Him enter your heart, let Him carry your daily struggles, and stop trying to manage life on your own? Surrender today.

Tune: Jesus is tenderly calling you home, calling today calling today
       Why from the sunshine of love will you roam
       Farther and farther away?

Father, You are the King of Glory, and the Lord of Lords. I wish to make you Lord of my life and I ask you to come into my heart. Forgive me where I fail you Lord and help me to live out my days for you.

Songs for Life – Day 48 – February 17

Text: Psalm 25:1-7

To you, O Lord, I lift up my soul.

[2] O my God, in you I trust; let me not be put to shame;
let not my enemies exult over me.

[3] Indeed, none who wait for you shall be put to shame;
they shall be ashamed who are wantonly treacherous.

[4] Make me to know your ways, O Lord; teach me your paths.

[5] Lead me in your truth and teach me,
for you are the God of my salvation;
for you I wait all the day long.

[6] Remember your mercy, O Lord, and your steadfast love,
for they have been from of old.

[7] Remember not the sins of my youth or my transgressions;
according to your steadfast love remember me,
for the sake of your goodness, O Lord!

Truth: In times of trial, our prayers can be more direct and personal. For the Psalmist (in this case, David) he understands that the key to being free from shame is to be right with God. He is asking for God to reveal Truth, to teach him His ways and paths, asking for His mercy and love, and most importantly, forgiveness of sins.

Thought: Perhaps one of the most challenging areas of the spiritual life for the Christian is to do some self-examination. We get so accustomed to our everyday living that sometimes our sinful acts and habits can get overlooked. David understood the need for repentance and cleansing.

Tune: O to grace how great a debtor, daily I'm constrained to be
Let Thy grace Lord like a fetter; bind my wand 'ring heart to Thee
Prone to wander Lord I feel it, prone to leave the God I love
Here's my heart Lord take and seal it, seal it for Thy courts above

Oh God, search my heart and reveal to me any ways or patterns in my heart that are not pleasing in your sight. I want to be clean before you so that I can be totally filled by the power of your Holy Spirit, God.

Songs for Life – Day 49 – February 18

Text: Psalm 25:8-15

[8] Good and upright is the Lord; therefore he instructs sinners in the way.
[9] He leads the humble in what is right,
    and teaches the humble his way.
[10] All the paths of the Lord are steadfast love and faithfulness,
    for those who keep his covenant and his testimonies.
[11] For your name's sake, O Lord, pardon my guilt, for it is great.
[12] Who is the man who fears the Lord?
    Him will he instruct in the way that he should choose.
[13] His soul shall abide in well-being,
    and his offspring shall inherit the land.
[14] The friendship of the Lord is for those who fear him,
    and he makes known to them his covenant.
[15] My eyes are ever toward the Lord,
    for he will pluck my feet out of the net.

Truth: No man is too far from the hand of Almighty God that He could not or would not seek to draw him into a right relationship. That goes for the unrepentant sinner who has never trusted Christ, or the Child of God who has wandered from the truth. Even David, as a man "after God's own heart" had to seek God for daily living with earnestness and humility.

Thought: What is the key to this right relationship with God? He makes it clear in verse 14 that relationship is His goal. "The friendship of the Lord is for those who fear him". A friend trusts his friend, a friend loves unconditionally, a friend shares, and a friend is stronger for doing so.

Tune: Praise to the Lord the Almighty the King of creation
O my soul praise Him, for He is thy health and salvation
All ye who hear now to His temple draw near
Praise Him in glad adoration

Father, I can only come to you because you have already loved me enough to draw me into a relationship with You. Father, I cannot get over your love for me, and I don't want to ever get over it.

Songs for Life – Day 50 – February 19

Text: Psalm 25:16-22

[16] Turn to me and be gracious to me, for I am lonely and afflicted.

[17] The troubles of my heart are enlarged;
  bring me out of my distresses.

[18] Consider my affliction and my trouble, and forgive all my sins.

[19] Consider how many are my foes,
  and with what violent hatred they hate me.

[20] Oh, guard my soul, and deliver me!
  Let me not be put to shame, for I take refuge in you.

[21] May integrity and uprightness preserve me, for I wait for you.

[22] Redeem Israel, O God, out of all his troubles.

Truth: The Psalmist is feeling the weight of his troubles and trials. He feels lonely, afflicted, his heart is troubled, and he feels vulnerable. David takes the right approach in understanding his current state. He is ripe for an attack by Satan. He asks God, not only for His protection, but His wisdom to make right decisions and live a righteous life.

Thought: It is never a wrong time to do the right thing or to live the right way. Understanding our spiritual vulnerability is often hard when we've been hurt, or we feel distant from God. Cry out to God! He hears His children like the mother hears her crying child. He runs to our aid.

Tune: In Christ alone, my hope is found
He is my light my strength my song
This Cornerstone this solid Ground
Firm through the fiercest drought and storm
What heights of love what depths of peace
When fears are stilled when strivings cease
My Comforter my All in All
Here in the love of Christ I stand

Holy Father, my only real hope is in Christ alone. You allowed Your Son to pay the price for my sins, to feel the weight of my sin. I know you love me. Today I cry out to you. Hear my heart, oh God.

Text: Psalm 26:1-7

Vindicate me, O Lord, for I have walked in my integrity,
  and I have trusted in the Lord without wavering.
[2] Prove me, O Lord, and try me;
  test my heart and my mind.
[3] For your steadfast love is before my eyes,
  and I walk in your faithfulness.
[4] I do not sit with men of falsehood,
  nor do I consort with hypocrites.
[5] I hate the assembly of evildoers,
  and I will not sit with the wicked.
[6] I wash my hands in innocence
  and go around your altar, O Lord,
[7] proclaiming thanksgiving aloud, and telling all your wondrous deeds.

Truth: No one can judge the spiritual condition of man but God alone. The only measure of integrity, the only measure of trusting in The Lord, the only measure of the condition of my heart and mind, the only measure of my faithfulness – these rest with God and God alone.

Thought: The world will give us various ideas of what is "living a good life." The trouble is, those ideas are based upon what the world looks at as acceptable, and not on striving for holiness. The only measure of "living a good life," truthfully, is striving for holiness, period!

Tune: This is the air I breathe. This is the air I breathe
Your holy presence living in me
This is my daily bread. This is my daily bread
Your very word spoken to me
And I I'm desperate for You, and I I'm lost without You

God, forgive me for looking at the world's evaluation of what is good and bad and being guilty of lowering the standards you have placed on my life for righteous living. Let Your Spirit and Your Word dwell within me freely.

Songs for Life – Day 52 – February 21

Text: Psalm 26:8-12

[8] O Lord, I love the habitation of your house
   and the place where your glory dwells.
[9] Do not sweep my soul away with sinners,
   nor my life with bloodthirsty men,
[10] in whose hands are evil devices,
   and whose right hands are full of bribes.
[11] But as for me, I shall walk in my integrity;
   redeem me, and be gracious to me.
[12] My foot stands on level ground;
   in the great assembly I will bless the Lord.

Truth: The psalmist is professing a love for the House of The Lord, His temple, His sanctuary – in other words, His Church. The Church serves as a place of refuge and protection, a source of instruction and guidance, the place where we can confidently approach the throne with other believers.

Thought: If I want to really build fellowship with someone, I have to spend time with them. If I want to spend time with them, I have to see them face-to-face. Phone calls, text messages, snap chats and e-mails are wonderful, but there is no substitute for face-to-face conversation. Such is the case with God's House. If you are going to fellowship with Him, go to where He is, where He has instructed us to go, to His house.

Tune: We have come into His house
And gathered in His name, to worship Him
We have come into His house
And gathered in His name to worship Him
We have come into His house
And gathered in His name to worship Christ the Lord
Worship Him Christ the Lord

Father, you gave Your Son for Your Church. Jesus loved the Church so much that He died for it. Help me to be faithful to be a part of Your church, both in worship and in service.

Text: Psalm 27:1-6

The Lord is my light and my salvation; whom shall I fear?
The Lord is the stronghold of my life; of whom shall I be afraid?
[2] When evildoers assail me to eat up my flesh,
my adversaries and foes, it is they who stumble and fall.
[3] Though an army encamp against me, my heart shall not fear;
though war arise against me, yet I will be confident.
[4] One thing have I asked of the Lord, that will I seek after:
that I may dwell in the house of the Lord all the days of my life,
to gaze upon the beauty of the Lord and to inquire in his temple.
[5] For he will hide me in his shelter in the day of trouble;
he will conceal me under the cover of his tent;
    he will lift me high upon a rock.
[6] And now my head shall be lifted up above my enemies all around me,
and I will offer in his tent sacrifices with shouts of joy;
I will sing and make melody to the Lord.

Truth: When the psalmist is attacked by enemies, he confidently knows that he is divinely protected by the Lord, who is the light, in contrast to the darkness of condemnation. There is no need for him to fear.

Thought: As believers, we must be faithful to and put our confidence in the Lord to help us in times of trouble. We will face trials, temptations and daily struggles, but we don't have to be afraid, or in darkness. We have God, who is THE LIGHT to offer us protection and shelter. Praise Him!

Tune: He hideth my soul in the cleft of the rock
That shadows a dry thirsty land
He hideth my life with the depths of His love
And covers me there with His hand
And covers me there with His hand

Dear Heavenly Father: Today, I just wish to delight myself in you, Lord, and the freedom and privilege we have to seek you and your shelter.

Songs for Life – Day 54 – February 23

Text: Psalm 27:7-14

[7] Hear, O Lord, when I cry aloud; be gracious to me and answer me!

[8] You have said, "Seek my face."

My heart says to you, "Your face, Lord, do I seek."

[9] Hide not your face from me.

Turn not your servant away in anger, O you who have been my help.

Cast me not off; forsake me not, O God of my salvation!

[10] For my father and my mother have forsaken me,

but the Lord will take me in.

[11] Teach me your way, O Lord, and lead me on a level path

because of my enemies.

[12] Give me not up to the will of my adversaries;

for false witnesses have risen against me,

and they breathe out violence.

[13] I believe that I shall look upon the goodness of the Lord

in the land of the living!

[14] Wait for the Lord; be strong, and let your heart take courage; wait for the Lord!

Truth: The prayer is for God's deliverance. The Psalmist is asking God to deliver and protect him from his enemies and to not forget about him, like even one's own family can sometimes. "Wait for the LORD" - while we are waiting on God to move, we still encourage others.

Thought: The word of the Lord is useless to us, if we don't accept it, obey it, believe it, AND believe that God will do what he says and that will be there for you, even when others leave you. You can count on the Lord for direction and protection. Remain strong and steadfast in your daily walk.

Tune: It is the cry of my heart to follow You

It is the cry of my heart to be close to You

It is the cry of my heart to follow - All of the days of my life

Dear Lord: I pray for your Word to penetrate my heart. Thank you, Father, for always being the one I can count on, no matter what.

Songs for Life – Day 55 – February 24

Text: Psalm 28:1-9

To you, O Lord, I call; my rock, be not deaf to me,

lest, if you be silent to me, I become like those who go down to the pit.

[2] Hear the voice of my pleas for mercy, when I cry to you for help,

when I lift up my hands toward your most holy sanctuary.

[3] Do not drag me off with the wicked, with the workers of evil,

who speak peace with their neighbors while evil is in their hearts.

[4] Give to them according to their work

and according to the evil of their deeds;

give to them according to the work of their hands;

render them their due reward.

[5] Because they do not regard the works of the Lord

or the work of his hands,

he will tear them down and build them up no more.

[6] Blessed be the Lord! For he has heard the voice of my pleas for mercy.

[7] The Lord is my strength and my shield;

in him my heart trusts, and I am helped;

my heart exults, and with my song I give thanks to him.

[8] The Lord is the strength of his people;

he is the saving refuge of his anointed.

[9] Oh, save your people and bless your heritage!

Be their shepherd and carry them forever.

Truth: There is no promise that tells us we will be free from struggles and trials. What God does promise is He will, if we will give Him control, be our strength to fight the battle and our shield of protection.

Thought: Fighting the battle gets us weary at times. We start asking "what did I do to deserve this?", or "why are they getting blessed and not me?" He is the saving refuge of his anointed! YOU are His anointed. Rejoice!

Tune: God is so good, God is so good
God is so good; He's so good to me

God, please be my saving refuge and shield today.

Songs for Life – Day 56 – February 25

Text: Psalm 29:1-6

Ascribe to the Lord, O heavenly beings,
  ascribe to the Lord glory and strength.
² Ascribe to the Lord the glory due his name;
  worship the Lord in the splendor of holiness.
³ The voice of the Lord is over the waters;
  the God of glory thunders, the Lord, over many waters.
⁴ The voice of the Lord is powerful;
  the voice of the Lord is full of majesty.
⁵ The voice of the Lord breaks the cedars;
  the Lord breaks the cedars of Lebanon.
⁶ He makes Lebanon to skip like a calf,
  and Sirion like a young wild ox.

Truth: Sometimes it is good just to be reminded of the Supremacy of God and of His mighty hand over the things and entities of this world. In this Psalm, we see that God is Supreme over Heavenly beings, over the forces of nature, and over humanity. God is God!

Thought: The majesty and glory of God Almighty is something that can be pondered but not truly understood. It can be pursued but never fully attained. Lest we get discouraged in this world, God has the final say. He has the final say in creation, in the world, and in your life.

Tune: Shout to the Lord all the earth let us sing
Power and majesty, Praise to the King
Mountains bow down and the seas will roar
At the sound of Your name
I sing for joy, at the work of Your hands
Forever I'll love You, forever I'll stand
Nothing compares to the promise I have in You

Father, your majesty and glory are beyond true comprehension, but I see Your handiwork in creation and in my life. Blessed be the name of Almighty God! Glory to the King of King and Lord of Lords.

Songs for Life – Day 57 – February 26

Text: Psalm 29:7-11

[7] The voice of the Lord flashes forth flames of fire.

[8] The voice of the Lord shakes the wilderness;
   the Lord shakes the wilderness of Kadesh.

[9] The voice of the Lord makes the deer give birth
   and strips the forests bare,
   and in his temple all cry, "Glory!"

[10] The Lord sits enthroned over the flood;
   the Lord sits enthroned as king forever.

[11] May the Lord give strength to his people!
   May the Lord bless his people with peace!

Truth: The voice of God is so powerful that He literally spoke creation into existence, piece by piece. His voice gave Moses the instruction in the burning bush. His voice called Saul to salvation on the Damascus road. It is His voice that tells the demons to flee. Whether it is the audible voice, the written Word, or the subtle nudge of the Holy Spirit, it is His voice that wields the most power and authority. It is also the voice of comfort for the hurting soul.

Thought: The worthy response to the voice of God in our lives is like that of those in the temple, described in verse 9. We cry "Glory!" We shout out the praise, whether we are by ourselves, in community, or in worship with fellow believers.

Tune: Can you hear it, the gentle voice of the Spirit
There's no reason to fear it
He's calling you to life - Just surrender
Run into the arms of the Father
The night is finally over
Take a step into the light

God, your voice is mighty and majestic. I want my voice to respond to your glory in a way that glorifies you, not only when it is just you and I, but when I'm with others in worship and in community. Empower me, God!

Songs for Life – Day 58 – February 27

Text: Psalm 30:1-7

I will extol you, O Lord, for you have drawn me up
 and have not let my foes rejoice over me.
² O Lord my God, I cried to you for help,
 and you have healed me.
³ O Lord, you have brought up my soul from Sheol;
 you restored me to life from among those who go down to the pit.
⁴ Sing praises to the Lord, O you his saints,
 and give thanks to his holy name.
⁵ For his anger is but for a moment,
 and his favor is for a lifetime.
Weeping may tarry for the night,
 but joy comes with the morning.
⁶ As for me, I said in my prosperity,
 "I shall never be moved."
⁷ By your favor, O Lord, you made my mountain stand strong;
you hid your face; I was dismayed.

Truth: David is thanking God for his deliverance from his enemies, for being an answered prayer in his life circumstances and for rescuing him from impending death. David realized he had been arrogant, because it was easy to trust in himself during the good times after so many victories.

Thought: Have you ever been like David, trusting in yourself and being somewhat arrogant during your good and prosperous times? Only God can offer us eternal salvation through his son, Jesus. Only God can save us from the enemy in our daily struggles and give us that peaceful joy.

Tune: And you stay the same through the ages, your love never changes,
There may be pain in the night, but joy comes in the morning,
And when the ocean rage, I don't have to be afraid,
Because I know that you love me.

Father, forgive me for my arrogant attitude. I know you are the deliverer of my enemies, my circumstances and my soul. I humble myself to you.

<u>Songs for Life – Day 59 – February 28</u>

Text: Psalm 30:8-12

[8] To you, O Lord, I cry,
   and to the Lord I plead for mercy:
[9] "What profit is there in my death,
   if I go down to the pit?
Will the dust praise you?
   Will it tell of your faithfulness?
[10] Hear, O Lord, and be merciful to me!
   O Lord, be my helper!"
[11] You have turned for me my mourning into dancing;
   you have loosed my sackcloth
   and clothed me with gladness,
[12] that my glory may sing your praise and not be silent.
   O Lord my God, I will give thanks to you forever!

Truth: In this Psalm, David had been in some dire circumstances and was praying and pleading to God, to extend his life. He wanted to share with others about God's faithfulness and to continue to give God all his praise.

Thought: Every day that we wake up is another day God has granted to us. Are we being faithful to spread the Good News and share with others all the wonderful blessings that God has so graciously given to us? Continue to give God credit for the things in your life, and share it with someone, today.

Tune: This is the day; this is the day
That the Lord hath made; that the Lord hath made
We will rejoice; we will rejoice
And be glad in it; And be glad in it

Father, I am so blessed to have your goodness and glory revealed to me daily. Please don't let me be silent but give me the strength and courage to sing your praises and share with those around me, so they too may praise your Holy Name.

Songs for Life – Day 60 – March 1

Text: Psalm 31:1-8

[1] Lord, I seek refuge in you; let me never be disgraced.
Save me by your righteousness.
[2] Listen closely to me; rescue me quickly.
Be a rock of refuge for me, a mountain fortress to save me.
[3] For you are my rock and my fortress;
you lead and guide me for your name's sake.
[4] You will free me from the net that is secretly set for me,
for you are my refuge.
[5] Into your hand I entrust my spirit;
you have redeemed me, Lord, God of truth.
[6] I hate those who are devoted to worthless idols, but I trust in the Lord.
[7] I will rejoice and be glad in your faithful love
because you have seen my affliction. You know the troubles of my soul
[8] and have not handed me over to the enemy.
You have set my feet in a spacious place.

Truth: David faced opposition regularly. David is calling on God to be his rock, refuge and fortress - a sure foundation, a place to hide and a place of protection. He acknowledges that God IS that rock, refuge and fortress. He can trust Him because He has been able to trust Him in the past.

Thought: Verse 5 is a very familiar statement from the last words of Christ on the cross, "Into your hand I entrust my spirit". It was at that moment of greatest vulnerability that Christ performed the greatest act in history. Sometimes it is at our greatest vulnerability that we find our greatest yielding. This is where God has the greatest freedom to work.

Tune: Praise the name of Jesus, praise the name of Jesus
He's my Rock, He's my Fortress,
He's my Deliverer, in Him will I trust
Praise the name of Jesus

Father, There has never been a time when you have not been faithful and true. I trust my spirit into Your hand.

Text: Psalm 31:9-13

⁹ Be gracious to me, Lord, because I am in distress;
my eyes are worn out from frustration—my whole being as well.
¹⁰ Indeed, my life is consumed with grief and my years with groaning;
my strength has failed because of my iniquity,
and my bones waste away.
¹¹ I am ridiculed by all my adversaries and even by my neighbors.
I am dreaded by my acquaintances;
those who see me in the street run from me.
¹² I am forgotten: gone from memory
like a dead person—like broken pottery.
¹³ I have heard the gossip of many; terror is on every side.
When they conspired against me, they plotted to take my life.

Truth: Perhaps the greatest toll on the individual going through troubles and trials happens beyond what others can see. The stress, the sadness, the grief, the uneasiness of spirit - these take a greater toll than the external stresses. Someone can look like they have it all together on the outside yet be torn up on the inside.

Thought: Do you ever feel alone, yet there are people all around? Does the noise in your head sometimes drown out the sounds of work and play around you? You can cry out like David did. "Be gracious to me Lord, because I am in distress". God always hears the cries of His children.

Tune: Why should I feel discouraged? Why should the shadows come?
Why should my heart be lonely, and long for heaven and home
When Jesus is my portion my constant friend is He
His eye is on the sparrow and I know He watches me
His eye is on the sparrow and I know He watches me

O Lord, be gracious to me. . . In times of distress as well as times of celebration, I need your grace. Lord, it is Your grace that enables me to take another breath, to walk another step. Cover me in Your grace, Lord.

Text: Psalm 31:14-20

[14] But I trust in you, Lord; I say, "You are my God."
[15] The course of my life is in your power;
rescue me from the power of my enemies and from my persecutors.
[16] Make your face shine on your servant;
save me by your faithful love.
[17] Lord, do not let me be disgraced when I call on you.
Let the wicked be disgraced; let them be quiet in Sheol.
[18] Let lying lips that arrogantly speak against the righteous
in proud contempt be silenced.
[19] How great is your goodness
that you have stored up for those who fear you
and accomplished in the sight of everyone
for those who take refuge in you.
[20] You hide them in the protection of your presence;
you conceal them in a shelter from human schemes,
from quarrelsome tongues.

Truth: "The course of my life is in your power" . . . What does that mean? David is saying his trust is fully in the Lord in the midst of his distress. He can count on God because God has never failed him in the past, and because God has promised to provide for and protect His children.

Thought: "The course of my life is in your power" . . . Why not now, Lord? Where are you, God? David reminds us that since we are God's children, we are no longer to evaluate success or failure based on our timetable. God's timing is perfect. We trust, and we wait.

Tune: Jesus, Jesus, how I trust Him
How I've proved Him o'er and o'er
Jesus, Jesus, precious Jesus
O for grace to trust Him more

Lord, You are the creator of time and You are the creator of me. Help me to rest in the knowledge that Your timing and Your ways are always best.

Text: Psalm 31:21-24

21 Blessed be the Lord,
for he has wondrously shown his faithful love to me
in a city under siege.
22 In my alarm I said,
"I am cut off from your sight."
But you heard the sound of my pleading
when I cried to you for help.
23 Love the Lord, all his faithful ones.
The Lord protects the loyal,
but fully repays the arrogant.
24 Be strong, and let your heart be courageous,
all you who put your hope in the Lord.

Truth: The phrase "love the Lord" appears a number of times in Scripture. It is love that enables us to trust God. It is love that enables us to receive redemption. Love is a response. Love is an action. It involves an intensity of emotion, thought and action. All of our experiences with God depend on our response to the command to "love the Lord".

Thought: Some of us struggle to really love the Lord intimately. For some, it is because our earthly examples of love have fallen short of the Biblical example. God's love is unconditional. It never stops. God extends love to us perpetually, which only asks for a response from Him to love Him back. It is in that love relationship that we experience God fully.

Tune: I love You Lord, and I lift my voice
To worship You, O my soul rejoice
Take joy my King in what You hear
May it be a sweet, sweet sound in Your ear

I love You, God! I know I say that many times, but I really do. My actions don't always reflect it, my heart sometimes contradicts it, but I really do love You! Help me live in such a way that I respond to the love that You have given me in a way that gives You my whole heart.

Songs for Life – Day 64 - March 5

Text: Psalm 32:1-5

[1] How joyful is the one whose transgression is forgiven,
whose sin is covered!
[2] How joyful is a person whom the Lord does not charge with iniquity
and in whose spirit is no deceit!
[3] When I kept silent, my bones became brittle
from my groaning all day long.
[4] For day and night your hand was heavy on me;
my strength was drained as in the summer's heat.
[5] Then I acknowledged my sin to you and did not conceal my iniquity.
I said, "I will confess my transgressions to the Lord,"
and you forgave the guilt of my sin.

Truth: David is writing this Psalm as if someone is asking him, "David, who is blessed by God?" David's answer is clear, "the one whose transgression is forgiven, whose sin is covered!" Verse 5 teaches us the process to go through in order to reach this blessed state: acknowledge our sin to God, confess and repent of it, and God will forgive.

Thought: In the middle verses of this passage, David describes what happens to us when we do not "come clean" with the Lord about what He already knows about us, our sin. David said his "bones became brittle", he groaned "all day long", he felt the heavy hand of God upon him, and his strength was gone. Sin tears us up from the inside out. Freedom does not come without a price, but the price we pay is nothing compared to what Jesus paid for our sin.

Tune: Out of my bondage sorrow and night, Jesus I come, Jesus I come
Into Thy freedom gladness and light, Jesus I come to Thee
Out of my sickness into Thy health, Out of my want and into Thy wealth
Out of my sin and into Thyself, Jesus I come to Thee

Father, I want nothing to stand between You and me. I want no sin, no barriers, no shame, to keep me from experiencing the fullness of your love and grace.

Songs for Life – Day 65 - March 6

Text: Psalm 32:6-11

[6] Therefore let everyone who is faithful pray to you immediately.
When great floodwaters come, they will not reach him.
[7] You are my hiding place; you protect me from trouble.
You surround me with joyful shouts of deliverance.
[8] I will instruct you and show you the way to go;
with my eye on you, I will give counsel.
[9] Do not be like a horse or mule, without understanding,
that must be controlled with bit and bridle
or else it will not come near you.
[10] Many pains come to the wicked,
but the one who trusts in the Lord will have faithful love surrounding him.
[11] Be glad in the Lord and rejoice, you righteous ones;
shout for joy, all you upright in heart.

Truth: Those who know the Lord and bring their sin, their trial, their tribulation, to the Lord will find Him to be a "hiding place". In that hiding place is a shelter from the storm, a protection from trouble, and the voice of His deliverance. In that shelter, the child of God who brings a true heart of confession will find steadfast love, gladness, rejoicing, and joy!

Thought: Sometimes our tendency, when we've been hurt or have found ourselves in a bad place we know we had a part in creating, is to retreat, recoil or resign. When we do that, we allow the pain to last longer, the healing to seem impossible, and we push God away. Acknowledging our true heart allows us to find that "hiding place", to experience that surrounding love from the gracious Father.

Tune: You are my hiding place
You always fill my heart with songs of deliverance, whenever I am afraid
I will trust in You, I will trust in You
Let the weak say I am strong in the strength of the Lord

Father, trust is sometimes hard for me. I know Your Word is true and I can trust it. Help me to trust YOU today all the way to the depths of my heart.

Songs for Life – Day 66 - March 7

Text: Psalm 33:1-12

[1] Rejoice in the Lord, you righteous ones;
praise from the upright is beautiful.
[2] Praise the Lord with the lyre; make music to him with a ten-stringed harp.
[3] Sing a new song to him; play skillfully on the strings, with a joyful shout.
[4] For the word of the Lord is right, and all his work is trustworthy.
[5] He loves righteousness and justice;
the earth is full of the Lord's unfailing love.
[6] The heavens were made by the word of the Lord,
and all the stars, by the breath of his mouth.
[7] He gathers the water of the sea into a heap;
he puts the depths into storehouses.
[8] Let the whole earth fear the Lord;
let all the inhabitants of the world stand in awe of him.
[9] For he spoke, and it came into being;
he commanded, and it came into existence.
[10] The Lord frustrates the counsel of the nations;
he thwarts the plans of the peoples.
[11] The counsel of the Lord stands forever,
the plans of his heart from generation to generation.
[12] Happy is the nation whose God is the Lord—
the people he has chosen to be his own possession!

Truth: We, the people of God, are called to praise him, and He gives us new reasons each day to sing songs of praise. God, who spoke the world into existence, rules it with His goodness, order and dependability.

Thought: Do you look for ways to praise God each day? Do you ever think about the fact that He created the world and everything in it and that He WILL rule over it forever and ever? He's worthy of all of our praise.

Tune: Sing unto the Lord a new song, Sing unto the Lord all the Earth, Sing unto the Lord a new song, Sing unto the Lord all the Earth.

Prayer: Father, today, create in me a new song to sing praises unto you.

Songs for Life – Day 67 - March 8

Text: Psalm 33:13-22

13 The Lord looks down from heaven;
he observes everyone.
14 He gazes on all the inhabitants of the earth
from his dwelling place.
15 He forms the hearts of them all;
he considers all their works.
16 A king is not saved by a large army;
a warrior will not be rescued by great strength.
17 The horse is a false hope for safety;
it provides no escape by its great power.
18 But look, the Lord keeps his eye on those who fear him—
those who depend on his faithful love
19 to rescue them from death
and to keep them alive in famine.
20 We wait for the Lord;
he is our help and shield.
21 For our hearts rejoice in him
because we trust in his holy name.
22 May your faithful love rest on us, Lord,
for we put our hope in you.

Truth: God's gaze sees all. He reigns over all the Earth, but He's never far away. Instead, He is observing everything, and His eye is on those of us who have put our hope and trust in Him. Rejoice in the Lord today.

Thought: Sometimes we forget just how close and personal God is to us. We think He's far away and just watching from a distance. But He is alive in us and there for each of us if we will just trust Him. Will you?

Tune: My Life is in YOU Lord, My Strength is in YOU Lord, My Hope is in YOU Lord, In YOU, It's in YOU, It's in YOU...

Prayer: Father, I know you are with me, Your Word tells me so. Please strengthen my trust and faith, and be upon me, as my hope is in you.

Songs for Life – Day 68 - March 9

Text: Psalm 34:1-10

[1] I will bless the Lord at all times; his praise will always be on my lips.

[2] I will boast in the Lord; the humble will hear and be glad.

[3] Proclaim the Lord's greatness with me; let us exalt his name together.

[4] I sought the Lord, and he answered me
and rescued me from all my fears.

[5] Those who look to him are radiant with joy;
their faces will never be ashamed.

[6] This poor man cried, and the Lord heard him
and saved him from all his troubles.

[7] The angel of the Lord encamps
around those who fear him, and rescues them.

[8] Taste and see that the Lord is good.
How happy is the person who takes refuge in him!

[9] You who are his holy ones, fear the Lord,
for those who fear him lack nothing.

[10] Young lions lack food and go hungry, but those who seek the Lord
will not lack any good thing.

Truth: David is giving this Psalm as a testimony. He has found the grace of God from the depths of his soul and desires to let praises continually come from his mouth. His testimony encourages the saints to look to God, for they will be "radiant" and their faces "shall never be ashamed".

Thought: "Oh, taste and see that the Lord is good!" Something that we desire to eat is not only something that looks good on the plate; it is something that tastes good when we take a bite. "Taste and see that the Lord is good" today.

Tune: O magnify, O magnify the Lord with me
And let us exalt His name together
O magnify the Lord, O magnify the Lord
And may His name be lifted high forever

Lord, I magnify Your name, I exalt You, I have tasted, and You are good!

<u>Songs for Life – Day 69 - March 10</u>

Text: Psalm 34:11-22

[11] Come, children, listen to me; I will teach you the fear of the Lord.

[12] Who is someone who desires life,
loving a long life to enjoy what is good?

[13] Keep your tongue from evil and your lips from deceitful speech.

[14] Turn away from evil and do what is good; seek peace and pursue it.

[15] The eyes of the Lord are on the righteous,
and his ears are open to their cry for help.

[16] The face of the Lord is set against those who do what is evil,
to remove all memory of them from the earth.

[17] The righteous cry out, and the Lord hears,
and rescues them from all their troubles.

[18] The Lord is near the brokenhearted; he saves those crushed in spirit.

[19] One who is righteous has many adversities,
but the Lord rescues him from them all.

[20] He protects all his bones; not one of them is broken.

[21] Evil brings death to the wicked,
and those who hate the righteous will be punished.

[22] The Lord redeems the life of his servants,
and all who take refuge in him will not be punished.

Truth: The troubles and trials in the life of the Christian have purpose. God uses them to refine us, but not destroy us.

Thought: There is never a right time for man to seek vengeance or take from God what is only in His power to do.

Tune: There is Love that came for us, Humbled to a sinner's cross
You broke my shame and sinfulness, You rose again victorious
You are stronger, You are stronger, Sin is broken, You have saved me
It is written, Christ is risen, Jesus You are Lord of all

Father, I see your blessings and enjoy them, but it seems sometimes the trials around them come more frequent and the hills are taller. But Father, I know You are stronger!

Text: Psalm 35:1-14

[1] Oppose my opponents, Lord; fight those who fight me.

[2] Take your shields—large and small—and come to my aid.

[3] Draw the spear and javelin against my pursuers,
and assure me: "I am your deliverance."

[4] Let those who intend to take my life be disgraced and humiliated;
let those who plan to harm me be turned back and ashamed.

[5] Let them be like chaff in the wind,
with the angel of the Lord driving them away.

[6] Let their way be dark and slippery,
with the angel of the Lord pursuing them.

[7] They hid their net for me without cause;
they dug a pit for me without cause.

[8] Let ruin come on him unexpectedly,
and let the net that he hid ensnare him; let him fall into it—to his ruin.

[9] Then I will rejoice in the Lord; I will delight in his deliverance.

[10] All my bones will say, "Lord, who is like you,
rescuing the poor from one too strong for him,
the poor or the needy from one who robs him?"

[11] Malicious witnesses come forward;
they question me about things I do not know.

[12] They repay me evil for good, making me desolate.

[13] Yet when they were sick, my clothing was sackcloth;
I humbled myself with fasting, and my prayer was genuine.

[14] I went about mourning as if for my friend or brother;
I was bowed down with grief, like one mourning for a mother.

Truth: In the midst of intense difficulty, David realizes his hope is totally in The Lord. His responsibility is simply to follow and obey. God will protect.

Thought: He alone is able to deliver. He alone is able to save.

Tune: Savior, He can move the mountains
My God is mighty to save, He is mighty to save
Forever, Author of salvation
He rose and conquered the grave, Jesus conquered the grave

Oh God, You alone are mighty to save. Thank You for including me.

Songs for Life – Day 71 - March 12

Text: Psalm 35:15-28

[15] But when I stumbled, they gathered in glee; they gathered against me.
Assailants I did not know tore at me and did not stop.

[16] With godless mockery they gnashed their teeth at me.

[17] Lord, how long will you look on? Rescue me from their ravages;
rescue my precious life from the young lions.

[18] I will praise you in the great assembly;
I will exalt you among many people.

[19] Do not let my deceitful enemies rejoice over me;
do not let those who hate me without cause wink at me maliciously.

[20] For they do not speak in friendly ways, but contrive fraudulent schemes
against those who live peacefully in the land.

[21] They open their mouths wide against me and say,"Aha, aha! We saw it!"

[22] You saw it, Lord; do not be silent. Lord, do not be far from me.

[23] Wake up and rise to my defense, to my cause, my God and my Lord!

[24] Vindicate me, Lord my God, in keeping with your righteousness,
and do not let them rejoice over me.

[25] Do not let them say in their hearts, "Aha! Just what we wanted."
Do not let them say, "We have swallowed him up!"

[26] Let those who rejoice at my misfortune be disgraced and humiliated;
let those who exalt themselves over me
be clothed with shame and reproach.

[27] Let those who want my vindication shout for joy and be glad;
let them continually say, "The Lord be exalted.
He takes pleasure in his servant's well-being."

[28] And my tongue will proclaim your righteousness,
your praise all day long.

Truth: David pledges to share his victory with the congregation.

Thought: Focus on the relationship, not the circumstance.

Tune: I'm trading my sorrows, I'm trading my shame
I'm laying them down for the joy of the Lord
I'm trading my sickness, I'm trading my pain,
I'm laying them down for the joy of the Lord

Father, You are the joy of my salvation. You are the port in the storm.

Songs for Life – Day 72 - March 13

Text: Psalm 36:1-6

[1] An oracle within my heart
concerning the transgression of the wicked person:
Dread of God has no effect on him.
[2] For with his flattering opinion of himself,
he does not discover and hate his iniquity.
[3] The words from his mouth are malicious and deceptive;
he has stopped acting wisely and doing good.
[4] Even on his bed he makes malicious plans.
He sets himself on a path that is not good, and he does not reject evil.
[5] Lord, your faithful love reaches to heaven,
your faithfulness to the clouds.
[6] Your righteousness is like the highest mountains,
your judgments like the deepest sea.
Lord, you preserve people and animals.

Truth: Wickedness and evil will speak to those who have no fear of God or His goodness. They end up being self absorbed and accountable to no one. They allow evil to dwell within themselves, pushing love away.

Thought: God's word tells us that we should meditate day and night, thus giving the evil thoughts and wickedness no place to dwell in our hearts and minds. We can't outrun God's righteousness or His judgments, for His love is boundless.

Tune: Your love O Lord, reaches to the heavens
Your faithfulness, stretches to the sky
Your righteousness,
Is like the mighty mountains
Your justice flows,
Like the ocean's tide

Father, I know my nature is sinful, and only by your saving grace are my sins covered through the blood of Jesus. Please remind me daily, to meditate on your word and allow your goodness and mercy to dwell in me.

Text: Psalm 36:7-12

[7] How priceless your faithful love is, God!
People take refuge in the shadow of your wings.
[8] They are filled from the abundance of your house.
You let them drink from your refreshing stream.
[9] For the wellspring of life is with you.
By means of your light we see light.
[10] Spread your faithful love over those who know you,
and your righteousness over the upright in heart.
[11] Do not let the foot of the arrogant come near me
or the hand of the wicked drive me away.
[12] There! The evildoers have fallen.
They have been thrown down and cannot rise.

Truth: There is nothing more precious than the amazing reliable love that God offers to his children. He offers us protection from those who would harm us. God is the source of spiritual and physical life and the sustainer of all light and life. The "refreshing stream" provided for us is the water of life through God's son, Jesus Christ.

Thought: Our God is an AWE-SOME God.... He freely gives us love, even when we don't deserve it... He freely gave his only Son to die for our sins and our eternal salvation, even though we did nothing to deserve it. He offers us protection from the enemy of the world. He is THE FOUNTAIN of LIFE for those who have trusted in Him. Will you?

Tune: Our God is an awesome God
He reigns from heaven above
With wisdom pow'r and love
Our God is an awesome God

God, my desire is to trust in you and your Word and to dwell in the safety and protection of the shadow of your wings. Cover me, Oh Lord, from my enemies. Allow me to acknowledge you as Lord of my life. Thank you for the provisions you have so freely provided for us.

Text: Psalm 37:1-6

[1] Do not be agitated by evildoers;
do not envy those who do wrong.
[2] For they wither quickly like grass
and wilt like tender green plants.
[3] Trust in the Lord and do what is good;
dwell in the land and live securely.
[4] Take delight in the Lord,
and he will give you your heart's desires.
[5] Commit your way to the Lord;
trust in him, and he will act,
[6] making your righteousness shine like the dawn,
your justice like the noonday.

Truth: Verse 4 is one of the more commonly quoted verses. Sometimes it is misapplied. Rather than the focus on the desires of the heart and asking the Lord to grant those, the intent of the verse really has more to do with the first part of the verse. If we take delight in the Lord, He will change our desires to be more in line with His desires. If our desires are more in line with His desires, then our heart's desires will be God-honoring. Looking at verse 4 this way enables you to see verse 5 more clearly.

Thought: What does it mean to take delight in the Lord? If delight means "a high degree of pleasure or enjoyment" then that means I'm seeking to find enjoyment in my relationship with The Lord. How do you find enjoyment in any relationship? In its simplest form, this comes in 1) time and 2) sharing experiences together. It is no different with The Lord.

Tune: So here I am to worship, here I am to bow down
Here I am to say that You're my God
You're altogether lovely, altogether worthy
Altogether wonderful to me

Heavenly Father, no longer do I want to ask you to bless me where I am but to take me to where You are blessing. Tune my desires to Yours.

Songs for Life – Day 75 - March 16

Text: Psalm 37:7-11

[7] Be silent before the Lord and wait expectantly for him;
do not be agitated by one who prospers in his way,
by the person who carries out evil plans.
[8] Refrain from anger and give up your rage;
do not be agitated—it can only bring harm.
[9] For evildoers will be destroyed,
but those who put their hope in the Lord
will inherit the land.
[10] A little while, and the wicked person will be no more;
though you look for him, he will not be there.
[11] But the humble will inherit the land
and will enjoy abundant prosperity.

Truth: Generally, we are people of activity. When something goes wrong, we want something to be done about it, immediately. We go through the fast food drive-through and get antsy if the food is not delivered fast enough. We have microwave ovens, instant messages, 24-hour news networks, yet God's Word still says, "Be silent before the Lord and wait expectantly for him;" Waiting is hard, but it is God's instruction to us.

Thought: Why do we have to wait? After all, isn't God able to do what He wants, when He wants, for as long as He wants? Absolutely! We must consider that since God is the Creator of time and space, He must have knowledge of the best use of that time. That includes when it is time for Him to act. What is God teaching you in the meantime? If you focus on His presence, He may reveal Himself in a fresh and new way.

Tune: Have Thine own way Lord, have Thine own way
Thou art the Potter, I am the clay
Mold me and make me after Thy will, while I am waiting, yielded and still

Lord, I confess that I get impatient sometimes. Sometimes I even want to pray "Lord, help me to learn whatever it is You are teaching me, and help me to learn it NOW!" But, I will wait on You. Your timing is best.

Text: Psalm 37:12-17

[12] The wicked person schemes against the righteous
and gnashes his teeth at him.
[13] The Lord laughs at him because he sees that his day is coming.
[14] The wicked have drawn the sword and strung the bow
to bring down the poor and needy
and to slaughter those whose way is upright.
[15] Their swords will enter their own hearts,
and their bows will be broken.
[16] The little that the righteous person has is better
than the abundance of many wicked people.
[17] For the arms of the wicked will be broken,
but the Lord supports the righteous.

Truth: Did anybody else read verse 16 and shout "AMEN!" after reading it? It is easy to get jealous of what many in the world seem to have. We see (seemingly) unrighteous people that appear prosperous to our eyes. It is easy to think "if I had what THEY have, I would be so much better off". The Word is clear here. Whatever we have, it has come from the Lord.

Thought: Can you imagine the picture that verse 13 depicts? What a sight - The Lord laughing at the wicked! Take comfort, child of God, God has the final word! A life sold out to God is a life free from regret.

Tune: Rock of ages cleft for me
Let me hide myself in Thee
Let the water and the blood
From Thy wounded side which flowed
Be of sin the double cure
Save from wrath and make me pure

God, You are my Rock of ages. You sent Your only begotten Son to redeem me. The water and the blood that flowed from His side on the cross poured out of His body but into my soul to give me life. What I have is from You and I know that You know exactly what I need.

Text: Psalm 37:18-24

[18] The Lord watches over the blameless all their days,
and their inheritance will last forever.
[19] They will not be disgraced in times of adversity;
they will be satisfied in days of hunger.
[20] But the wicked will perish;
the Lord's enemies, like the glory of the pastures,
will fade away—they will fade away like smoke.
[21] The wicked person borrows and does not repay,
but the righteous one is gracious and giving.
[22] Those who are blessed by the Lord will inherit the land,
but those cursed by him will be destroyed.
[23] A person's steps are established by the Lord,
and he takes pleasure in his way.
[24] Though he falls, he will not be overwhelmed,
because the Lord supports him with his hand.

Truth: The righteous will have abundance in the time of famine, they are generous and giving, and shall inherit the land of promise. In contrast, the wicked (those who have not trusted in The Lord – not simply wicked in behavior) will perish, will vanish, borrow but never repay, and most importantly, they shall be cut off. It's quite a contrast!

Thought: Living in the center of God's will comes down to understanding that our steps "are established by The Lord". This doesn't mean we will never falter or fail, but the grace and mercy of God gives us assurance of a hope and future. The true believer will endure! He loves us THAT much!

Tune: Open the eyes of my heart, Lord. Open the eyes of my heart
I want to see You, I want to see You.
Open the eyes of my heart, Lord. Open the eyes of my heart
I want to see You, I want to see You

Lord, I pray today that you might help me see the steps YOU have for me today and not my own. Open my eyes to your direction.

Text: Psalm 37:25-29

[25] I have been young and now I am old,
yet I have not seen the righteous abandoned
or his children begging for bread.
[26] He is always generous, always lending,
and his children are a blessing.
[27] Turn away from evil, do what is good,
and settle permanently.
[28] For the Lord loves justice
and will not abandon his faithful ones.
They are kept safe forever,
but the children of the wicked will be destroyed.
[29] The righteous will inherit the land
and dwell in it permanently.

Truth: The Psalmist is giving testimony of the faithfulness of God. Through a lifetime of serving God, He says not only has God never failed him, but He's never seen any of God's children abandoned.

Thought: Faith has been described as the substance of things hoped for but not seen. While that is a true statement, let us never think that faith is ever blind. Though you may have never been through a particular situation before, the believer can always go back and realize that God has never failed them in the past, so while the circumstance you are going into may be different, the God you serve is not.

Tune: The steadfast love of the Lord never ceases
His mercies, they never come to an end
They are new every morning, new every morning
Great is Thy faithfulness, O Lord
Great is Thy faithfulness

Holy Father, You have met every need of my life. Help me to see the difference in wants and needs. Wherever You lead me today, Father, I will follow. Whatever You provide is what I need.

Text: Psalm 37:30-34

30 The mouth of the righteous utters wisdom;
his tongue speaks what is just.
31 The instruction of his God is in his heart;
his steps do not falter.
32 The wicked one lies in wait for the righteous
and intends to kill him;
33 the Lord will not leave him
in the power of the wicked one
or allow him to be condemned when he is judged.
34 Wait for the Lord and keep his way,
and he will exalt you to inherit the land.
You will watch when the wicked are destroyed.

Truth: The righteous man, the believer, lives in a privilege that the unbeliever could never understand until he comes to The Lord. The Holy Spirit equips us with wisdom to face our situations and places the law of God in our hearts so that we can make right decisions. The Lord understands that the wicked want to bring down the righteous, yet they never can, because the Lord will never abandon the righteous man.

Thought: Sometimes we can get so discouraged that we may start to believe the lie from Satan that through some poor decision-making we can find ourselves away from the hand of the Lord. Nothing could be further from the truth. God will take care of the wicked, and God will continue to love you with an everlasting love that will never be less than unconditional.

Tune: Knowing You Jesus, knowing You
There is no greater thing
You're my all, You're the best
You're my joy, my righteousness
And I love You, Lord, love You, Lord

God, help me not to stress about following You today, but just to trust the Holy Spirit's work within me.

Text: Psalm 37:35-40

[35] I have seen a wicked, violent person
well-rooted, like a flourishing native tree.
[36] Then I passed by and noticed he was gone;
I searched for him, but he could not be found.
[37] Watch the blameless and observe the upright,
for the person of peace will have a future.
[38] But transgressors will all be eliminated;
the future of the wicked will be destroyed.
[39] The salvation of the righteous is from the Lord,
their refuge in a time of distress.
[40] The Lord helps and delivers them;
he will deliver them from the wicked and will save them
because they take refuge in him.

Truth: If you have been saved, if you are a Christian, then this statement is absolutely true: salvation pursued you. You did not pursue salvation without a drawing of the Holy Spirit. Our text declares it this way: "The salvation of the righteous is from the Lord".

Thought: How in the world did The Lord give you an individual call to salvation? Have you ever thought of it that way? The Lord created the heavens and the earth. The Lord created the trees and the seas. The Lord created YOU! He created you, knowing that you needed a redeemer. How wonderful it is to have the Creator pursue a love relationship with us!!

Tune: I stand amazed in the presence of Jesus the Nazarene
And wonder how He could love me, a sinner, condemned, unclean
How marvelous, how wonderful, and my song shall ever be
How marvelous, how wonderful, is my Savior's love for me

Father, I'm amazed by Your love for me. I am undeserving, unworthy, and at times, unlovable – yet, You love me with an everlasting love. Father, I thank You for Your love for me and I receive it gladly. Thank You for loving me in spite of myself.

Songs for Life – Day 81 - March 22

Text: Psalm 38:1-8

[1] Lord, do not punish me in your anger
or discipline me in your wrath.
[2] For your arrows have sunk into me,
and your hand has pressed down on me.
[3] There is no soundness in my body because of your indignation;
there is no health in my bones because of my sin.
[4] For my iniquities have flooded over my head;
they are a burden too heavy for me to bear.
[5] My wounds are foul and festering because of my foolishness.
[6] I am bent over and brought very low;
all day long I go around in mourning.
[7] For my insides are full of burning pain,
and there is no soundness in my body.
[8] I am faint and severely crushed;
I groan because of the anguish of my heart.

Truth: While God most certainly is a God of love, He also is a God of wrath. He is holy, therefore He commands us to pursue holiness. The fact is, sometimes we find ourselves in consequences of our sin. We just need to call sin what it is . . . sin. We must flee from sin and deal with it.

Thought: When we gloss over the sinful things in our lives as "God loves me anyway" without dealing with them, we are minimizing sin and taking God for granted. Dealing with sin is not pleasant, but the freedom that comes from repentance and forgiveness brings forth an incredible joy!

Tune: Alas and did my Savior bleed, and did my Sovereign die?
Would He devote that sacred head for sinners such as I?
At the cross, at the cross, where I first saw the light
And the burden of my heart rolled away
It was there by faith I received my sight
And now I am happy all the day

Father, reveal any sinful way in my life so that I may leave it at the cross.

Songs for Life – Day 82 - March 23

Text: Psalm 38:9-16

[9] Lord, my every desire is in front of you;
my sighing is not hidden from you.
[10] My heart races, my strength leaves me,
and even the light of my eyes has faded.
[11] My loved ones and friends stand back from my affliction,
and my relatives stand at a distance.
[12] Those who intend to kill me set traps,
and those who want to harm me threaten to destroy me;
they plot treachery all day long.
[13] I am like a deaf person; I do not hear.
I am like a speechless person who does not open his mouth.
[14] I am like a man who does not hear and has no arguments in his mouth.
[15] For I put my hope in you, Lord; you will answer me, my Lord, my God.
[16] For I said, "Don't let them rejoice over me—
those who are arrogant toward me when I stumble."

Truth: Among the people you have interactions with on a daily basis, it is likely that you have some who are committed believers, some who claim to be Christians but have lost their fire, as well as those who have never yet trusted Christ as Savior. To face the battles in life, it is best to let the Holy Spirit do the work and only respond as He gives us direction.

Thought: Waiting on the Lord . . . that is a concept many of us struggle with. However, the answer that God will give in His perfect time, the response to your accusers that He will deliver, will be much more effective and will not leave behind a mess that we have to clean up. Today, make a commitment to think and pray before speaking and reacting.

Tune: They that wait upon the Lord shall renew their strength
They shall mount up with wings as eagles
They shall run and not be weary; they shall walk and not faint
Teach me Lord, teach me Lord to wait

Dear Lord, where You lead, You will meet every need and where You guide, You will provide.

Text: Psalm 38:17-22

[17] For I am about to fall, and my pain is constantly with me.
[18] So I confess my iniquity;
I am anxious because of my sin.
[19] But my enemies are vigorous and powerful;
many hate me for no reason.
[20] Those who repay evil for good
attack me for pursuing good.
[21] Lord, do not abandon me;
my God, do not be far from me.
[22] Hurry to help me, my Lord, my salvation.

Truth: Where does our help come from? Our help comes from The Lord. Even as we confess our sin to our Father, He brings us help in the form of forgiveness. Even when we feel we cannot make it one more day, He brings us help. Life is a series of struggles, separated by victories. All of them bear the marks of Almighty God.

Thought: The Psalmist has an incredibly intimate love relationship with the Lord. That is His design for us. He is pursuing an intimate love relationship with you constantly. Through that relationship, He will provide you all the help you need.

Tune: You are God alone, from before time began
You were on Your throne, You are God alone
And right now in the good times and bad
You are on Your throne, You are God alone
You're unchangeable, You're unshakable
You're unstoppable, that's what You are
You're unchangeable, You're unshakable
You're unstoppable, that's what You are

Lord, teach me how to love you with a love so personal that there is no separation between You speaking to me and me hearing Your voice. I want to sense every nudge, hear every whisper, and receive every Word.

Songs for Life – Day 84 - March 25

Text: Psalm 39:1-6

[1] I said, "I will guard my ways so that I may not sin with my tongue;
I will guard my mouth with a muzzle
as long as the wicked are in my presence."
[2] I was speechless and quiet;
I kept silent, even from speaking good,and my pain intensified.
[3] My heart grew hot within me;
as I mused, a fire burned.
I spoke with my tongue:
[4] "Lord, make me aware of my end
and the number of my days
so that I will know how short-lived I am.
[5] In fact, you have made my days just inches long,
and my life span is as nothing to you.
Yes, every human being stands as only a vapor.Selah
[6] Yes, a person goes about like a mere shadow.
Indeed, they rush around in vain,
gathering possessions
without knowing who will get them.

Truth: "I will" being used twice here are very strong words that David is using to show his commitment to God about guarding his words and not complaining about God in the presence of his enemies. We can still take our griefs to God, or course, but in private. Our life here on earth is but a fleeting shadow, too short to live in constant turmoil.

Thought: Do you air your grief's in public? Today with our social media you can see daily someone's rants about their life. If we take our troubles to God, privately, we could deal with them and move on to God's glory.

Tune: All to Jesus I surrender; All to Him I freely give
I will ever love and trust Him; In His presence daily live

Father, today "I will" watch my words in public and learn how to take my grievances to You and let You help me in my situations.

Text: Psalm 39:7-13

[7] "Now, Lord, what do I wait for? My hope is in you.
[8] Rescue me from all my transgressions;
do not make me the taunt of fools.
[9] I am speechless; I do not open my mouth
because of what you have done.
[10] Remove your torment from me.
Because of the force of your hand I am finished.
[11] You discipline a person with punishment for iniquity,
consuming like a moth what is precious to him;
yes, every human being is only a vapor.Selah
[12] "Hear my prayer, Lord,
and listen to my cry for help;
do not be silent at my tears.
For I am here with you as an alien,
a temporary resident like all my ancestors.
[13] Turn your angry gaze from me so that I may be cheered up
before I die and am gone."

Truth: David boldly declares that his Hope is in God and he is asking God to deliver him from his sins. He begs for God to hear him, to give him peace. David knows the shortness of life here on earth and cries out to God for help while he is here, before he leaves this world.

Thought: No Jesus - No Hope
                Know Jesus - Know Hope

Tune: This world is not my home I'm only passing through
My treasures are laid up Somewhere beyond the blue
The angels beckon me From heaven's open door
And I can't feel at home In this world anymore

God, Please forgive me for my sins and allow my short time on earth to serve you and love you and when the time is right, come dwell with you in Your house for all eternity.

Songs for Life – Day 86 - March 27

Text: Psalm 40:1-8

[1] I waited patiently for the Lord,
and he turned to me and heard my cry for help.
[2] He brought me up from a desolate pit, out of the muddy clay,
and set my feet on a rock, making my steps secure.
[3] He put a new song in my mouth, a hymn of praise to our God.
Many will see and fear, and they will trust in the Lord.
[4] How happy is anyone who has put his trust in the Lord
and has not turned to the proud or to those who run after lies!
[5] Lord my God, you have done many things—
your wondrous works and your plans for us; none can compare with you.
If I were to report and speak of them, they are more than can be told.
[6] You do not delight in sacrifice and offering; you open my ears to listen.
You do not ask for a whole burnt offering or a sin offering.
[7] Then I said, "See, I have come; in the scroll it is written about me.
[8] I delight to do your will, my God, and your instruction is deep within me."

Truth: We come into this world already condemned to separation from God. Through His incredible work of redemption through Christ on the cross, we no longer abide in the pit of destruction, but on The Rock.

Thought: Take a moment and read verses 1-3. Wherever it says something about the Lord, He or God, say the word "You". Then make it your prayer today. An example is shown in the prayer below.

Tune: In times like these you need a Savior
In times like these you need an anchor
Be very sure be very sure your anchor holds and grips the solid Rock
This Rock is Jesus yes, He's the One, this Rock is Jesus, the only One
Be very sure, be very sure, your anchor holds and grips the solid Rock

I waited patiently for You, Lord. You turned to me and heard my cry for help. You brought me up from a desolate pit, out of the muddy clay, and set my feet on a rock, making my steps secure. You put a new song in my mouth, a hymn of praise to God. Thank You, Lord!

Songs for Life – Day 87 - March 28

Text: Psalm 40:9-17

[9] I proclaim righteousness in the great assembly;
see, I do not keep my mouth closed—as you know, Lord.
[10] I did not hide your righteousness in my heart;
I spoke about your faithfulness and salvation;
I did not conceal your constant love and truth from the great assembly.
[11] Lord, you do not withhold your compassion from me.
Your constant love and truth will always guard me.
[12] For troubles without number have surrounded me;
my iniquities have overtaken me; I am unable to see.
They are more than the hairs of my head, and my courage leaves me.
[13] Lord, be pleased to rescue me; hurry to help me, Lord.
[14] Let those who intend to take my life
be disgraced and confounded.
Let those who wish me harm be turned back and humiliated.
[15] Let those who say to me, "Aha, aha!"
be appalled because of their shame.
[16] Let all who seek you rejoice and be glad in you;
let those who love your salvation continually say, "The Lord is great!"
[17] I am oppressed and needy; may the Lord think of me.
You are my helper and my deliverer; my God, do not delay.

Truth: God IS great! He doesn't just do great things, He IS great!

Thought: Who in your world needs to hear about the greatness of God?

Tune: Great is the Lord, He is holy and just
By His power we trust in His love
Great is the Lord, He is faithful and true
By His mercy He proves He is love
Great is the Lord and worthy of glory
Great is the Lord and worthy of praise
Great is the Lord, now lift up your voice
Now lift up your voice. Great is the Lord

You are everything I need and so much more. I lift my voice to You, Lord.

<u>Songs for Life – Day 88 - March 29</u>

Text: Psalm 41:1-7

[1] Happy is one who is considerate of the poor;
the Lord will save him in a day of adversity.
[2] The Lord will keep him and preserve him;
he will be blessed in the land.
You will not give him over to the desire of his enemies.
[3] The Lord will sustain him on his sickbed;
you will heal him on the bed where he lies.
[4] I said, "Lord, be gracious to me;
heal me, for I have sinned against you."
[5] My enemies speak maliciously about me:
"When will he die and be forgotten?"
[6] When one of them comes to visit, he speaks deceitfully;
he stores up evil in his heart; he goes out and talks.
[7] All who hate me whisper together about me; they plan to harm me.

Truth: In the Sermon on the Mount in Matthew 5-7, Jesus speaks of the poor in spirit and says they are blessed. Part of that blessing comes when the family of God surrounds that person with the love of God. God honors the one who seeks to be used by God to minister to those in need.

Thought: We do not have to go far to find anyone in need. People are hurting because of trials in relationships, in finances, in addictions, in loneliness and in many other areas. Where can God use you today to help meet a need in someone's life?

Tune: Let others see Jesus in you
Let others see Jesus in you
Keep telling the story, be faithful and true
Let others see Jesus in you

Father, today I ask you to help me take my eyes off of myself. Help me to see others as You see them. If you have someone in mind for me to help today, open my eyes and my heart to see that and I will trust You for the wisdom as to how to minister in that situation.

Songs for Life – Day 89 - March 30

Text: Psalm 41:8-13

[8] "Something awful has overwhelmed him,
and he won't rise again from where he lies!"
[9] Even my friend in whom I trusted,
one who ate my bread,
has raised his heel against me.
[10] But you, Lord, be gracious to me and raise me up;
then I will repay them.
[11] By this I know that you delight in me:
my enemy does not shout in triumph over me.
[12] You supported me because of my integrity
and set me in your presence forever.
[13] Blessed be the Lord God of Israel,
from everlasting to everlasting.
Amen and amen.

Truth: In this passage, David writes of the betrayal by his close companion. Some might even say David was "kicked" when he was down. That can be a lonely place when we feel like those closest to us have turned against us.

Thought: The tendency, when we are hurt, is to either 1) lash out at those around us or 2) turn inward and just let our hurt grow within us. It is in those times that we can feel lonely in a crowded room. God's grace is sufficient to minister to you in time of need. His mercy is sufficient to do the work of restoration. Let His grace and mercy minister to you today!

Tune: Oh His grace is sufficient for me, and His love is abundant and free
And what joy fills my soul, just to know, just to know
That His grace is sufficient for me

Father, when I'm hurting all I want to do is feel better. I know You are the only one that can heal those hurts. Sometimes I just want the ones to hurt in the same way that they hurt me, but I know that's not Your plan. Your ways are best.

Songs for Life – Day 90 - March 31

Text: Psalm 42:1-5

[1] As a deer longs for flowing streams,
so I long for you, God.
[2] I thirst for God, the living God.
When can I come and appear before God?
[3] My tears have been my food day and night,
while all day long people say to me,
"Where is your God?"
[4] I remember this as I pour out my heart:
how I walked with many,
leading the festive procession to the house of God,
with joyful and thankful shouts.
[5] Why, my soul, are you so dejected?
Why are you in such turmoil?
Put your hope in God, for I will still praise him,
my Savior and my God.

Truth: David remembers when he would go to the Temple to worship God. Now, no longer able, his soul thirsts for God. His enemies laughed at him and told him he had left God. Even though his heart was heavy burdened, David still had his hope in God.

Thought: Water is a basic necessity of all life. Does your soul "thirst" for the water of life that only the one true God can offer? We can worship and praise God through prayer, songs or reading scripture. Put your hope in God and thirst no more!

Tune: As the deer panteth for the water, so my soul longs after You, You alone are my heart's desire and I long to worship You.

Father, I see you for the life-giving water that I can only receive from you. May I always thank you for the many gifts from above. Fill me, Father, as I worship you.

<u>Songs for Life – Day 91 – April 1</u>

Text: Psalm 42:6-11

[6] I am deeply depressed;
therefore I remember you from the land of Jordan
and the peaks of Hermon, from Mount Mizar.
[7] Deep calls to deep in the roar of your waterfalls;
all your breakers and your billows have swept over me.
[8] The Lord will send his faithful love by day;
his song will be with me in the night—
a prayer to the God of my life.
[9] I will say to God, my rock,
"Why have you forgotten me?
Why must I go about in sorrow because of the enemy's oppression?"
[10] My adversaries taunt me, as if crushing my bones,
while all day long they say to me, "Where is your God?"
[11] Why, my soul, are you so dejected?
Why are you in such turmoil?
Put your hope in God, for I will still praise him,
my Savior and my God.

Truth: David is in the land of Northern Palestine, far away from Jerusalem where the sanctuary was located. He feels that he is drowning in deep water. At this point he is blaming God for his troubles. In Verse 11 he acknowledges that his hope and salvation are in God.

Thought: Do you ever feel that you are far away from God and drowning in a sea of troubles? It's easy to let ourselves get disheartened over our troubles and trials. Take comfort, for you can go to God and find hope. "Put your hope in God, for I will still praise him, my Savior and my God."

Tune: Blessed assurance Jesus is mine;
O what a foretaste of glory divine;
Heir of salvation purchase of God;
Born of His Spirit washed in His blood.

Father, I am thankful that I can meet you any time and any place and for any reason. I have such blessed assurance in You.

Text: Psalm 43:1-5

[1] Vindicate me, God, and champion my cause against an unfaithful nation;
rescue me from the deceitful and unjust person.
[2] For you are the God of my refuge.
Why have you rejected me?
Why must I go about in sorrow
because of the enemy's oppression?
[3] Send your light and your truth; let them lead me.
Let them bring me to your holy mountain,
to your dwelling place.
[4] Then I will come to the altar of God,
to God, my greatest joy.
I will praise you with the lyre, God, my God.
[5] Why, my soul, are you so dejected?
Why are you in such turmoil?
Put your hope in God, for I will still praise him,
my Savior and my God.

Truth: The Psalmist reminds us that the path to holiness, the path into the glorious presence of God, is paved with two things: The Truth (God's Word), and the light (the Holy Spirit). The Holy Spirit gives us understanding, or light, to Truth.

Thought: There are so many resources that people choose to draw from in order to find God's direction for their lives. There is no substitute for the Word of God and the Holy Spirit helping us to understand it. Meditate on God's Word today and call on the Holy Spirit for understanding.

Tune: Sing them over again to me, Wonderful words of life
Let me more of their beauty see, Wonderful words of life
Words of life and beauty, Teach me faith and duty
Beautiful words wonderful words, Wonderful words of life
Beautiful words wonderful words, Wonderful words of life

O Lord, draw me to Your Word today. Give me understanding & wisdom.

Songs for Life – Day 93 - April 3

Text: Psalm 44:1-8

[1] God, we have heard with our ears—our ancestors have told us—
the work you accomplished in their days, in days long ago:
[2] In order to plant them, you displaced the nations by your hand;
in order to settle them, you brought disaster on the peoples.
[3] For they did not take the land by their sword—
their arm did not bring them victory—
but by your right hand, your arm, and the light of your face,
because you were favorable toward them.
[4] You are my King, my God, who ordains victories for Jacob.
[5] Through you we drive back our foes;
through your name we trample our enemies.
[6] For I do not trust in my bow, and my sword does not bring me victory.
[7] But you give us victory over our foes
and let those who hate us be disgraced.
[8] We boast in God all day long;
we will praise your name forever. Selah

Truth: The psalmist is rejoicing in the protection the children of Israel have received from The Lord. He recounts the times God drove out the nations and afflicted people with plagues and diseases. He acknowledges that God was the power behind the sword of victory for the Israelites. He is bold in his testimony that the victory was by the hand of God.

Thought: Trusting God for the future is made easier when we remember the victories of the past. Whatever your affliction is today, have you totally entrusted it to God? He was there before your affliction was created. He will be there through the trial, and He will stand with you

Tune: I'm pressing on the upward way, new heights I'm gaining ev'ry day
Still praying as I'm onward bound, Lord plant my feet on higher ground
Lord lift me up and let me stand, by faith on heaven's table-land
A higher plane than I have found,
Lord plant my feet on higher ground

Lord, teach me to trust You today. I don't want to just say it, I want to do it!

Text: Psalm 44:9-16

[9] But you have rejected and humiliated us;
you do not march out with our armies.
[10] You make us retreat from the foe, and those who hate us
have taken plunder for themselves.
[11] You hand us over to be eaten like sheep
and scatter us among the nations.
[12] You sell your people for nothing;
you make no profit from selling them.
[13] You make us an object of reproach to our neighbors,
a source of mockery and ridicule to those around us.
[14] You make us a joke among the nations,
a laughingstock among the peoples.
[15] My disgrace is before me all day long, and shame has covered my face,
[16] because of the taunts of the scorner and reviler,
because of the enemy and avenger.

Truth: The psalmist is describing the feeling of rejection that he and the people of Israel now feel by the hand of The Lord. Recently he recounted the victories that God has brought forth for them, yet now he feels like they are "to be eaten like sheep", being left for destruction.

Thought: Have you ever felt that you were trying to do everything right, yet the blessings are not coming? As a believer, even our trials, tribulations and defeats are in the hand of The Lord. God has something to teach us through every trial. What is He teaching you today?

Tune: 'Cause what if Your blessings come through raindrops
What if Your healing comes through tears
And what if a thousand sleepless nights
Are what it takes to know You're near
And what if trials of this life are Your mercies in disguise

I need Your presence today to comfort me through my trial, and to teach me more about You today. I know that You work all things for my good.

Songs for Life – Day 95 - April 5

Text: Psalm 44:17-26

[17] All this has happened to us, but we have not forgotten you
or betrayed your covenant.
[18] Our hearts have not turned back;
our steps have not strayed from your path.
[19] But you have crushed us in a haunt of jackals
and have covered us with deepest darkness.
[20] If we had forgotten the name of our God
and spread out our hands to a foreign god,
[21] wouldn't God have found this out,
since he knows the secrets of the heart?
[22] Because of you we are being put to death all day long;
we are counted as sheep to be slaughtered.
[23] Wake up, Lord! Why are you sleeping? Get up! Don't reject us forever!
[24] Why do you hide and forget our affliction and oppression?
[25] For we have sunk down to the dust; our bodies cling to the ground.
[26] Rise up! Help us! Redeem us because of your faithful love.

Truth: There are many things in this life that are unexplainable. The psalmist is trying to make sense of a situation where God's children have continued to trust Him, yet they feel forsaken.

Thought: Perhaps you have felt forsaken, even by The Lord. Even when it seems God is a million miles away, He never fails to hear the cry of His children, like a parent hearing the cry of their hurting child.

Tune: I don't know about tomorrow, I just live from day to day
I don't borrow from its sunshine, for its skies may turn to gray
I don't worry o'er the future, for I know what Jesus said
And today I'll walk beside Him, For He knows what is ahead
Many things about tomorrow I don't seem to understand
But I know who holds tomorrow, and I know who holds my hand

Father, there are so many things about today, about tomorrow, even about yesterday, that I do not understand. However, I know WHO holds tomorrow and I know YOU hold my hand. I trust You, Father!

Text: Psalm 45:1-9

[1] My heart is moved by a noble theme as I recite my verses to the king;
my tongue is the pen of a skillful writer.
[2] You are the most handsome of men; grace flows from your lips.
Therefore God has blessed you forever.
[3] Mighty warrior, strap your sword at your side.
In your majesty and splendor—
[4] in your splendor ride triumphantly in the cause of truth, humility, and justice.
May your right hand show your awe-inspiring acts.
[5] Your sharpened arrows pierce the hearts of the king's enemies;
the peoples fall under you.
[6] Your throne, God, is forever and ever;
the scepter of your kingdom is a scepter of justice.
[7] You love righteousness and hate wickedness;
therefore God, your God, has anointed you with the oil of joy
more than your companions.
[8] Myrrh, aloes, and cassia perfume all your garments;
from ivory palaces harps bring you joy.
[9] Kings' daughters are among your honored women;
the queen, adorned with gold from Ophir, stands at your right hand.

Truth: A wedding celebration is about to take place. Look at all the words describing the groom!! The emotions of his heart are being poured out as he anticipates the event. All believers will celebrate this. Revelation 19:9b, "Blessed are those invited to the marriage feast of the Lamb!"

Thought: The Church is the Bride of Christ, and the Groom is Christ. One day, Jesus will return for us. We, as believers, are to be making ourselves ready for the groom by keeping ourselves pure and holy.

Tune: Majesty worship His majesty;
unto Jesus be all glory honor and praise;
Majesty kingdom authority;
flow from His throne, unto His own His anthem raise

Father, I exalt you and praise You and Your Holy Name.

Text: Psalm 45:10-17

[10] Listen, daughter, pay attention and consider:
forget your people and your father's house,
[11] and the king will desire your beauty.
Bow down to him, for he is your lord.
[12] The daughter of Tyre, the wealthy people,
will seek your favor with gifts.
[13] In her chamber, the royal daughter is all glorious,
her clothing embroidered with gold.
[14] In colorful garments she is led to the king;
after her, the virgins, her companions, are brought to you.
[15] They are led in with gladness and rejoicing;
they enter the king's palace.
[16] Your sons will succeed your ancestors;
you will make them princes throughout the land.
[17] I will cause your name to be remembered for all generations;
therefore the peoples will praise you forever and ever.

Truth: As in the first part of this Psalm, the bride, in her pure white robe (symbolizing purity), is now ready to be united with her love. Revelation 19:7 tells of this glorious event. Let us rejoice!!

Thought: Imagine all the anticipation that comes before a wedding. The bride makes many preparations and excitedly looks forward to wearing the dress and walking the aisle. We are to be like that new bride, making our preparations on earth, by sharing the good news of Jesus and showing others the love of Christ, inviting them to the great wedding.

Tune: Refiner's fire; My heart's one desire is to be holy;
Set apart for You Lord, I choose to be holy;
Set apart for You my Master
Ready to do Your will

Lord Jesus, I ask you to give me the courage and strength to show Your love and goodness to others.

Text: Psalm 46:1-7

[1] God is our refuge and strength, a helper who is always found
in times of trouble.
[2] Therefore we will not be afraid, though the earth trembles
and the mountains topple into the depths of the seas,
[3] though its water roars and foams
and the mountains quake with its turmoil. Selah
[4] There is a river—its streams delight the city of God,
the holy dwelling place of the Most High.
[5] God is within her; she will not be toppled.
God will help her when the morning dawns.
[6] Nations rage, kingdoms topple;
the earth melts when he lifts his voice.
[7] The Lord of Armies is with us;
the God of Jacob is our stronghold. Selah

Truth: Refuge = shelter or protection from danger or trouble. Strength = power by reason of influence, authority, resources or numbers. Help = contribute strength or means to; render assistance to. God IS our refuge. God IS our strength. God IS our help. Even if the mountains be thrown into the sea, God IS our refuge, God IS our strength, and He IS a VERY present help.

Thought: Do you feel like the raging waters are about to overwhelm you? Does life have some mountains that seem to be right in your path? Do not fear, child of God. God is your Refuge, Strength, and very present Help.

Tune: God is my refuge, and God is my strength
A very present help in trouble
God is my refuge, and God is my strength
A very present help in trouble
Therefore, I will not fear, though the earth be removed
And though the mountains be carried into the midst of the sea

God, help me in these times of trouble to come to know You better.

Text: Psalm 46:8-11

[8] Come, see the works of the Lord,
who brings devastation on the earth.
[9] He makes wars cease throughout the earth.
He shatters bows and cuts spears to pieces;
he sets wagons ablaze.
[10] "Stop your fighting, and know that I am God,
exalted among the nations, exalted on the earth."
[11] The Lord of Armies is with us;
the God of Jacob is our stronghold. Selah

Truth: "Stop your fighting (be still), and know that I am God" is really a two-fold command. First, it is a command not to panic. When we are frustrated or worried, the tendency can be to get out of control. Being still is the antidote. The second part of the command is to recognize the sovereignty of God ("I am God"). For the believer, this is an assurance, a promise, and a comfort. Nothing escapes His grasp or His control.

Thought: With all of the noises in our lives - voices, phones, televisions, computers, radios, machinery, and so much more, the challenge to "Be still" is great. However, prayer was designed to be a dialogue, rather than a monologue. He wants to speak to us and not just listen. Give Him time & opportunity to speak to you today.

Tune: There is a place of quiet rest, near to the heart of God
A place where sin cannot molest, near to the heart of God

O Jesus blest Redeemer
Sent from the heart of God
Hold us who wait before Thee
Near to the heart of God

Lord, today I will try to "be still" before You and let You speak. Teach me to before You today and to recognize Your still, small voice.

Songs for Life – Day 100 - April 10

Text: Psalm 47:1-9

[1] Clap your hands, all you peoples; shout to God with a jubilant cry.

[2] For the Lord, the Most High, is awe-inspiring,
a great King over the whole earth.

[3] He subdues peoples under us and nations under our feet.

[4] He chooses for us our inheritance—
the pride of Jacob, whom he loves. Selah

[5] God ascends among shouts of joy,
the Lord, with the sound of trumpets.

[6] Sing praise to God, sing praise;
sing praise to our King, sing praise!

[7] Sing a song of wisdom, for God is King of the whole earth.

[8] God reigns over the nations;
God is seated on his holy throne.

[9] The nobles of the peoples have assembled
with the people of the God of Abraham.
For the leaders of the earth belong to God; he is greatly exalted.

Truth: This psalm celebrates God's kingship and His rule over all the earth. The promise to Abraham, that all peoples will be blessed in Him, is based on the fact that there is only one true God, to whom all mankind owes love and loyalty.

Thought: There is a time to "be still' before God, and there is a time to clap your hands, shout and rejoice! Take some time today to sing praises to God! Glorify Him! Magnify Him! He is worthy!

Tune: Worthy is the Lamb Who was slain, Holy holy is He
Sing a new song to Him Who sits on Heaven's mercy seat
Holy holy holy, is the Lord God Almighty
Who was and is and is to come
With all creation I sing praise to the King of kings
You are my ev'rything, and I will adore You

Almighty God, my voice sings in honor of Your name. I worship You alone.

Text: Psalm 48:1-8

[1] The Lord is great and highly praised in the city of our God.
His holy mountain, [2] rising splendidly, is the joy of the whole earth.
Mount Zion—the summit of Zaphon—
is the city of the great King.
[3] God is known as a stronghold
in its citadels.
[4] Look! The kings assembled;
they advanced together.
[5] They looked and froze with fear;
they fled in terror.
[6] Trembling seized them there,
agony like that of a woman in labor,
[7] as you wrecked the ships of Tarshish
with the east wind.
[8] Just as we heard, so we have seen
in the city of the Lord of Armies,
in the city of our God; God will establish it forever. Selah

Truth: While praising the greatness of God, an event is being retold of kings gathering to attack Jerusalem, the magnificent "city of our God!" That is like attacking God Himself!

Thought: Perhaps there have been times when we have been under attack from the enemy and trembled in fear or panic, but through the greatness of our God, we prevailed. For great is the LORD and greatly to be praised.

Tune: God is great and His praise; Fills the earth fills the heavens
And Your name will be praised; Through all the world
God is great sing His praise; All the earth all the heavens
'Cause we're living for the glory; Of Your name

Lord God, Your name is great, and greatly to be praised. Help me to remember that each and every day.

Text: Psalm 48:9-14

[9] God, within your temple,
we contemplate your faithful love.
[10] Like your name, God, so your praise
reaches to the ends of the earth;
your right hand is filled with justice.
[11] Mount Zion is glad.
Judah's villages rejoice
because of your judgments.
[12] Go around Zion, encircle it;
count its towers,
[13] note its ramparts; tour its citadels
so that you can tell a future generation:
[14] "This God, our God forever and ever—
he will always lead us."

Truth: The Psalmist is reflecting on God's steadfast love and how the preservation of His people is allowing the knowledge of Him and His righteousness to be spread all over the earth. We are encouraged to share God's love to the next generation.

Thought: Are you active in sharing your faith and what God has done in your life with your next generation and your church family? In the book Experiencing God, Henry Blackaby says, "If the members are not talking about what they sense God is doing in their midst, the whole body will be disoriented to God." What is God doing in your midst? Can you share it?

Tune: Amazing love, how can it be?
That you, my king would die for me
Amazing love, I know it's true
It's my joy to honor you
In all I do, I honor you.

Father, I am so thankful for your steadfast love that you have so freely given to me. Please help me to share it with others as an encouragement.

Text: Psalm 49:1-9

[1] Hear this, all you peoples; listen, all who inhabit the world,
[2] both low and high, rich and poor together.
[3] My mouth speaks wisdom;
my heart's meditation brings understanding.
[4] I turn my ear to a proverb;
I explain my riddle with a lyre.
[5] Why should I fear in times of trouble?
The iniquity of my foes surrounds me.
[6] They trust in their wealth
and boast of their abundant riches.
[7] Yet these cannot redeem a person
or pay his ransom to God—
[8] since the price of redeeming him is too costly,
one should forever stop trying—
[9] so that he may live forever and not see the Pit.

Truth: Though we don't like to think about it often, death is a part of life. The ratio is 1:1 for people to death. The psalm not only gives the certainty of death, but also the reminder that no material means gathered in this life will mean anything at the time our life on earth ends. No man can die for another, save Christ, due to the sinful state of our lives. Only Jesus Christ, the Holy One, can ransom our lives with His.

Thought: Why should we wait until our life seems in the balance to embrace the most important things: Christ, family, love, and relationships? Have you evaluated your life recently to see what is really important and what you are holding on to that is truly temporary?

Tune: I'll fly away O glory; I'll fly away (in the morning)
When I die hallelujah by and by, I'll fly away

Father, help me today to see what is really important in my life, and where I might have things out of balance. I want Your priorities to be my priorities.

Songs for Life – Day 104 - April 14

Text: Psalm 49:10-15

[10] For one can see that the wise die; the foolish and stupid also pass away. Then they leave their wealth to others.
[11] Their graves are their permanent homes,
their dwellings from generation to generation,
though they have named estates after themselves.
[12] But despite his assets, mankind will not last;
he is like the animals that perish.
[13] This is the way of those who are arrogant, and of their followers,
who approve of their words. Selah
[14] Like sheep they are headed for Sheol; Death will shepherd them.
The upright will rule over them in the morning,
and their form will waste away in Sheol, far from their lofty abode.
[15] But God will redeem me from the power of Sheol,
for he will take me. Selah

Truth: No person, regardless of his means, is able to escape death; it is inevitable. However, the one who trusts Christ with His life, that one is redeemed by the only Redeemer, God Himself. The psalmist is expressing his confidence in God, that He would raise him to eternal life.

Thought: There is nothing wrong in this life with chasing our dreams. However, we need to be sure that God is the Author of those dreams that we pursue. If our priorities reflect God's priorities for our lives, then our dreams will be His dreams for us. Focus on God as your Redeemer.

Tune: Who taught the sun where to stand in the morning
And who told the ocean you can only come this far
And who showed the moon where to hide 'til evening
Whose words alone can catch a falling star
Well I know my Redeemer lives, I know my Redeemer lives
All of creation testifies this life within me cries
I know my Redeemer lives

God, place the dreams in my heart that glorify You and follow Your plan for my life. Thank You for being my Redeemer and loving me!

Songs for Life – Day 105 - April 15

Text: Psalm 49:16-20

[16] Do not be afraid when a person gets rich,
when the wealth of his house increases.
[17] For when he dies, he will take nothing at all;
his wealth will not follow him down.
[18] Though he blesses himself during his lifetime—
and you are acclaimed when you do well for yourself—
[19] he will go to the generation of his fathers; they will never see the light.
[20] Mankind, with his assets but without understanding,
is like the animals that perish.

Truth: When the body dies, the soul is immediately transported. For the believer, the soul is present with the Lord immediately. However, the soul will not be accompanied by any "things". The accumulation of things in this life is not necessarily bad, but it has no lasting value.

Thought: It is easy for man to try to evaluate his success in comparison to other men. Sometimes we may even see others who live ungodly lifestyles, who (seem to) have plenty of the things of the world. We wonder what it is we have done wrong because we feel we have less. Be not afraid, child of God, while your prosperity may not come in this life, neither will the ungodly man be able to take his riches with him. However, your retirement will be out of this world!

Tune: I'm looking now across the river
Where my faith will end in sight
There's just a few more days to labor
Then I will take my heav'nly flight
Beulah land (Beulah land) I am longing for you
And someday (and someday) on Thee I'll stand
Where my home (where my home) shall be eternal
Beulah land sweet Beulah land

Heavenly Father, help me not to place my trust in the things of this life, but to put my hope in eternal things.

Songs for Life – Day 106 - April 16

Text: Psalm 50:1-11

[1] The Mighty One, God, the Lord, speaks; he summons the earth
from the rising of the sun to its setting.
[2] From Zion, the perfection of beauty, God appears in radiance.
[3] Our God is coming; he will not be silent!
Devouring fire precedes him, and a storm rages around him.
[4] On high, he summons heaven and earth in order to judge his people:
[5] "Gather my faithful ones to me,
those who made a covenant with me by sacrifice."
[6] The heavens proclaim his righteousness, for God is the Judge. Selah
[7] "Listen, my people, and I will speak;
I will testify against you, Israel. I am God, your God.
[8] I do not rebuke you for your sacrifices
or for your burnt offerings, which are continually before me.
[9] I will not take a bull from your household or male goats from your pens,
[10] for every animal of the forest is mine, the cattle on a thousand hills.
[11] I know every bird of the mountains,
and the creatures of the field are mine.

Truth: God is not only the God of love, but He is also the God of wrath.
He is not concerned with our list of works as much as He is about our
hearts. Here, He proclaims that He will refuse the sacrifices and burnt
offerings that come from an impure heart.

Thought: God will not expose His children to His wrath. Though He
disciplines who He loves, we will never feel the wrath that those who only
followed Him with their works and not their hearts. God owns the cattle on
a thousand hills, yet He will drop everything and run to the one who brings
his heart to Him.

Tune: He leadeth me He leadeth me
By His own hand He leadeth me
His faithful follower I would be
For by His hand He leadeth me

Lord, I'm so thankful that Your love for me is not based on my works.

Text: Psalm 50:12-18

[12] If I were hungry, I would not tell you,
for the world and everything in it is mine.
[13] Do I eat the flesh of bulls or drink the blood of goats?
[14] Sacrifice a thank offering to God, and pay your vows to the Most High.
[15] Call on me in a day of trouble;
I will rescue you, and you will honor me."
[16] But God says to the wicked:
"What right do you have to recite my statutes
and to take my covenant on your lips?
[17] You hate instruction and fling my words behind you.
[18] When you see a thief,
you make friends with him, and you associate with adulterers.

Truth: God is addressing those who are tempted to think that He somehow needs the sacrifices, that they can be used somehow as a bribe to satisfy Him. What God desires here are the sacrifices of the heart, expressed in verse 14 as thank offerings and vows of the heart. These are illustrations of the Lord's Supper to come, which, for the partaker, are both thanksgiving and a commitment of heart to continue to let the body and blood of Christ dwell within us.

Thought: Even on our darkest days, Christians have much to express thanks for. We have grace that covers our sin debt, mercy that keeps us from experiencing the real consequences of our sinful actions, the love of Christ that fills us, the blessing of His church, and so much more. What do you have to be thankful for today?

Tune: Lord prepare me to be a sanctuary
Pure and holy, tried and true
With thanksgiving I'll be a living
Sanctuary for You

Help me to look at my life through Your eyes. I know that by doing that I will be able to see how much I have to be thankful for. Thank You, God.

Songs for Life – Day 108 - April 18

Text: Psalm 50:19-23

[19] You unleash your mouth for evil and harness your tongue for deceit.
[20] You sit, maligning your brother, slandering your mother's son.
[21] You have done these things, and I kept silent;
you thought I was just like you.
But I will rebuke you
and lay out the case before you.
[22] "Understand this, you who forget God,
or I will tear you apart,
and there will be no one to rescue you.
[23] Whoever sacrifices a thank offering honors me,
and whoever orders his conduct,
I will show him the salvation of God."

Truth: This passage is directed members of the covenant people, the ones who despise the privileges of the covenant. While they say they are followers, they reject the fatherly discipline that God gives His children. Rather than bringing people together, these people cause division. The one who exalts God is the one who offers thanksgiving as his sacrifice.

Thought: The tongue is, perhaps, the most destructive force available to man. The external scars of physical damage can often heal, while the emotional scars of the destructive tongue often do not. Just as the tongue that offers thanksgiving to God glorifies Him, so man is encouraged by the positive power of the tongue. Encourage someone today.

Tune: Down at the cross where my Savior died
Down where for cleansing from sin I cried
There to my heart was the blood applied, glory to His name
Glory to His name, Glory to His name
There to my heart was the blood applied, glory to His name

Lord, may You use my mouth to glorify You today. Put the words in my mouth that would glorify You and encourage others today.

Songs for Life – Day 109 - April 19

Text: Psalm 51:1-12

[1] Be gracious to me, God, according to your faithful love;
according to your abundant compassion, blot out my rebellion.
[2] Completely wash away my guilt and cleanse me from my sin.
[3] For I am conscious of my rebellion, and my sin is always before me.
[4] Against you—you alone—I have sinned and done this evil in your sight.
So you are right when you pass sentence;you are blameless when you judge.
[5] Indeed, I was guilty when I was born;
I was sinful when my mother conceived me.
[6] Surely you desire integrity in the inner self,
and you teach me wisdom deep within.
[7] Purify me with hyssop, and I will be clean;
wash me, and I will be whiter than snow.
[8] Let me hear joy and gladness; let the bones you have crushed rejoice.
[9] Turn your face away from my sins and blot out all my guilt.
[10] God, create a clean heart for me and renew a steadfast spirit within me.
[11] Do not banish me from your presence or take your Holy Spirit from me.
[12] Restore the joy of your salvation to me,
and sustain me by giving me a willing spirit.

Truth: David realizes that he was born a sinner. He is seeking restoration and renewal in his relationship to God. He desires to have his heart cleansed and have the joy of his fellowship with God restored. What he is expressing is one of the best illustrations of repentance in God's Word.

Thought: II Corinthians 6:14 says, "For what fellowship has righteousness with lawlessness?" If God is righteousness, having true fellowship with God means coming to Him with a pure heart. As we examine our hearts daily, we can bring our heart, our sin, and our unrighteous behavior before God. This opens the door for Him to cleanse and restore us.

Tune: Purify my heart, cleanse me from within and make me holy, Purify my heart, cleanse me from my sin, deep within....

Father God, help me to cleanse my heart from sin, so I that I can be restored in holy fellowship with you.

Text: Psalm 51:13-19

[13] Then I will teach the rebellious your ways,
and sinners will return to you.
[14] Save me from the guilt of bloodshed, God—
God of my salvation—
and my tongue will sing of your righteousness.
[15] Lord, open my lips,
and my mouth will declare your praise.
[16] You do not want a sacrifice, or I would give it;
you are not pleased with a burnt offering.
[17] The sacrifice pleasing to God is a broken spirit.
You will not despise a broken and humbled heart, God.
[18] In your good pleasure, cause Zion to prosper;
build the walls of Jerusalem.
[19] Then you will delight in righteous sacrifices, whole burnt offerings;
then bulls will be offered on your altar.

Truth: Notice the words, "my tongue will sing", "declare your praise", and "sacrifice." These are words of action in public worship. We must have the right attitude toward God and a humble heart when we are asking forgiveness for our sins. "Cause Zion to prosper" refers to being a strong body of God's people. We must maintain our own spiritual well-being to be an effective community of believers.

Thought: "It's all about relationships", right? We must strive to keep a close daily personal relationship with God. This allows us to, when we come together as a church body, build strong relationships with each other, to be united as the body of Christ.

Tune: Make us one Lord; Make us one
Holy Spirit make us one; Let Your love flow
So the world will know; We are one in You

God, please give me the right attitude when I seek forgiveness from You. My desire is to have a strong and personal relationship with You.

Songs for Life – Day 111 - April 21

Text: Psalm 52:1-9

[1] Why boast about evil, you hero! God's faithful love is constant.

[2] Like a sharpened razor, your tongue devises destruction,
working treachery.

[3] You love evil instead of good, lying instead of speaking truthfully. Selah

[4] You love any words that destroy, you treacherous tongue!

[5] This is why God will bring you down forever.
He will take you, ripping you out of your tent;
he will uproot you from the land of the living. Selah

[6] The righteous will see and fear,
and they will derisively say about that hero,

[7] "Here is the man who would not make God his refuge,
but trusted in the abundance of his riches,
taking refuge in his destructive behavior."

[8] But I am like a flourishing olive tree in the house of God;
I trust in God's faithful love forever and ever.

[9] I will praise you forever for what you have done.
In the presence of your faithful people,
I will put my hope in your name, for it is good.

Truth: It's an epic battle of good vs. evil. On the good shoulder you have the "God's faithful love", which will never show any decrease. On the evil shoulder you have. . . the tongue?? In just the first 4 verses, we see that the tongue is a boaster, a destroyer, like a sharp razor, a worker of deceit.

Thought: "I'd sure like to give him a piece of my mind!" "Say that one more time!" The tongue is such a potentially destructive force, but it doesn't have to be. The difference is in the power behind it. Ask God to control your tongue today.

Tune: We worship You, Hallelujah hallelujah
We worship You for who You are
We worship You, Hallelujah hallelujah
We worship You for who You are, For You are good

Father, may my tongue be only used to bring glory to Your name today!

Songs for Life – Day 112 - April 22

Text: Psalm 53:1-6

[1] The fool says in his heart, "There's no God."
They are corrupt, and they do vile deeds.
There is no one who does good.
[2] God looks down from heaven on the human race
to see if there is one who is wise, one who seeks God.
[3] All have turned away; all alike have become corrupt.
There is no one who does good, not even one.
[4] Will evildoers never understand?
They consume my people as they consume bread;
they do not call on God.
[5] Then they will be filled with dread— dread like no other—
because God will scatter the bones of those who besiege you.
You will put them to shame, for God has rejected them.
[6] Oh, that Israel's deliverance would come from Zion!
When God restores the fortunes of his people,
let Jacob rejoice, let Israel be glad.

Truth: Twice in this Psalm we are told that there are none who do good, none who can seek after God. What does that mean? Since the fall of man in the Garden of Eden in Genesis, there is no man who can be righteous on his own, who can come to God on his own. We all must be drawn by God through the Holy Spirit to Himself.

Thought: If I cannot come to God on my own, where does my hope lie? It lies in the hands, in the power, and in the love, of Almighty God. God pursues a loving relationship with YOU continually. Yes, YOU! Yes, continually! There has never been a moment He has not loved you.

Tune: Your love never fails,
it never gives up
Never runs out on me

Father, I don't really understand why You would pursue a love relationship with me continually. I'm not worthy of it, but I accept it gladly.

Text: Psalm 54:1-7

[1] God, save me by your name,
and vindicate me by your might!
[2] God, hear my prayer;
listen to the words from my mouth.
[3] For strangers rise up against me,
and violent men intend to kill me.
They do not let God guide them. Selah
[4] God is my helper;
the Lord is the sustainer of my life.
[5] He will repay my adversaries for their evil.
Because of your faithfulness, annihilate them.
[6] I will sacrifice a freewill offering to you.
I will praise your name, Lord,
because it is good.
[7] For he has rescued me from every trouble,
and my eye has looked down on my enemies.

Truth: "God, save me by your name", from verse 1, indicates to us that God's name is our salvation. Acts 4:12 says "And there is salvation in no one else, for there is no other name under heaven given among men by which we must be saved."

Thought: We see people all the time who seem to have little or no respect for God. Verse 3 calls them "violent men." God is all knowing, all seeing and ever present. One day, EVERY knee will bow, and EVERY tongue will confess that Jesus Christ is LORD! THERE IS NO OTHER!!!

Tune: No other name but the name of Jesus
No other name but the name of the Lord
No other name but the name of Jesus
Is worthy of glory and worthy of honor
And worthy of power and all praise

Father, there is no other name, but yours, that can save me.

Text: Psalm 55:1-8

[1] God, listen to my prayer and do not hide from my plea for help.
[2] Pay attention to me and answer me.
I am restless and in turmoil with my complaint,
[3] because of the enemy's words, because of the pressure of the wicked.
For they bring down disaster on me and harass me in anger.
[4] My heart shudders within me; terrors of death sweep over me.
[5] Fear and trembling grip me;
horror has overwhelmed me.
[6] I said, "If only I had wings like a dove!
I would fly away and find rest.
[7] How far away I would flee;
I would stay in the wilderness. Selah
[8] I would hurry to my shelter
from the raging wind and the storm."

Truth: For much of David's ministry, he was an obedient "man after God's heart". While he pursued obedience and God's hand, he had many who opposed him, even within his own camp. Rather than try to avenge his accusers himself, David let God handle them. Still, while he waited on God to act, the intensity of his prayers demonstrates the anguish he felt.

Thought: Sometimes it seems like only the wicked prosper. We face opposition and it seems God has forgotten us. It is easy to forget that God not only knows your everyday battles, but also your hope and future. What is He teaching you through this trial? Is it trust? Is it dependence on Him? Is it surrendering control to Him? You can depend on God.

Tune: Through it all through it all
I've learned to trust in Jesus, I've learned to trust in God
Through it all through it all
I've learned to depend upon His word

Lord, when my patience grows thin, when my strength becomes weakness, I must trust You. Teach me to trust You today.

Text: Psalm 55:9-16

[9] Lord, confuse and confound their speech,
for I see violence and strife in the city;
[10] day and night they make the rounds on its walls.
Crime and trouble are within it;
[11] destruction is inside it;
oppression and deceit never leave its marketplace.
[12] Now it is not an enemy who insults me—otherwise I could bear it;
it is not a foe who rises up against me—otherwise I could hide from him.
[13] But it is you, a man who is my peer, my companion and good friend!
[14] We used to have close fellowship;
we walked with the crowd into the house of God.
[15] Let death take them by surprise; let them go down to Sheol alive,
because evil is in their homes and within them.
[16] But I call to God, and the Lord will save me.

Truth: This passage begins with a reference to the Tower of Babel experience, where God came down to a group of people who had built a tower. They built this tower to make a name for themselves. When God came down, he responded in such a way that He confused their language. This confusion caused them to scatter throughout the region. David even laments that he is being taunted by a former trusted friend. David is certain that his accusers will not repent. He calls on God for action.

Thought: Insult is such a strong word. Have you ever felt the sting of insults by a friend, a family member, even a spouse? When we act out on those feelings we only answer hurt for hurt. We practically ensure that the end result will be more hurt for ourselves. Crying out to God, trusting in His Word, those are the steps to healing.

Tune: There is none like You
No one else can touch my heart like You do
I could search for all eternity long and find, there is none like You

Father, only You can heal my hurts, the pains of my past. I bring those things to You today, and I ask that you help me not to lash out today.

Text: Psalm 55:17-23

[17] I complain and groan morning, noon, and night,
and he hears my voice.
[18] Though many are against me,
he will redeem me from my battle unharmed.
[19] God, the one enthroned from long ago,
will hear and will humiliate them. Selah
because they do not change and do not fear God.
[20] My friend acts violently against those at peace with him;
he violates his covenant.
[21] His buttery words are smooth, but war is in his heart.
His words are softer than oil, but they are drawn swords.
[22] Cast your burden on the Lord, and he will sustain you;
he will never allow the righteous to be shaken.
[23] God, you will bring them down to the Pit of destruction;
men of bloodshed and treachery will not live out half their days.
But I will trust in you.

Truth: The word for burden in verse 22 implies one's circumstances, one's lot. The psalmist promises that the Lord will uphold the believer in the struggles of life.

Thought: When a fisherman puts his line into the water, he "casts" his line out away from himself, so that he can reach the good stuff which is beyond his own reach. Cast your burden on the Lord today, and He can reach the good stuff that is way beyond your reach. Your burden is well within His reach, to heal and to restore.

Tune: Would you be free from your burden of sin
There's power in the blood, power in the blood
Would you o'er evil a victory win
There's wonderful power in the blood

God, it is so easy to hold on to my "line", to my burdens. Teach me how to cast my burdens on You, so I can "reel in" the good stuff.

Text: Psalm 56:1-7

[1] Be gracious to me, God, for a man is trampling me;
he fights and oppresses me all day long.
[2] My adversaries trample me all day,
for many arrogantly fight against me.
[3] When I am afraid, I will trust in you.
[4] In God, whose word I praise, in God I trust; I will not be afraid.
What can mere mortals do to me?
[5] They twist my words all day long;
all their thoughts against me are evil.
[6] They stir up strife, they lurk; they watch my steps
while they wait to take my life.
[7] Will they escape in spite of such sin?
God, bring down the nations in wrath.

Truth: The psalmist makes a choice to replace his fear with trust. Trust is the antidote of fear. For a child who gets separated from his parent in a store, the embrace when they are re-connected brings a trust that helps dispel the fear. Confidence, or trust, in the Lord, is a conscientious decision, not an emotional one, and can help heal troublesome emotions.

Thought: There is just something about having someone with you in an uncertain situation. I knew of a young girl who was afraid of thunder and was afraid to walk outside in the dark, yet as long as she had her baby sister with her, she was ok. Her baby sister could do nothing to protect her, but her presence made all the difference. God's presence makes all of the difference in an uncertain situation.

Tune: When all You are is glorious oh God
Victorious and strong, whom shall I fear
When all You are is powerful and true
And good in all You do, whom shall I fear, whom shall I fear

Lord, when I am afraid, I will put my trust in You. Let the warmth of Your presence fill my heart and soul today, so I will not be alone.

Text: Psalm 56:8-13

[8] You yourself have recorded my wanderings.
Put my tears in your bottle.
Are they not in your book?
[9] Then my enemies will retreat on the day when I call.
This I know: God is for me.
[10] In God, whose word I praise,
in the Lord, whose word I praise,
[11] in God I trust; I will not be afraid.
What can mere humans do to me?
[12] I am obligated by vows to you, God;
I will make my thank offerings to you.
[13] For you rescued me from death,
even my feet from stumbling,
to walk before God in the light of life.

Truth: Whose word is praiseworthy? Only God's Word is praiseworthy. The psalmist is placing his trust in the Word of God. The Word of God promises protection for the child of God. The Word of God promises deliverance for the child of God. The Word of God is Truth, and Truth destroys deception.

Thought: Have you ever had a verse stick in your head or heart for a period of time? God is bringing that verse to remembrance for you at that moment. Meditating on the Word of God soothes the soul and arms you for battle.

Tune: From the breaking of the dawn to the setting of the sun
I will stand on ev'ry promise of Your word
Words of power strong to save that will never pass away
I will stand on ev'ry promise of Your word
For Your covenant is sure and on this I am secure
I can stand on ev'ry promise from Your word

God, Your Word is sufficient. Your word is complete. I stand today on it.

Text: Psalm 57:1-5

[1] Be gracious to me, God, be gracious to me,
for I take refuge in you.
I will seek refuge in the shadow of your wings
until danger passes.
[2] I call to God Most High,
to God who fulfills his purpose for me.
[3] He reaches down from heaven and saves me,
challenging the one who tramples me. Selah
God sends his faithful love and truth.
[4] I am surrounded by lions;
I lie down among devouring lions—
people whose teeth are spears and arrows,
whose tongues are sharp swords.
[5] God, be exalted above the heavens;
let your glory be over the whole earth.

Truth: David had been pursued by Saul and was hiding out. He was seeking refuge in God, to calm the storms of his life. David knew that God had never removed his involvement in his life and was confident that God would honor his request for mercy. David wanted to be sure that God was exalted and received the Glory!

Thought: Do you ever feel overwhelmed by the circumstances in your life? Do you feel as if you've hit rock bottom? When we're at the bottom, God is there! HE IS OUR ROCK!! We can cry out to and rest in God's grace and mercy till the "danger" passes by.

Tune: 'Til the storm passes over, 'Til the thunder sounds no more;
'Til the clouds roll forever from the sky,
Hold me fast, let me stand, in the hollow of thy hand;
Keep me safe 'til the storm passes by.

Father, Sometimes I am overwhelmed by life circumstances. Please help me to seek You and to feel your loving arms of protection around me.

Text: Psalm 57:6-11

[6] They prepared a net for my steps; I was despondent.
They dug a pit ahead of me, but they fell into it! Selah
[7] My heart is confident, God, my heart is confident.
I will sing; I will sing praises.
[8] Wake up, my soul! Wake up, harp and lyre!
I will wake up the dawn.
[9] I will praise you, Lord, among the peoples;
I will sing praises to you among the nations.
[10] For your faithful love is as high as the heavens;
your faithfulness reaches the clouds.
[11] God, be exalted above the heavens;
let your glory be over the whole earth.

Truth: The Psalmist is preparing his heart for praise. He is so excited that he wants to wake up the dawn! He desires to share his praise and thanks to God "among the peoples," meaning everyone, AND to those who don't know God. He is anticipating the spread of the gospel message of salvation. The Psalmist also knows that God's mercy, truth and glory are unfathomable, or "above the heavens!"

Thought: Wow! Imagine being so excited to praise God and share the Gospel with someone that you can't even sleep or wait for the dawn of the new day! Ask God to stir passion for Him today. Commit to praise our Father in Heaven today.

Tune: Praise Him praise Him, Jesus our blessed Redeemer
Sing O earth His wonderful love proclaim
Hail Him hail Him highest archangels in glory
Strength and honor give to His holy name
Like a shepherd Jesus will guard His children
In His arms He carries them all day long

Lord, fill me and mold me. Make me that kind of person who joyfully rises with full anticipation to praise You.

Text: Psalm 58:1-5

[1] Do you really speak righteously, you mighty ones?
Do you judge people fairly?
[2] No, you practice injustice in your hearts;
with your hands you weigh out violence in the land.
[3] The wicked go astray from the womb;
liars wander about from birth.
[4] They have venom like the venom of a snake,
like the deaf cobra that stops up its ears,
[5] that does not listen to the sound of the charmers
who skillfully weave spells.

Truth: In verse 3, the psalmist says that the unbelievers, or the wicked, are "astray from the womb". We come into this life under the curse of sin, in need of a Savior. It is only through the drawing of the Holy Spirit that we can come to know God. John 6:44, "No one can come to me unless the Father who sent me draws him." When the Father draws us in, He transforms us from one who is "astray" to become a child of the King.

Thought: Have you expressed to God lately how thankful you are to be saved? Just think...you have had opportunity for eternal life, for a relationship with the Creator of the world, simply because He loved you enough to invite you into a relationship with Him. The unbelievers are fighting a battle with flesh. As a child of God, you don't have to depend on yourself. You have the Holy Spirit to rely on as your Teacher.

Tune: And I'm forever grateful to You
I'm forever grateful for the cross
I'm forever grateful to You
That You came to seek and save the lost

Father, you weren't obligated to love me, but You did. You weren't obligated to save me, but You've offered it to me. You aren't obligated to give me grace and mercy, yet they are new every morning. Thank you, Father, for loving me, for calling me to Yourself, and for being my Savior.

<u>Songs for Life – Day 122 - May 2</u>

Text: Psalm 58:6-11

[6] God, knock the teeth out of their mouths;
Lord, tear out the young lions' fangs.
[7] May they vanish like water that flows by;
may they aim their blunted arrows.
[8] Like a slug that moves along in slime,
like a woman's miscarried child, may they not see the sun.
[9] Before your pots can feel the heat of the thorns—
whether green or burning—he will sweep them away.
[10] The righteous one will rejoice when he sees the retribution;
he will wash his feet in the blood of the wicked.
[11] Then people will say, "Yes, there is a reward for the righteous!
There is a God who judges on earth!"

Truth: Between the time that David was anointed to be King and his
actual sitting on the throne, David was pursued by the previous King,
Saul. Saul made over 15 attempts on David's life, out of jealousy and fear.
David had many opportunities to kill Saul, but each time, he would
remember that he would be taking vengeance that God did not ordain.

Thought: The human temptation is to strike back when we are hurt. We
see people who (seem to) have everything that life has to offer, yet their
hearts seem wicked. We must leave vengeance in God's hand.

Tune: He giveth more grace when the burdens grow greater
He sendeth more strength when the labors increase
To added affliction, He addeth His mercy
To multiplied trials His multiplied peace
His love has no limit, His grace has no measure
His pow'r has no boundary known unto men
For out of His infinite riches in Jesus
He giveth and giveth and giveth again

*O Lord, You have said that vengeance belongs to You, Your ways are
best. Help me to respond as You would have me to.*

Songs for Life – Day 123 - May 3

Text: Psalm 59:1-7

[1] Rescue me from my enemies, my God;
protect me from those who rise up against me.
[2] Rescue me from those who practice sin,
and save me from men of bloodshed.
[3] Because look, Lord, they set an ambush for me.
Powerful men attack me, but not because of any sin or rebellion of mine.
[4] For no fault of mine, they run and take up a position.
Awake to help me, and take notice.
[5] Lord God of Armies, you are the God of Israel.
Rise up to punish all the nations;
do not show favor to any wicked traitors. Selah
[6] They return at evening, snarling like dogs and prowling around the city.
[7] Look, they spew from their mouths—
sharp words from their lips. "For who," they say, "will hear?"

Truth: Opposition comes in many forms, not the least of which is from the Devil. Scripture is clear that "Your adversary the devil prowls around like a roaring lion, seeking someone to devour." (I Peter 5:8) Devour is a pretty strong word, but it also is descriptive of what Satan wants to do to us.

Thought: Life is a battle. All of these battles are made more understandable when we are fighting with the right tools. We must put on the belt of truth, the breastplate of righteousness, and shod our feet with the gospel of peace. We must take up the shield of faith, the helmet of salvation and the sword of the Spirit. Let God go before you and fight.

Tune: Onward Christian soldiers marching as to war
With the cross of Jesus going on before
Christ the royal Master leads against the foe
Forward into battle see His banner go
Onward Christian soldiers marching as to war
With the cross of Jesus going on before

Lord, equip me today for battle, for I know that my adversary is ready.

Text: Psalm 59:8-17

[8] But you laugh at them, Lord; you ridicule all the nations.

[9] I will keep watch for you, my strength, because God is my stronghold.

[10] My faithful God will come to meet me;

God will let me look down on my adversaries.

[11] Do not kill them; otherwise, my people will forget.

By your power, make them homeless wanderers and bring them down,

Lord, our shield.

[12] For the sin of their mouths and the words of their lips,

let them be caught in their pride. They utter curses and lies.

[13] Consume them in rage; consume them until they are gone.

Then people will know throughout the earth

that God rules over Jacob.Selah

[14] And they return at evening, snarling like dogs

and prowling around the city.

[15] They scavenge for food; they growl if they are not satisfied.

[16] But I will sing of your strength and will joyfully proclaim

your faithful love in the morning.

For you have been a stronghold for me, a refuge in my day of trouble.

[17] To you, my strength, I sing praises,

because God is my stronghold— my faithful God.

Truth: God is exalted as stronghold, faithful, powerful, shield, love and refuge. The psalmist has faith that God will be all of those for him.

Thought: Do you sometimes feel like you are in a never-ending battle? God's Word says he will meet you in his steadfast love. Take some time to meet Him today and share your hurts and heartaches. He is your refuge!

Tune: Open our eyes Lord, We want to see Jesus
To reach out and touch Him, and say that we love Him
Open our ears Lord, and help us to listen
Open our eyes Lord, We want to see Jesus

God, I know You are ready to meet with me. I need Your wisdom today.

Text: Psalm 60:1-5

[1] God, you have rejected us;
you have broken us down;
you have been angry. Restore us!
[2] You have shaken the land and split it open.
Heal its fissures, for it shudders.
[3] You have made your people suffer hardship;
you have given us wine to drink
that made us stagger.
[4] You have given a signal flag to those who fear you,
so that they can flee before the archers. Selah
[5] Save with your right hand, and answer me,
so that those you love may be rescued.

Truth: God's people felt as though they had been abandoned during this military attack. They knew that God had set up his "signal flag" to serve as a rallying point. What did they need to achieve success in their in their next military endeavors? They needed God's "right hand", His strength, His power and His might!

Thought: For a moment I ask you to think about our military, our American patriotism, about those who are protecting our lands, about our love for our great nation, and how it was originally founded on Biblical principles. We need God as OUR "banner", OUR "rallying point" with His "right hand" of protection on our nation.

Tune: God Bless America, land that I love.
Stand beside her and guide her
Thru the night with a light from above.
From the mountains, to the prairies,
To the oceans, white with foam
God bless America, My home sweet home

Father, We ask for your right hand of protection on our nation and our families. We pray that You would reveal Yourself to our leaders.

Songs for Life – Day 126 - May 6

Text: Psalm 60:6-12

6 God has spoken in his sanctuary:

"I will celebrate! I will divide up Shechem.

I will apportion the Valley of Succoth.

7 Gilead is mine, Manasseh is mine,

and Ephraim is my helmet;

Judah is my scepter.

8 Moab is my washbasin.

I throw my sandal on Edom; I shout in triumph over Philistia."

9 Who will bring me to the fortified city?

Who will lead me to Edom?

10 God, haven't you rejected us?

God, you do not march out with our armies.

11 Give us aid against the foe,

for human help is worthless.

12 With God we will perform valiantly;

he will trample our foes.

Truth: Shechem, Succoth, Gilead, Ephrain, and Judah are all areas occupied by Israelites. They are also key areas that belong to God. Moab, Edom and Philistia are principle enemies surrounding the Israelites. God's chosen people are seeking God's help. They know that to rely on themselves would be useless and be a rejection of God's call.

Thought: Our enemies today are the foes of sin, death and Satan. But Praise GOD, Verse 12 says He will "trample our foes"! We can rest in the knowledge that our enemies are subdued for all time.

Tune: You are the everlasting God; The everlasting God

You do not faint, You won't grow weary

You're the defender of the weak

You comfort those in need

You lift us up on wings like eagles

Father, Today, I admit that I need You, I need Your saving Grace!

Songs for Life – Day 127 - May 7

Text: Psalm 61:1-8

[1] God, hear my cry; pay attention to my prayer.

[2] I call to you from the ends of the earth when my heart is without strength.
Lead me to a rock that is high above me,

[3] for you have been a refuge for me,
a strong tower in the face of the enemy.

[4] I will dwell in your tent forever
and take refuge under the shelter of your wings. Selah

[5] God, you have heard my vows;
you have given a heritage to those who fear your name.

[6] Add days to the king's life; may his years span many generations.

[7] May he sit enthroned before God forever.
Appoint faithful love and truth to guard him.

[8] Then I will continually sing of your name,
fulfilling my vows day by day.

Truth: Trust . . . so hard to earn, so easy to lose, and so very difficult to regain once it is broken. This passage describes the perfect place where you can always place your trust - in God. He is described here as rock, refuge, strong tower, and a tent. He has wings big enough to cover you.

Thought: Sometimes people have trouble trusting God because they have been let down by people - maybe a parent, spouse, friend, leader, or family member. God will never let you down - He's never failed, not even once. His ways are higher than ours. Look up! Trust God! Seek refuge!

Tune: In the eye of the storm, You remain in control
And in the middle of the war, You guard my soul
You alone are the anchor, when my sails are torn
Your love surrounds me, in the eye of the storm
Lord Jesus, I open my heart to trust You. Whatever areas I have held back in the past, reveal them to me so that I can trust You fully.

Lord, be my Refuge today. Lead me to the Rock that is higher than I. You are my Shelter and my Port in the storm.

Songs for Life – Day 128 - May 8

Text: Psalm 62:1-7

[1] I am at rest in God alone; my salvation comes from him.
[2] He alone is my rock and my salvation,
my stronghold; I will never be shaken.
[3] How long will you threaten a man?
Will all of you attack as if he were a leaning wall or a tottering fence?
[4] They only plan to bring him down from his high position.
They take pleasure in lying;
they bless with their mouths, but they curse inwardly. Selah
[5] Rest in God alone, my soul,
for my hope comes from him.
[6] He alone is my rock and my salvation,
my stronghold; I will not be shaken.
[7] My salvation and glory depend on God, my strong rock.
My refuge is in God.

Truth: David was anointed to be king at a very early age and continued to live a life of a man "after God's heart", waiting patiently for God's timing to put him in place. Though it was hard to be patient at times, David knew that God's timing was best.

Thought: Does it ever seem like God is never going to come through? David probably felt that way at times, but we see the truth here in verse 1-2, a truth that you can also embrace. David had to wait on the Lord because his salvation, His rescue, comes from God and God alone.

Tune: You are the source of life, and I can't be left behind
No one else will do, and I will take hold of You
'Cause I need You Jesus, To come to my rescue
Where else can I go?
There's no other name, By which I am saved
Capture me with grace, I will follow You

God, grant me the depths of Your love so that while I am waiting on You, I can feel Your presence and know that I am protected.

Text: Psalm 62:8-12

[8] Trust in him at all times, you people;
pour out your hearts before him.
God is our refuge. Selah
[9] Common people are only a vapor;
important people, an illusion.
Together on a scale,
they weigh less than a vapor.
[10] Place no trust in oppression, or false hope in robbery.
If wealth increases, don't set your heart on it.
[11] God has spoken once;
I have heard this twice:
strength belongs to God,
[12] and faithful love belongs to you, Lord.
For you repay each according to his works.

Truth: Once again, we see a theme of trust. Verse 9 reminds us that people of all walks of life, all shapes and sizes, can let us down from time to time. Beyond that, God warns us here not to trust in things like riches, for they can disappear faster than they came. We are to "Trust in him at all times", for God is the only true and trustworthy one.

Thought: A song once said, "When Jesus is all that I have, He's all that I need." Once He has your full surrender, He can then fully guide you exactly where He wants you to go and how He wants to get you there.

Tune: Where You go I'll go, where You stay I'll stay
When You move I'll move, I will follow You
Whom You love I'll love, how You serve I'll serve
If this life I lose, I will follow (You)

Lord, teach me to trust. I don't mean to say "I trust You", but to really TRUST You. I want to surrender control and give it to You, Lord.

Text: Psalm 63:1-4

[1] God, you are my God; I eagerly seek you.
I thirst for you;
my body faints for you
in a land that is dry, desolate, and without water.
[2] So I gaze on you in the sanctuary
to see your strength and your glory.
[3] My lips will glorify you
because your faithful love is better than life.
[4] So I will bless you as long as I live;
at your name, I will lift up my hands.

Truth: David is out in the wilderness and is eagerly seeking the Lord. He knows that God's continuous love is worth more than anything else in life. He determines to lift up his hands as an outward sign of his prayer to God. He is making himself ready to receive blessings from God.

Thought: Are you in the "wilderness" or perhaps in a dry and weary land? God is ALL you need! Let Him be your God and eagerly seek Him, as David did. Raise your hands and praise God with your fingers and hands open wide. Whatever you receive from God will be good and will show your trust in God, and God alone. There can be no other.

Tune: God, You are my God
And I will ever praise you
Oh God, You are my God
And I will ever praise you

I will seek You in the morning
And I will learn to walk in Your ways
And step by step You'll lead me
And I will follow You all of my days

Almighty God, Holy Father, my Lord, I praise your Holy name. I stand with hands and arms open wide, in submission to you, to put my trust in You.

Text: Psalm 63:5-11

[5] You satisfy me as with rich food;
my mouth will praise you with joyful lips.
[6] When I think of you as I lie on my bed,
I meditate on you during the night watches
[7] because you are my helper;
I will rejoice in the shadow of your wings.
[8] I follow close to you; your right hand holds on to me.
[9] But those who intend to destroy my life
will go into the depths of the earth.
[10] They will be given over to the power of the sword;
they will become a meal for jackals.
[11] But the king will rejoice in God;
all who swear by him will boast, for the mouths of liars will be shut.

Truth: There is a comparison that is revealed here of spiritual satisfaction to that of filling and comforting food at a fancy banquet. David enjoys spiritual satisfaction because he clings or holds fast to his unfailing commitment to God. David's troubles from wicked people will be taken care of by God, who protects His people and His anointed king.

Thought: What gives you satisfaction or fills your soul like your favorite tasty meal fills your appetite? Perhaps your spiritual appetite needs some attention? Spend time with your Heavenly Father by reading His word, praying, and attending services with fellow believers. Cling to God in your time of need and let God give you the peace that your soul longs for.

Tune: Who can satisfy my soul like You
Who on earth could comfort me
And love me like You do
Who could ever be more faithful true
I will trust in You, Lord, I will trust in You my God

Lord God, only You can satisfy my soul and love me unconditionally. Lord, I cling to You and Your Word which fills me with joy!

Text: Psalm 64:1-6

[1] God, hear my voice when I am in anguish.
Protect my life from the terror of the enemy.
[2] Hide me from the scheming of wicked people, from the mob of evildoers,
[3] who sharpen their tongues like swords
and aim bitter words like arrows,
[4] shooting from concealed places at the blameless.
They shoot at him suddenly and are not afraid.
[5] They adopt an evil plan;
they talk about hiding traps and say, "Who will see them?"
[6] They devise crimes and say,
"We have perfected a secret plan."
The inner man and the heart are mysterious.

Truth: The psalmist uses several words and phrases which depict the forces that oppose us as we seek to follow Christ. "Enemy", "wicked", "evildoers", "tongues like swords", and "bitter words like arrows" are very descriptive terms. Our opposition is fierce and active, both from the outside and on the inside. Recognizing that helps us to fight the battle

Thought: Do you ever feel that, as a Christian, you are in the minority? Consider this… Christians are opposed by Satan, by the world, and even by our own flesh. It's no wonder we get tired from fighting! Do not be concerned with the external forces until you get your internal forces aligned with the power of the Holy Spirit. He will equip you for battle.

Tune: In heavenly armor we'll enter the land
The battle belongs to the Lord
No weapon that's fashioned against us will stand
The battle belongs to the Lord
And we sing glory honor, Power and strength to the Lord
We sing glory honor, Power and strength to the Lord

Holy Spirit, I know that my battle is not fought alone. The battle belongs to You. I need you to protect my soul, my spirit, with Your battle armor.

Songs for Life – Day 133 - May 13

Text: Psalm 64:7-10

⁷ But God will shoot them with arrows;
suddenly, they will be wounded.
⁸ They will be made to stumble;
their own tongues work against them.
All who see them will shake their heads.
⁹ Then everyone will fear
and will tell about God's work,
for they will understand what he has done.
¹⁰ The righteous one rejoices in the Lord and takes refuge in him;
all those who are upright in heart will offer praise.

Truth: If God be for us, who can be against us? The answer to that is . . . no one! For the Christian, sometimes the struggle is not in realizing that God has the power to destroy our enemies, both external and within ourselves, but in wondering when He is going to step in to fight that battle with and for us.

Thought: Have you ever wondered, "is God still there"? Maybe you are in a place right now where you have been waiting on an answer from God, waiting for Him to demonstrate His power over the things and circumstances which trouble you, or simply waiting on His assurance that things are going to be ok. This passage reminds us that when God acts, He acts swiftly, "suddenly, they will be wounded". Rejoice in the Lord! Take refuge in Him! God will be with you through the battle . . . today!

Tune: I am weak, but Thou art strong; Jesus, keep me from all wrong;
I'll be satisfied as long as I walk, let me walk close to Thee.
Just a closer walk with Thee,
Grant it, Jesus, is my plea,
Daily walking close to Thee,
Let it be, dear Lord, let it be.

Father, I know in my heart that You are always there, yet sometimes I feel you are a million miles away. Let me have a closer walk with You today.

Text: Psalm 65:1-8

[1] Praise is rightfully yours, God, in Zion; vows to you will be fulfilled.

[2] All humanity will come to you, the one who hears prayer.

[3] Iniquities overwhelm me;

only you can atone for our rebellions.

[4] How happy is the one you choose and bring near to live in your courts!

We will be satisfied with the goodness of your house,

the holiness of your temple.

[5] You answer us in righteousness, with awe-inspiring works,

God of our salvation,

the hope of all the ends of the earth and of the distant seas.

[6] You establish the mountains by your power;

you are robed with strength.

[7] You silence the roar of the seas, the roar of their waves,

and the tumult of the nations.

[8] Those who live far away are awed by your signs;

you make east and west shout for joy.

Truth: Praise, vows, prayers, come to you, atonement, courts, house, temple - all of these are terms, in this passage, which indicate what happens in worship. The worshippers have come to celebrate the unlimited kindness and mercy of God to His people. It is a privilege to come into His presence, into His house, and offer expressions of worship.

Thought: The temptation for the child of God is to sometimes withdraw from God when we have been hurt, or when we are weary from the battle. Saints of God have been fighting battles for ages upon ages. Let us learn from their example and come to God in all times. Let us never withdraw from worship but enter into His presence even more in times of trouble.

Tune: He's alive alive, alive Hallelujah, alive praise and glory to the Lamb Alive alive, alive hallelujah, alive forever amen

God, You are the Balm for my hurts, yet sometimes my first instinct is to pull away. I praise You today and see Your presence and Your touch.

Text: Psalm 65:9-13

[9] You visit the earth and water it abundantly,
enriching it greatly.
God's stream is filled with water,
for you prepare the earth in this way,
providing people with grain.
[10] You soften it with showers and bless its growth,
soaking its furrows and leveling its ridges.
[11] You crown the year with your goodness;
your carts overflow with plenty.
[12] The wilderness pastures overflow,
and the hills are robed with joy.
[13] The pastures are clothed with flocks
and the valleys covered with grain.
They shout in triumph; indeed, they sing.

Truth: Every blessing, every privilege, every bit of joy, has come at the hand of our Heavenly Father. He provides rain for the crops and showers of blessing for our soul. He provides the grain for food, and the nourishment for our heart. God could have left us to our own destruction many times, yet His love for us is so great that He continues to provide what we do not deserve. His mercies are great; His grace unending.

Thought: Have you ever had someone tell you thank you for something that you just did because they care about you? Have you ever had someone come and say, "I love you", just when you needed to hear it? Those are responses to the Holy Spirit providing you what you needed, just when you needed it. Trust God for His provision today. Nothing we have comes because of our own effort, but because He has provided it.

Tune: Showers of blessing, Showers of blessing we need
Mercy drops round us are falling, but for the showers we plead

Heavenly Father, I need my life to feel the drenching rain of Your showers of blessing. Pour out on me today, Heavenly Father.

Songs for Life – Day 136 - May 16

Text: Psalm 66:1-7

[1] Let the whole earth shout joyfully to God!

[2] Sing about the glory of his name; make his praise glorious.

[3] Say to God, "How awe-inspiring are your works!

Your enemies will cringe before you because of your great strength.

[4] The whole earth will worship you and sing praise to you.

They will sing praise to your name." Selah

[5] Come and see the wonders of God;

his acts for humanity are awe-inspiring.

[6] He turned the sea into dry land,

and they crossed the river on foot.

There we rejoiced in him.

[7] He rules forever by his might; he keeps his eye on the nations.

The rebellious should not exalt themselves. Selah

Truth: Verses 1-4 serve as a reminder to acknowledge the one true God who created everything! We should "shout joyfully to God", thanking God daily for his awesome deeds. Verses 5-7 tell of how God brought his chosen Israelites out of bondage and provided many miraculous events.

Thought: God created everything!! The planet we live on, the stars, moon and sun. God created the animals, vegetation, land and oceans. He created it ALL. God created you and me. God provides us a world to live in and people to enrich and fill our lives. He is with us and protects us; just He did for the Israelites so long ago.

Tune: Mighty is our God; Mighty is our King

Mighty is our Lord; Ruler of ev'rything

Glory to our God; Glory to our King

Glory to our Lord; Ruler of ev'rything

His name is higher; Higher than any other name

His pow'r is greater; For He has created ev'rything

Father, Thank You for your unending love and the provisions you have so graciously given me. I love you, Lord.

Songs for Life – Day 137 - May 17

Text: Psalm 66:8-15

[8] Bless our God, you peoples; let the sound of his praise be heard.
[9] He keeps us alive
and does not allow our feet to slip.
[10] For you, God, tested us;
you refined us as silver is refined.
[11] You lured us into a trap; you placed burdens on our backs.
[12] You let men ride over our heads;
we went through fire and water,
but you brought us out to abundance.
[13] I will enter your house with burnt offerings;
I will pay you my vows
[14] that my lips promised and my mouth spoke during my distress.
[15] I will offer you fattened sheep as burnt offerings,
with the fragrant smoke of rams;
I will sacrifice bulls with goats. Selah

Truth: The Psalmist begins by thanking God for His protection, safety and security. He is telling the people to thank God for taking them through a difficult situation, and for refining them like silver through purifying trials. God is using his chosen people to spread the news to the Gentiles of everything He has done. The passage shifts from corporate praise and worship to one individual with the words, "I will".

Thought: We are called to gather in corporate worship with our fellow believers and unite as one to worship God. We must be faithful to do our part as God is ALWAYS faithful to us. Along with worship, we bring our offerings in the "house" or church as we are also commanded.

Tune: Come Thou Almighty King; Help us Thy name to sing
Help us to praise; Father all glorious
O'er all victorious; Come and reign over us; Ancient of Days

Heavenly Father, I thank you for Your love and protection, and for the refinement that I endure. Come and reign over me and in my life.

Text: Psalm 66:16-20

16 Come and listen, all who fear God,
and I will tell what he has done for me.
17 I cried out to him with my mouth,
and praise was on my tongue.
18 If I had been aware of malice in my heart,
the Lord would not have listened.
19 However, God has listened;
he has paid attention to the sound of my prayer.
20 Blessed be God!
He has not turned away my prayer
or turned his faithful love from me.

Truth: "Come and listen, all who fear God," says the Psalmist. He was very excited to share that God had listened to his prayers and cries for help in his time of need. The Psalmist knew not to have sin in his heart, and to be cleansed before he went to God in prayer for help for his difficult situations.

Thought: Who do you cry out to in your time of need? Have you checked your heart for sin that might need to be confessed so you can enjoy pure fellowship with God? God will be faithful to you. What about you? Are you faithful to God? Share your blessings of what God has done in your life with someone today.

Tune: He's been faithful, faithful to me
Looking back, His love and mercy I see
Though in my heart, I have questioned
Even failed to believe
Yet He's been faithful, faithful to me

Father God...Please cleanse my heart and reveal to me the areas of sin in my life. Please forgive me where I fail you Lord. I know You will be faithful to me; and I desire Your love, grace and mercy.

Text: Psalm 67:1-7

[1] May God be gracious to us and bless us;
may he make his face shine upon us. Selah
[2] so that your way may be known on earth,
your salvation among all nations.
[3] Let the peoples praise you, God;
let all the peoples praise you.
[4] Let the nations rejoice and shout for joy,
for you judge the peoples with fairness
and lead the nations on earth. Selah
[5] Let the peoples praise you, God, let all the peoples praise you.
[6] The earth has produced its harvest; God, our God, blesses us.
[7] God will bless us,
and all the ends of the earth will fear him.

Truth: In this Psalm, we see the prayer for divine mercy (v. 1-2), the plea for universal worship (v. 3-5) and the prospect of divine blessings (v. 6-7). As His mercy is displayed, people are drawn to Him and come to know Him. As He is worshipped, the believers are exalting the One who has given life and are drawn into His presence. This helps put into perspective where our blessings come from, from God and God alone.

Thought: What could happen if a congregation of people came together on any given time of worship and had no hindrances to worship? We perhaps could see an evidence of what we see described in the Old Testament, where the glory of God was so present that the priests could not lead in worship. Let that start within you today, right where you are.

Tune: Praise God from whom all blessings flow
Praise Him all creatures here below
Praise Him above ye heavenly host
Praise Father Son and Holy Ghost - Amen

Father God, I know that You are the Source of all blessings, the Source of everything in the world. I worship You today with all of my heart.

Songs for Life – Day 140 - May 20

Text: Psalm 68:1-6

[1] God arises. His enemies scatter,
and those who hate him flee from his presence.
[2] As smoke is blown away,
so you blow them away.
As wax melts before the fire,
so the wicked are destroyed before God.
[3] But the righteous are glad;
they rejoice before God and celebrate with joy.
[4] Sing to God! Sing praises to his name.
Exalt him who rides on the clouds—
his name is the Lord—and celebrate before him.
[5] God in his holy dwelling is a father of the fatherless
and a champion of widows.
[6] God provides homes for those who are deserted.
He leads out the prisoners to prosperity,
but the rebellious live in a scorched land.

Truth: The words "God arises" were the first words Moses spoke each day before Israel marched during the wilderness period. As he spoke, the ark of the covenant would be raised to lead the process. What did the ark of the covenant represent? It was the Word of God. It was God's Word that led them, sustained them, and freed them from bondage.

Thought: One of these days, perhaps very soon, "God arises" from His throne and say to Jesus, "Son of Man, go and bring my children home". God always has the final word, and He is undefeated.

Tune: Let God arise
Let God arise
Our God reigns now and forever
He reigns now and forever

God, I'm ready for the day when You will arise and bring all of Your children home. Thank You for the promise of eternal life with You.

Text: Psalm 68:7-14

[7] God, when you went out before your people,
when you marched through the desert, Selah
[8] the earth trembled and the skies poured rain
before God, the God of Sinai, before God, the God of Israel.
[9] You, God, showered abundant rain;
you revived your inheritance when it languished.
[10] Your people settled in it;
God, you provided for the poor by your goodness.
[11] The Lord gave the command;
a great company of women brought the good news:
[12] "The kings of the armies flee—they flee!"
She who stays at home divides the spoil.
[13] While you lie among the sheep pens,
the wings of a dove are covered with silver,
and its feathers with glistening gold.
[14] When the Almighty scattered kings in the land, it snowed on Zalmon.

Truth: "The Lord gave the command" . . . Though the usage here is primarily a military term, think of what has happened when The Lord has given "the command" over the course of history. Light came from darkness, waters came into existence, plants and trees were birthed. When God speaks, things happen immediately and according to His command.

Thought: God's design for His Word is that we would read it, ingest it, and obey it immediately. His Word is the nourishment for our soul, direction for our lives, and source of our salvation.

Tune: Break Thou the bread of life dear Lord to me
As Thou didst break the loaves beside the sea
Beyond the sacred page I seek Thee Lord
My spirit pants for Thee O Living Word

Father, give me a thirst for Your Word that never ceases.

Text: Psalm 68:15-23

15 Mount Bashan is God's towering mountain;
Mount Bashan is a mountain of many peaks.
16 Why gaze with envy, you mountain peaks,
at the mountain God desired for his abode?
The Lord will dwell there forever!
17 God's chariots are tens of thousands, thousands and thousands;
the Lord is among them in the sanctuary as he was at Sinai.
18 You ascended to the heights, taking away captives;
you received gifts from people, even from the rebellious,
so that the Lord God might dwell there.
19 Blessed be the Lord!
Day after day he bears our burdens; God is our salvation. Selah
20 Our God is a God of salvation,
and escape from death belongs to the Lord my Lord.
21 Surely God crushes the heads of his enemies,
the hairy brow of one who goes on in his guilty acts.
22 The Lord said, "I will bring them back from Bashan;
I will bring them back from the depths of the sea
23 so that your foot may wade in blood
and your dogs' tongues may have their share from the enemies."

Truth: Verses 19-20 remind us that God does not provide our salvation, He IS our salvation. You can read vs. 19-20 and make it personal - saying "my" in place of "our".

Thought: Salvation is not in a process, a prayer, or following a code of conduct. Our God IS salvation!

Tune: He touched me, Oh He touched me
And oh the joy that floods my soul
Something happened and now I know
He touched me and made me whole

Father, You are my salvation, not only for eternity, but for every day.

Text: Psalm 68:24-31

24 People have seen your procession, God,
the procession of my God, my King, in the sanctuary.
25 Singers lead the way, with musicians following;
among them are young women playing tambourines.
26 Bless God in the assemblies;
bless the Lord from the fountain of Israel.
27 There is Benjamin, the youngest, leading them,
the rulers of Judah in their assembly,
the rulers of Zebulun, the rulers of Naphtali.
28 Your God has decreed your strength.
Show your strength, God, you who have acted on our behalf.
29 Because of your temple at Jerusalem,
kings will bring tribute to you.
30 Rebuke the beast in the reeds,
the herd of bulls with the calves of the peoples.
Trample underfoot those with bars of silver.
Scatter the peoples who take pleasure in war.
31 Ambassadors will come from Egypt;
Cush will stretch out its hands to God.

Truth: The scene described here is when the ark of the covenant was being brought to Mount Zion. Imagine the celebration for the entrance of the Word of God . . . singers, musicians, saints praising Almighty God.

Thought: Should this be any less when we get together to worship on any given Sunday? How about whenever we sit down individually to read the Word? How can you prepare for the entrance of The Word?

Tune: How firm a foundation ye saints of the Lord
Is laid for your faith in His excellent word
What more can He say, than to you He hath said
To you who for refuge to Jesus have fled

Dear Lord, Your Word is life. Give me an unquenchable thirst for it.

Text: Psalm 68:32-35

[32] Sing to God, you kingdoms of the earth;
sing praise to the Lord, Selah
[33] to him who rides in the ancient, highest heavens.
Look, he thunders with his powerful voice!
[34] Ascribe power to God.
His majesty is over Israel,
his power is among the clouds.
[35] God, you are awe-inspiring in your sanctuaries.
The God of Israel gives power and strength to his people.
Blessed be God!

Truth: In this closing call to praise for this Psalm, the call goes out to all of the kingdoms of the earth to sing to God. God's majesty is over Israel, and He has chosen them to be the vehicle to spread the love of God throughout the world. What a privilege! In the same way, in the New Testament age, we who know the love of Christ have been given the command to share the Gospel with the world.

Thought: With great privilege comes great responsibility. God has given us the greatest privilege in the world, the privilege of opportunity to know Him and to be saved from eternal separation from Him. However, it was not intended to end with us - we must share the good news! Who in your life needs to know the power of the Gospel today?

Tune: And I thank God for the lighthouse, I owe my life to Him
For Jesus is the lighthouse, and from the rocks of sin
He has shone a light around me that I could clearly see
If it wasn't for the lighthouse
Tell me where would this ship be

Lord, just as someone shared the good news about You with me, I must also share with others the fact that You are salvation. Burden my heart with the names of those You desire for me to share Your love with.

Text: Psalm 69:1-5

[1] Save me, God,
for the water has risen to my neck.
[2] I have sunk in deep mud, and there is no footing;
I have come into deep water,
and a flood sweeps over me.
[3] I am weary from my crying;
my throat is parched.
My eyes fail, looking for my God.
[4] Those who hate me without cause
are more numerous than the hairs of my head;
my deceitful enemies, who would destroy me, are powerful.
Though I did not steal, I must repay.
[5] God, you know my foolishness,
and my guilty acts are not hidden from you.

Truth: "Save me, God!" Can't you just hear the desperate cries of this psalmist? His voice is weary, and he is exhausted. His enemies have falsely accused him. Though he may be innocent from those circumstances, he has sin in his heart that cannot be hidden from God.

Thought: Desperate times call for desperate measures. When you're desperate and feel the enemy attacking you, cry out, "Save me, God!" The enemy will falsely accuse you, and, try to bring you down. Don't let it happen. Be strong! God Loves You! He sent His son Jesus to save you from your sins and to give you eternal life. When you are down and out, just cry to Jesus!

Tune: Sometimes the way is lonely
And steep and filled with pain
So if your sky is dark and pours the rain
Then cry to Jesus
Cry to Jesus; Cry to Jesus and live.

Oh Lord, Save me. Forgive me. I love You and I desperately need You!

Text: Psalm 69:6-12

[6] Do not let those who put their hope in you be disgraced because of me,
Lord God of Armies; do not let those who seek you
be humiliated because of me, God of Israel.
[7] For I have endured insults because of you,
and shame has covered my face.
[8] I have become a stranger to my brothers
and a foreigner to my mother's sons
[9] because zeal for your house has consumed me,
and the insults of those who insult you
have fallen on me.
[10] I mourned and fasted, but it brought me insults.
[11] I wore sackcloth as my clothing, and I was a joke to them.
[12] Those who sit at the city gate talk about me,
and drunkards make up songs about me.

Truth: David felt that his shame and suffering would reflect poorly on God and might cause others to stumble. But he loved God so much that he would fast and mourn with grief over his sins. His own family would reject him. Others would ridicule him and make up drinking songs about him during this time of suffering.

Thought: Do you love God so much that your heart is burdened or saddened by those who dishonor God? Have you ever thought that your sins could be a stumbling block for new or weak Christians? Maybe it's time to examine your life and your heart. Today IS the day.

Tune: I'm casting my cares aside; I'm leaving my past behind
I'm setting my heart and mind on You, Jesus
I'm reaching my hands to Yours; Believing there's so much more
Knowing that all You have in store for me is good, It's good
Today is the day You have made; I will rejoice and be glad in it!
Today is the day You have made; I will rejoice and be glad in it!

Today, I'm seeking YOU with all my heart. I will rejoice and be glad in it.

Songs for Life – Day 147 - May 27

Text: Psalm 69:13-18

[13] But as for me, Lord, my prayer to you is for a time of favor.
In your abundant, faithful love, God, answer me with your sure salvation.
[14] Rescue me from the miry mud; don't let me sink.
Let me be rescued from those who hate me
and from the deep water.
[15] Don't let the floodwaters sweep over me
or the deep swallow me up;
don't let the Pit close its mouth over me.
[16] Answer me, Lord,
for your faithful love is good.
In keeping with your abundant compassion, turn to me.
[17] Don't hide your face from your servant, for I am in distress.
Answer me quickly!
[18] Come near to me and redeem me; ransom me because of my enemies.

Truth: "But as for me, Lord, my prayer to you is for a time of favor." Do you hear the intensity of the psalmist's cry? He is telling us that he is expressing his total reliance on, and trust in, God. He is urgently crying out to God to be near to him. God's very presence will redeem and deliver him.

Thought: Who do you cry out to? Do you pray to God and ask him to "come near?" Do you fully accept that God's very presence will redeem and deliver you in difficult times? God's love is steadfast and good.

Tune: Draw me close to You, never let me go
I lay it all down again; To hear You say that I'm Your friend
You are my desire no one else will do;
'Cause nothing else could take Your place
To feel the warmth of Your embrace;
Help me find the way bring me back to You

Heavenly Father, Draw me into your loving arms. I need you today. You are my one desire. Fill me with your presence.

Songs for Life – Day 148 - May 28

Text: Psalm 69:19-28

[19] You know the insults I endure—my shame and disgrace.
You are aware of all my adversaries.
[20] Insults have broken my heart, and I am in despair.
I waited for sympathy, but there was none;
for comforters, but found no one.
[21] Instead, they gave me gall for my food, and for my thirst
they gave me vinegar to drink.
[22] Let their table set before them be a snare,
and let it be a trap for their allies.
[23] Let their eyes grow too dim to see, and let their hips continually quake.
[24] Pour out your rage on them, and let your burning anger overtake them.
[25] Make their fortification desolate; may no one live in their tents.
[26] For they persecute the one you struck
and talk about the pain of those you wounded.
[27] Charge them with crime on top of crime;
do not let them share in your righteousness.
[28] Let them be erased from the book of life
and not be recorded with the righteous.

Truth: "Shame", "disgrace" "despair", those are heartfelt emotions that the psalmist was feeling. The people he thought were friends and would be supportive, turned against him. He turns to God and prays the plots of the wicked would be justly punished.

Thought: Do you ever feel "shame, dishonor and despair," in your heart? Those are emotions that aren't necessarily visible to man. They can live in your heart and the enemy can use them against you. There is One who knows what is in your heart, the secret place behind your walls of protection. Verse 19 says, "You know." God knows.

Tune: He knows my name; He knows my every thought
He sees each tear that falls, and he hears me when I call

God, You know my heart and my hurts. I need you today.

Songs for Life – Day 149 - May 29

Text: Psalm 69:29-36

^{29} But as for me—poor and in pain—let your salvation protect me, God.
^{30} I will praise God's name with song
and exalt him with thanksgiving.
^{31} That will please the Lord more than an ox,
more than a bull with horns and hooves.
^{32} The humble will see it and rejoice.
You who seek God, take heart!
^{33} For the Lord listens to the needy
and does not despise his own who are prisoners.
^{34} Let heaven and earth praise him,
the seas and everything that moves in them,
^{35} for God will save Zion and build up the cities of Judah.
They will live there and possess it.
^{36} The descendants of his servants will inherit it,
and those who love his name will live in it.

Truth: The psalmist was in pain, yet he asked God for salvation. He praised God's name for all to see. He knew that glorifying the Lord with thanksgiving was more valuable than bringing any material possession, no matter how valuable. God intended for the whole world to praise Him.

Thought: "Let heaven and earth praise him." Can you imagine what that would be like? It's hard because we see so much wickedness and evil in the world that corrupt the life of God's people. Why not stop right now and praise your Heavenly Father? He is worthy of all our praise.

Tune: Let everything that, everything that,
Everything that has breath Praise the Lord.
Praise You in the morning; Praise You in the evening
Praise You when I'm young; And when I'm old
Praise You when I'm laughing; Praise You when I'm grieving
Praise You ev'ry season of the soul

Father, be glorified in my life and let others see You through me.

Text: Psalm 70:1-5

[1] God, hurry to rescue me.
Lord, hurry to help me!
[2] Let those who seek to kill me
be disgraced and confounded;
let those who wish me harm
be turned back and humiliated.
[3] Let those who say, "Aha, aha!"
retreat because of their shame.
[4] Let all who seek you rejoice and be glad in you;
let those who love your salvation
continually say, "God is great!"
[5] I am oppressed and needy; hurry to me, God.
You are my help and my deliverer; Lord, do not delay.

Truth: David, the author of many of the Psalms, was anointed to be King at an early age, yet was attacked regularly, both by his enemies, as well as by his king. Yet, God put a heart of praise within David and always delivered him right on time, even when David was vulnerable.

Thought: The last verse of this Psalm puts things in perspective. When it all comes down to it, we have nothing of our own accord, we've earned nothing, and we are due nothing. We are poor and needy. However, God did not create us to leave us stranded without a lifeline. He is our help and deliverer. If He created you, He knows how to keep you and sustain you. He knows how to save you. He knows how to deliver you, and His timing is always perfect.

Tune: Jesus what a Friend for sinners, Jesus Lover of my soul
Friends may fail me foes assail me, He my Savior makes me whole
Hallelujah what a Savior, Hallelujah what a Friend
Saving, helping, keeping, loving, He is with me to the end

Lord, I have nothing without You. I am poor and needy. Only You know really what I need. Meet my needs today and I will be thankful.

Songs for Life – Day 151 – May 31

Text: Psalm 71:1-6

[1] Lord, I seek refuge in you; let me never be disgraced.

[2] In your justice, rescue and deliver me;
listen closely to me and save me.

[3] Be a rock of refuge for me, where I can always go.
Give the command to save me, for you are my rock and fortress.

[4] Deliver me, my God, from the power of the wicked,
from the grasp of the unjust and oppressive.

[5] For you are my hope, Lord God,
my confidence from my youth.

[6] I have leaned on you from birth;
you took me from my mother's womb.
My praise is always about you.

Truth: The righteousness of God does not permit Him to fail, or to fail to keep even one of His promises. God is indeed our hope, our trust, our rock, our refuge. If He led you to it, He'll lead you through it.

Thought: The will of God will never take you where the grace of God will not protect you. Just as David certainly must have felt alone at times and perhaps even wondered why God allowed him to go through such trials and tribulations, the righteousness of God never failed, even for a moment. He is our only hope.

Tune: And can it be that I should gain
An interest in the Savior's blood
Died He for me who caused His pain
For me who Him to death pursued
Amazing love how can it be
That Thou my God shouldst die for me
Amazing love how can it be
That Thou my God shouldst die for me

Lord, Your righteousness is better than life itself. Let Your righteousness shine through me today so that others may see You in me.

<u>Songs for Life – Day 152 – June 1</u>

Text: Psalm 71:7-16

[7] I am like a miraculous sign to many, and you are my strong refuge.

[8] My mouth is full of praise and honor to you all day long.

[9] Don't discard me in my old age.
   As my strength fails, do not abandon me.

[10] For my enemies talk about me, and those who spy on me plot together,

[11] saying, "God has abandoned him;
   chase him and catch him, for there is no one to rescue him."

[12] God, do not be far from me; my God, hurry to help me.

[13] May my adversaries be disgraced and destroyed;
   may those who intend to harm me
   be covered with disgrace and humiliation.

[14] But I will hope continually and will praise you more and more.

[15] My mouth will tell about your righteousness
   and your salvation all day long, though I cannot sum them up.

[16] I come because of the mighty acts of the Lord God;
   I will proclaim your righteousness, yours alone.

Truth: The word refuge in verse 7 refers to the Psalmist's own acknowledgement that he has had some colossal failures in his life. He has been a living demonstration at times of what God's consequences can bring, YET God has continued to be a help and a stronghold.

Thought: The true test of the inner man is what we do when failures come. The question is not IF failures will come, but WHEN. Our true character comes out in how we deal with them. God uses our struggles to demonstrate His glory. Will You give Him your struggles today?

Tune: Years I spent in vanity and pride
Caring not my Lord was crucified
Knowing not it was for me He died on Calvary
Mercy there was great, and grace was free
Pardon there was multiplied to me
There my burdened soul found liberty at Calvary

Father, help me to see your glory, even in my struggles.

Songs for Life – Day 153 - June 2

Text: Psalm 71:17-24

[17] God, you have taught me from my youth,
and I still proclaim your wondrous works.
[18] Even while I am old and gray, God, do not abandon me,
while I proclaim your power to another generation,
your strength to all who are to come.
[19] Your righteousness reaches the heights, God,
you who have done great things; God, who is like you?
[20] You caused me to experience many troubles and misfortunes,
but you will revive me again.
You will bring me up again, even from the depths of the earth.
[21] You will increase my honor and comfort me once again.
[22] Therefore, I will praise you with a harp for your faithfulness, my God;
I will sing to you with a lyre, Holy One of Israel.
[23] My lips will shout for joy when I sing praise to you
because you have redeemed me.
[24] Therefore, my tongue will proclaim your righteousness all day long,
for those who intend to harm me will be disgraced and confounded.

Truth: Revival . . . a need, a cry, a desire . . . The Psalmist is crying out for revival. He acknowledges God as the God who teaches, as well as the God who allows "troubles and misfortunes" to come. He knows that God will eventually revive him again. He knows this because God has demonstrated this repeatedly from the time of his youth.

Thought: Our need for God is really best understood in the tough times. When things are rocking along smoothly, it is easy to lose sight of the One who brought us those victories. In our troubles, God strips away all of the distractions, and we have laser-like focus on asking God to deliver us.

Tune: We praise Thee O God for the Son of Thy love
For Jesus who died and is now gone above
Hallelujah Thine the glory, Hallelujah amen
Hallelujah Thine the glory, revive us again

O Lord, take the brokenness of my heart and revive it again! I need it!

Text: Psalm 72:1-7

[1] God, give your justice to the king
and your righteousness to the king's son.
[2] He will judge your people with righteousness
and your afflicted ones with justice.
[3] May the mountains bring well-being to the people
and the hills, righteousness.
[4] May he vindicate the afflicted among the people,
help the poor, and crush the oppressor.
[5] May they fear you while the sun endures
and as long as the moon, throughout all generations.
[6] May the king be like rain that falls on the cut grass,
like spring showers that water the earth.
[7] May the righteous flourish in his days
and well-being abound until the moon is no more.

Truth: The plea or prayer is that the king would seek God, to give him the righteousness and justice to preside over God's people for their well-being. When kings would rule with justice and compassion, the whole earth itself would be overcome with goodness. The psalmist is asking God to allow the kings to see as He sees, and to judge as He judges.

Thought: What would it be like in our nation today if our president, governors, senators and others who are in places of authority always sought God in prayer before making decisions that affect me and you? II Chronicles 7:14 calls on the people of God to call on Him, seek Him.

Tune: Great is Thy faithfulness; O God my Father
There is no shadow; Of turning with Thee
Thou changest not; Thy compassions they fail not
As Thou hast been; Thou forever wilt be

Heavenly Father, we are your people. We pray for our leaders to seek Your face. We ask you to bless and heal our land, as only You can.

Text: Psalm 72:8-14

[8] May he rule from sea to sea
  and from the Euphrates to the ends of the earth.
[9] May desert tribes kneel before him
  and his enemies lick the dust.
[10] May the kings of Tarshish
  and the coasts and islands bring tribute,
  the kings of Sheba and Seba offer gifts.
[11] Let all kings bow in homage to him, all nations serve him.
[12] For he will rescue the poor who cry out
  and the afflicted who have no helper.
[13] He will have pity on the poor and helpless
  and save the lives of the poor.
[14] He will redeem them from oppression and violence,
  for their lives are precious in his sight.

Truth: The prayer asks God to send blessings beyond Israel's borders for the desert tribes and people in other remote places to submit and serve Israel's King. It is a plea for unity and protection. Verses 12-14 ask the king in power to protect the weak from oppression because they are precious to God.

Thought: *"for their lives are precious in His sight,"* - reflect on that. I Samuel 26:24 says *"Behold, as your life was precious this day in my sight, so may my life be precious in your eyes this day."* As born-again believers, we are precious in God's eyes. God dearly loves His creation, His people.

Tune: Jesus loves the little children, all the children of the world.
Red and yellow, black and white,
They are precious in His sight,
Jesus loves the little children of the world.

Lord, thank you that I am precious in Your sight. I'm thankful that you love me, that You sent Your son to be my ultimate redeemer from sin.

Songs for Life – Day 156 - June 5

Text: Psalm 72:15-20

[15] May he live long!
  May gold from Sheba be given to him.
  May prayer be offered for him continually,
  and may he be blessed all day long.
[16] May there be plenty of grain in the land;
  may it wave on the tops of the mountains.
  May its crops be like Lebanon.
  May people flourish in the cities
  like the grass of the field.
[17] May his name endure forever;
  as long as the sun shines, may his fame increase.
  May all nations be blessed by him and call him blessed.
[18] Blessed be the Lord God, the God of Israel,
  who alone does wonders.
[19] Blessed be his glorious name forever;
  the whole earth is filled with his glory.
  Amen and amen.
[20] The prayers of David son of Jesse are concluded.

Truth: This is the end of the prayer by the Israelites, asking God for His hand on their land and crops, and for an increase in their number. It concludes with a heartfelt praise to God and asking Him to fill the whole earth with His glory.

Thought: Today - Focus on verses 18-19. Meditate on it. Re-read it several times, maybe even memorize it. Let Him fill you with His glory.

Tune: I see the Lord seated on the throne, exalted,
And the train of His robe fills the temple with glory,
And the whole earth is filled; And the whole earth is filled;
And the whole earth is filled, with His glory.

Father, You are blessed! You do wondrous things! Blessed be Your glorious name forever; and may the whole earth be filled with Your glory!

<u>Songs for Life – Day 157 - June 6</u>

Text: Psalm 73:1-15

[1] God is indeed good to Israel, to the pure in heart.

[2] But as for me, my feet almost slipped; my steps nearly went astray.

[3] For I envied the arrogant; I saw the prosperity of the wicked.

[4] They have an easy time until they die, and their bodies are well fed.

[5] They are not in trouble like others; they are not afflicted like most people.

[6] Therefore, pride is their necklace, and violence covers them like a garment.

[7] Their eyes bulge out from fatness; the imaginations of their hearts run wild.

[8] They mock, and they speak maliciously;
   they arrogantly threaten oppression.

[9] They set their mouths against heaven,
   and their tongues strut across the earth.

[10] Therefore his people turn to them and drink in their overflowing words.

[11] The wicked say, "How can God know?
   Does the Most High know everything?"

[12] Look at them—the wicked!
   They are always at ease, and they increase their wealth.

[13] Did I purify my heart and wash my hands in innocence for nothing?

[14] For I am afflicted all day long and punished every morning.

[15] If I had decided to say these things aloud,
   I would have betrayed your people.

Truth: This passage reminds us that things that adorn us are just external things. What matters is the condition of the heart.

Thought: If the inner man is sin-sick, no measure of external decoration or adornment is going to change his destination, or his attitude once he gets there. God's plan for growth is from the inside out.

Tune: You dance over me, while I am unaware
You sing all around, but I never hear the sound
Lord I'm amazed by You, Lord I'm amazed by You
Lord I'm amazed by You, How You love me

Father, look into the depths of my heart and see if there is anything that is contrary to your plan for my life. Reveal it to me so I can confess it.

Songs for Life – Day 158 - June 7

Text: Psalm 73:16-22

[16] When I tried to understand all this,
 it seemed hopeless

[17] until I entered God's sanctuary.
 Then I understood their destiny.

[18] Indeed, you put them in slippery places;
 you make them fall into ruin.

[19] How suddenly they become a desolation!
 They come to an end, swept away by terrors.

[20] Like one waking from a dream,
 Lord, when arising, you will despise their image.

[21] When I became embittered and my innermost being was wounded,

[22] I was stupid and didn't understand;
 I was an unthinking animal toward you.

Truth: The psalmist was struggling with trying to understand how it seems that the wicked seem to prosper, or how so many have it "together" on the outside. It remained a mystery "until I entered God's sanctuary". When we go to the sanctuary of God, He takes the blinders off, gives us the truth, and comforts the weary soul.

Thought: You can deal with every situation in life by going into "God's sanctuary". It is a sanctuary of refuge, a place where we worship, and is a place where all is revealed before Almighty God. Sometimes it's painful to go a few layers deep, but the results are worth it.

Tune: Alleluia alleluia, For the Lord God Almighty reigns
Alleluia alleluia, For the Lord God Almighty reigns, Alleluia
(You are) Holy holy, are You Lord God Almighty
Worthy is the Lamb, Worthy is the Lamb
You are holy holy, are You Lord God Almighty
Worthy is the Lamb, Worthy is the Lamb, Amen

Lord Jesus, bring me today into Your sanctuary. Surround me with Your presence; fill the space where I am with the fullness of Your glory.

Text: Psalm 73:23-28

[23] Yet I am always with you; you hold my right hand.

[24] You guide me with your counsel,
and afterward you will take me up in glory.

[25] Who do I have in heaven but you?
And I desire nothing on earth but you.

[26] My flesh and my heart may fail,
but God is the strength of my heart, my portion forever.

[27] Those far from you will certainly perish;
you destroy all who are unfaithful to you.

[28] But as for me, God's presence is my good.
I have made the Lord God my refuge, so I can tell about all you do.

Truth: Whatever the appearance on the outside, those who abandon God to live a life on their own, will eventually endure eternal death. No amount of riches, power, fame, or friendships can come anywhere close to the value of a personal relationship with Christ. Once we get to where we desire nothing on earth besides Christ, we will have things in perspective.

Thought: Do you have battles of the flesh that you fight every day? You are not alone. David is known as a "man after God's own heart", yet he says, "my flesh and my heart may fail". God may not choose to take away your sinful desires permanently, but He will give you grace to get through today. Tomorrow is another day.

Tune: Have you been to Jesus for the cleansing power
Are you washed in the blood of the Lamb
Are you fully trusting in His grace this hour?
Are you washed in the blood of the Lamb?
Are you washed in the blood?
In the soul cleansing blood of the Lamb
Are your garments spotless are they white as snow?
Are you washed in the blood of the Lamb?

God, Your grace is sufficient today. Give me the grace to embrace today.

Text: Psalm 74:1-8

¹ Why have you rejected us forever, God?
  Why does your anger burn against the sheep of your pasture?
² Remember your congregation, which you purchased long ago
  and redeemed as the tribe for your own possession.
  Remember Mount Zion where you dwell.
³ Make your way to the perpetual ruins,
  to all that the enemy has destroyed in the sanctuary.
⁴ Your adversaries roared in the meeting place where you met with us.
  They set up their emblems as signs.
⁵ It was like men in a thicket of trees, wielding axes,
⁶ then smashing all the carvings with hatchets and picks.
⁷ They set your sanctuary on fire; they utterly desecrated
  the dwelling place of your name.
⁸ They said in their hearts, "Let us oppress them relentlessly."
  They burned every place throughout the land where God met with us.

Truth: There is something truly special about God's. "congregation". He created it, He owns it, and through Christ, He purchased it through shed blood. The congregation (the church) is the environment in which God intended to grow His Kingdom. No Christian can fully grow, apart from a close relationship with a local church.

Thought: Periodically, someone will call the church office and ask to speak to the "owner of the business". It always brings a chuckle, but the right response would be "you have to pray to talk to the Owner of the church, but you can't reach Him by telephone". The church is vitally important to Christ, so much so that He died for it. Are you living as one who loves the church like Jesus does?

Tune: All hail the pow'r of Jesus' name, Let angels prostrate fall
Bring forth the royal diadem, and crown Him Lord of all
Bring forth the royal diadem, and crown Him Lord of all

Jesus, Give me love like You have for the church, which you love with Your whole heart and gave Your entire life for.

Songs for Life – Day 161 - June 10

Text: Psalm 74:9-17

[9] There are no signs for us to see. There is no longer a prophet.
   And none of us knows how long this will last.
[10] God, how long will the enemy mock?
   Will the foe insult your name forever?
[11] Why do you hold back your hand?
   Stretch out your right hand and destroy them!
[12] God my King is from ancient times, performing saving acts on the earth.
[13] You divided the sea with your strength;
   you smashed the heads of the sea monsters in the water;
[14] you crushed the heads of Leviathan;
   you fed him to the creatures of the desert.
[15] You opened up springs and streams;
   you dried up ever-flowing rivers.
[16] The day is yours, also the night; you established the moon and the sun.
[17] You set all the boundaries of the earth; you made summer and winter.

Truth: The previous passage speaks of how the enemies of the "congregation" destroyed the sanctuary. The facility was attacked, torn apart, yet God remained silent. However, the Psalmist is comforted by remembering God's work in the past and confident that He will act in His time.

Thought: When we ask someone a question and silence is the response, it can be very defeating. When we are seeking God's direction in a situation, the last thing we want to experience is silence. However, God is always at work, and His silence is even a part of His work. Perhaps He is waiting for the right time to act or taking time to shape your heart.

Tune: At the cross I bow my knee, where Your blood was shed for me
There's no greater love than this
You have overcome the grave; Your glory fills the highest place
What can separate me now?

Father God, I need to hear Your voice today. Tune my heart to hear You.

Text: Psalm 74:18-23

[18] Remember this: the enemy has mocked the Lord,
  and a foolish people has insulted your name.
[19] Do not give to beasts the life of your dove;
  do not forget the lives of your poor people forever.
[20] Consider the covenant,
  for the dark places of the land are full of violence.
[21] Do not let the oppressed turn away in shame;
  let the poor and needy praise your name.
[22] Rise up, God, champion your cause!
  Remember the insults
  that fools bring against you all day long.
[23] Do not forget the clamor of your adversaries,
  the tumult of your opponents that goes up constantly.

Truth: Throughout the history of Old Testament Israel, the church was seldom all on the same page. Sure, they had times when they all shouted for joy, and times, such as at the dedication of the Temple or the dedication of the rebuilt wall in Nehemiah where the unity in worship was incredible. Still the church was faced with attacks from outsiders as well as from the inside, by people turning to idols or becoming self-righteous.

Thought: Aren't you glad God never gives up on us? As many times, as we try to do things our own way, God is always the Father who welcomes the prodigal back with open arms. Going back to the covenant with Abraham, God has promised us He will always be there for us to run to.

Tune: Holy Spirit rain down, rain down
O Comforter and Friend, how we need Your touch again
Holy Spirit rain down rain down
Let Your power fall let Your voice be heard
Come and change our hearts as we stand on Your Word
Holy Spirit rain down

Lord, hold me close to You today. I want to be near You like never before.

Text: Psalm 75:1-5

¹ We give thanks to you, God;
  we give thanks to you, for your name is near.
  People tell about your wondrous works.
² "When I choose a time,
  I will judge fairly.
³ When the earth and all its inhabitants shake,
  I am the one who steadies its pillars. Selah
⁴ I say to the boastful, 'Do not boast,'
  and to the wicked, 'Do not lift up your horn.
⁵ Do not lift up your horn against heaven
  or speak arrogantly.'"

Truth: Rock steady! Balance! Control! God is the firm foundation to all that exists. When I begin to waver... He is there. When I grow weak, He is there... He is my strength. He was there for the children of Israel, through every challenge they faced.

Thought: Do you lift up God to others and tell of all His greatness? Have you committed every area of your life to him? Maybe you have not given God all the glory for the things He has done in your life. Seek God and His heart. Then give God the glory and "boast in the Lord."

Tune: So, pull me a little closer
Take me a little deeper
I want to know Your heart, I want to know Your heart
'Cause Your love is so much sweeter
Than anything I've tasted
I want to know Your heart
I want to know Your heart
(I want to know Your heart)

Heavenly Father, I praise you for all you have done in my life. I praise you for sending Your son, to die on that cross, for me. I feel so unworthy, yet you love me enough to offer eternal life with you. I love you, Lord.

Text: Psalm 75:6-10

[6] Exaltation does not come
  from the east, the west, or the desert,
[7] for God is the Judge:
  He brings down one and exalts another.
[8] For there is a cup in the Lord's hand,
  full of wine blended with spices, and he pours from it.
  All the wicked of the earth will drink,
  draining it to the dregs.
[9] As for me, I will tell about him forever;
  I will sing praise to the God of Jacob.
[10] "I will cut off all the horns of the wicked,
  but the horns of the righteous will be lifted up."

Truth: It is very clear that God will execute His judgments on the just and the unjust. He will use His divine authority to put down and humble the wicked. All of this will happen in God's timing.

Thought: God will always protect His children. Sometimes we may ask of God, "When are you going to reveal Yourself in this situation, God?" We concern ourselves with the timing of God's movement, because we identify things through time. The palmist gives us a promise from the heart of God, "but the horns of the righteous will be lifted up." Get ready!

Tune: Worthy of worship, worthy of praise,
Worthy of honor and glory.
Worthy of all the glad songs we can sing....
Worthy of all of the off'rings we bring.
You are worthy! Father, Creator
You are worthy! Savior, Sustainer
You are worthy, worthy and wonderful,
Worthy of worship and praise

Father, I know you see my heart. Please forgive me when I question you and your motives.

Text: Psalm 76:1-6

[1] God is known in Judah; his name is great in Israel.

[2] His tent is in Salem, his dwelling place in Zion.

[3] There he shatters the bow's flaming arrows,
the shield, the sword, and the weapons of war. Selah

[4] You are resplendent and majestic
coming down from the mountains of prey.

[5] The brave-hearted have been plundered;
they have slipped into their final sleep.
None of the warriors was able to lift a hand.

[6] At your rebuke, God of Jacob,
both chariot and horse lay still.

Truth: The psalmist describes a particular battle here, where God destroyed the weapons of Israel's enemies: their arrows, their shields, their swords and their weapons of war. God is willing to use His power to protect His people and give them victory.

Thought: What are the weapons of war that you face? Is it a temptation that is so easy for you to slip into? Is it certain people, who you never feel you can be yourself around because you feel attacked? Maybe you simply feel that you are inadequate? God will give you the weapons you need when you need them. What weapons do you need today?

Tune: God sent His Son they called Him Jesus
He came to love heal and forgive
He bled and died to buy my pardon
An empty grave is there to prove My Savior lives
Because He lives I can face tomorrow
Because He lives all fear is gone
Because I know He holds the future
And life is worth the living just because He lives

God, equip me with the armor of God today. I know that whatever I face, I am not alone, for You are with me. Equip me and protect me today, God.

Text: Psalm 76:7-12

[7] And you—you are to be feared.
  When you are angry, who can stand before you?
[8] From heaven you pronounced judgment.
  The earth feared and grew quiet
[9] when God rose up to judge
  and to save all the lowly of the earth. Selah
[10] Even human wrath will praise you;
  you will clothe yourself with the wrath that remains.
[11] Make and keep your vows to the Lord your God;
  let all who are around him bring tribute to the awe-inspiring one.
[12] He humbles the spirit of leaders;
  he is feared by the kings of the earth.

Truth: In the story of David versus Goliath, David is described as a very young man, not particularly large in stature. Goliath was the best warrior the Philistines had. Being about 9 feet tall certainly didn't hurt. Yet, David was the only one who volunteered to slay the giant. Why? Because He knew that God would be the one actually doing the fighting.

Thought: In places where there is fear, there is often a lack of trust. Where there is worry, there is often a lack of faith. When God stands with us, there is no enemy that can defeat us. Are you hiding yourself in the depths of His love today?

Tune: My hope is built on nothing less
Than Jesus' blood and righteousness
I dare not trust the sweetest frame
But wholly trust in Jesus' Name
Christ alone cornerstone
Weak made strong in the Savior's love
Through the storm He is Lord
Lord of all

Father, replace my fear with trust. Replace my worry with faith.

Songs for Life – Day 167 - June 16

Text: Psalm 77:1-9

¹ I cry aloud to God, aloud to God, and he will hear me.

² I sought the Lord in my day of trouble.
  My hands were continually lifted up all night long;
  I refused to be comforted.

³ I think of God; I groan; I meditate; my spirit becomes weak. Selah

⁴ You have kept me from closing my eyes;
  I am troubled and cannot speak.

⁵ I consider days of old, years long past.

⁶ At night I remember my music;
  I meditate in my heart, and my spirit ponders.

⁷ "Will the Lord reject forever and never again show favor?

⁸ Has his faithful love ceased forever?
  Is his promise at an end for all generations?

⁹ Has God forgotten to be gracious?
  Has he in anger withheld his compassion?" Selah

Truth: Some describe this passage as coming from a place of depression; others describe it as an earnest prayer coming from a troubled heart. In either event, it seems the deeper the sorrow, the louder the cry. You can almost feel the frustration and sadness of the psalmist as he speaks of being so troubled that he says he cannot speak.

Thought: When you are troubled, does your cry to God get louder, or does it become less fervent, closer to silence? Does your spirit get weak from the struggle? God inhabits the praises of His people and always hears the cries of His children. Cry out in praise to Almighty God!

Tune: Wonderful so wonderful is Your unfailing love
Your cross has spoken mercy over me
No eye has seen no ear has heard, no heart could fully know
How glorious how beautiful You are
Beautiful One I love, Beautiful One I adore
Beautiful One my soul must sing

Father, take what is wrong in my heart and make it right.

Songs for Life – Day 168 - June 17

Text: Psalm 77:10-15

10 So I say, "I am grieved
   that the right hand of the Most High has changed."
11 I will remember the Lord's works;
   yes, I will remember your ancient wonders.
12 I will reflect on all you have done and meditate on your actions.
13 God, your way is holy. What god is great like God?
14 You are the God who works wonders;
   you revealed your strength among the peoples.
15 With power you redeemed your people,
   the descendants of Jacob and Joseph. Selah

Truth: In the midst of his depressive state, the psalmist remembers the blessings of the Lord. As he prays, as he cries out to God, God brings those gentle reminders of the blessings he has received.

Thought: Even on our darkest days, we can thank God for His call on our lives to salvation, the grace to live another day, and breath in our bodies. There are always things we could wish were better, but God has been more than faithful to His children. He is our Redeemer, our Guide, our Source of salvation, our Rock, our Fortress and Deliverer. Lift Him up!

Tune: O for a thousand tongues to sing
Blessed be the name of the Lord
The glories of my God and King
Blessed be the name of the Lord

Blessed be the name, blessed be the name
Blessed be the name of the Lord
Blessed be the name, blessed be the name
Blessed be the name of the Lord

Father, Your name is high above all others. You are my Redeemer, my Guide, my Source of salvation, my Rock, my Fortress and Deliverer.

Text: Psalm 77:16-20

[16] The water saw you, God.
   The water saw you; it trembled. Even the depths shook.
[17] The clouds poured down water.
   The storm clouds thundered; your arrows flashed back and forth.
[18] The sound of your thunder was in the whirlwind;
   lightning lit up the world.
   The earth shook and quaked.
[19] Your way went through the sea
   and your path through the vast water,
   but your footprints were unseen.
[20] You led your people like a flock by the hand of Moses and Aaron.

Truth: When God shows up, things happen. The psalmist recalls God's presence at the Red Sea, when the waters parted. He recalls God providing rain in time of drought, and even perhaps prophesying about the earth trembling and shaking at the tearing of the temple veil at Jesus' crucifixion. When God shows up, things happen.

Thought: We often pray for God to fix circumstances, and there is nothing wrong with that. However, experiencing the fullness of God's presence gives us spiritual eyes to see circumstances as He sees them. Rather than focusing on your circumstances, seek God's presence today.

Tune: This is my desire, to honor You
Lord with all my heart, I worship You
All I have within me, I give You praise
All that I adore is in You
Lord I give You my heart, I give You my soul
I live for You alone
Ev'ry breath that I take, Ev'ry moment I'm awake
Lord have Your way in me

Father, nothing else matters in my life if I don't have You with me. Fill me and surround me with Your presence today so I can see with Your eyes.

Text: Psalm 78:1-8

[1] My people, hear my instruction; listen to the words from my mouth.

[2] I will declare wise sayings; I will speak mysteries from the past—

[3] things we have heard and known
and that our fathers have passed down to us.

[4] We will not hide them from their children, but will tell a future generation
the praiseworthy acts of the Lord,
his might, and the wondrous works he has performed.

[5] He established a testimony in Jacob and set up a law in Israel,
which he commanded our fathers to teach to their children

[6] so that a future generation—children yet to be born—might know.
They were to rise and tell their children

[7] so that they might put their confidence in God
and not forget God's works, but keep his commands.

[8] Then they would not be like their fathers,
a stubborn and rebellious generation,
a generation whose heart was not loyal
and whose spirit was not faithful to God.

Truth: "Hear my instruction!" The Lord is speaking a message to YOU, His child! Tell everyone you know, tell your children, tell their children!

Thought: I heard someone once say that they were riding to heaven on the coat tails of another faithful believer. Friends, it just doesn't work like that. We can't save our kids or anyone. Only God can. Each person must come to the knowledge and saving grace of Christ on his own. We believers must continue to share our faith, pray for and encourage others.

Tune: Oh, may all who come behind us find us faithful
May the fire of our devotion light their way
May the footprints that we leave, lead them to believe
And the lives we live inspire them to obey
Oh may all who come behind us find us faithful

Father God, give me the courage to share my faith with those around me.

Text: Psalm 78:9-16

[9] The Ephraimite archers turned back on the day of battle.

[10] They did not keep God's covenant and refused to live by his law.

[11] They forgot what he had done,
the wondrous works he had shown them.

[12] He worked wonders in the sight of their fathers
in the land of Egypt, the territory of Zoan.

[13] He split the sea and brought them across;
the water stood firm like a wall.

[14] He led them with a cloud by day
and with a fiery light throughout the night.

[15] He split rocks in the wilderness
and gave them drink as abundant as the depths.

[16] He brought streams out of the stone
and made water flow down like rivers.

Truth: The Ephraimites were the leading tribe of Israel. They were well equipped and furnished with the best weapons. However, they failed in faith and trust. They ran away from the enemy. They forsook God even after he had performed miracles in front of them: parting the Red Sea, leading them by a cloud and fire, and providing them water from rocks.

Thought: We go into battle every day. These battles may not be physical, but spiritual. How do we prepare to be ready? We must spend time each day with our Father. We must cultivate our relationship with the Almighty. I encourage you to read God's word and pray and reflect on the things God has done for you in your life. Then you will be reday.

Tune: O victory in Jesus; My Savior forever
He sought me and bought me; With His redeeming blood
He loved me ere I knew Him; and all my love is due Him
He plunged me to victory; Beneath the cleansing flood

Almighty God, I seek you daily to prepare myself for my spiritual battles and struggles so I may have victory over the enemy.

Songs for Life – Day 172 - June 21

Text: Psalm 78:17-20

[17] But they continued to sin against him,
   rebelling in the desert against the Most High.
[18] They deliberately tested God,
   demanding the food they craved.
[19] They spoke against God, saying,
   "Is God able to provide food in the wilderness?
[20] Look! He struck the rock and water gushed out;
   torrents overflowed.
   But can he also provide bread
   or furnish meat for his people?"

Truth: The Israelites are wandering in the wilderness and are grumbling and complaining about their choices of food. They were not being grateful for they had or what the Lord had provided them. They were continuing in sin against God and Moses. They ask a ridiculous sarcastic question in verse 19, showing their lack of faith.

Thought: Everyone is guilty sometimes of grumbling about what we wish we had, rather than being grateful for what the Lord has provided us. Perhaps you think you need a better job, but how about being thankful that you have a job? What about your home? Think about all the homeless people who have no bed or place to call home. The Lord has richly blessed us and sometimes we just need to stop and take stock of what we DO have, rather than what we don't have.

Tune: When upon life's billows you are tempest tossed
When you are discouraged, thinking all is lost
Count your many blessings, name them one by one
And it will surprise you what the Lord hath done

Father, forgive me for not being more thankful for what You have provided me. Thank You for loving me and allowing me such rich blessings as the gift of eternal life with you.

Text: Psalm 78:21-25

[21] Therefore, the Lord heard and became furious;
   then fire broke out against Jacob,
   and anger flared up against Israel
[22] because they did not believe God
   or rely on his salvation.
[23] He gave a command to the clouds above
   and opened the doors of heaven.
[24] He rained manna for them to eat;
   he gave them grain from heaven.
[25] People ate the bread of angels.
   He sent them an abundant supply of food.

Truth: The Lord was upset at the children of Israel for their lack of belief and trust in Him, yet He heard their cries. As a reminder of His great faithfulness, He provided them manna from Heaven - the bread of angels. God didn't just meagerly provide, verse 25 says, "He sent them an abundant supply of food."

Thought: God Provides. Genesis 22:14, "So Abraham called that place The LORD Will Provide." Notice it says "will".... not can, maybe, or partially, but WILL. The Greek translation of "God will provide" is Jehovah-Jireh. Maybe you need God's sufficient grace poured on you today. Let God be your Jehovah-Jireh.

Tune: Jehovah-Jireh my Provider
His grace is sufficient for me, for me, for me
Jehovah-Jireh my Provider
His grace is sufficient for me
My God shall supply all my need, according to His riches in glory
He gives His angels charge over me
Jehovah-Jireh cares for me, for me, for me,
Jehovah-Jireh cares for me

Father God, You are my Jehovah-Jireh, my Provider. You are all I need.

Text: Psalm 78:26-31

26 He made the east wind blow in the skies
and drove the south wind by his might.
27 He rained meat on them like dust,
and winged birds like the sand of the seas.
28 He made them fall in the camp,
all around the tents.
29 The people ate and were completely satisfied,
for he gave them what they craved.
30 Before they had turned from what they craved,
while the food was still in their mouths,
31 God's anger flared up against them,
and he killed some of their best men.
He struck down Israel's fit young men.

Truth: While the Israelites were still wandering around in the desert, they were being supplied manna from God, but were dissatisfied with that and wanted meat. So once again, God heard them and sent quail. So much quail that it seemed like meat literally rained on them. But God was angered toward them and put to death the mightiest from among them.

Thought: If God is providing for you, even if it's not as much as what you want, should you keep persisting for something else? God will cut off the disbelieving along the way. It may not always be easy, but we must learn to be satisfied with what the Lord has provided and stop the grumbling and complaining. Move on. Our rewards await us in Heaven!

Tune: I'm satisfied with just a cottage below
A little silver and a little gold
But in that city where the ransomed will shine
I want a gold one that's silver lined

Dear Lord, help me to be content with all you have given me. It all came from you. I ask forgiveness for my sins and trust that You know what's best for me. You have a mansion waiting for me, just over the hilltop.

Text: Psalm 78:32-38

[32] Despite all this, they kept sinning
   and did not believe his wondrous works.
[33] He made their days end in futility,
   their years in sudden disaster.
[34] When he killed some of them, the rest began to seek him;
   they repented and searched for God.
[35] They remembered that God was their rock,
   the Most High God, their Redeemer.
[36] But they deceived him with their mouths,
   they lied to him with their tongues,
[37] their hearts were insincere toward him,
   and they were unfaithful to his covenant.
[38] Yet he was compassionate;
   he atoned for their iniquity and did not destroy them.
   He often turned his anger aside and did not unleash all his wrath.

Truth: The Israelites continued to sin and didn't believe in God even though they had seen miraculous wonders. God put some to death and others sought God, but not wholeheartedly. But God showed compassion and accepted their sacrifices and held back on His wrath.

Thought: We serve such a kind hearted and compassionate God. He could really show His wrath on all sinners; BUT GOD - chooses to forgive when we repent and even when we show our unbelief. We are fortunate that we don't get what we deserve. BUT GOD - full of grace and mercy.

Tune: Lord we stand by grace in Your presence
Cleansed by the blood of the Lamb; We are Your children
Called by Your name; Humbly we bow, and we pray
Release Your power; to work in us and through us
'Til we are changed to be more like You; Then all the nations will see
Your glory revealed; And worship You

Father God... thank You for the BUT GOD moments in my life!

Text: Psalm 78:39-44

[39] He remembered that they were only flesh,
 a wind that passes and does not return.
[40] How often they rebelled against him in the wilderness
 and grieved him in the desert.
[41] They constantly tested God
 and provoked the Holy One of Israel.
[42] They did not remember his power shown
 on the day he redeemed them from the foe,
[43] when he performed his miraculous signs in Egypt
 and his wonders in the territory of Zoan.
[44] He turned their rivers into blood,
 and they could not drink from their streams.

Truth: "They did not remember his power." We have seen several times these words referring to the Israelites' short-term memory. They even saw God's mighty power time and again. They witnessed many miraculous events, such as the parting of the Red Sea and seeing their pursuers drown, yet they rebelled, and tested God again and again.

Thought: I ask you, "What was wrong with those people?" How could they forget in such a short time of all the provisions of manna and water from rocks; events they had witnessed first-hand? They became rebellious and unbelieving people. Yet God chose to still protect them and provide for them, time and time again. How blessed we are to serve a patient and loving God.

Tune: All the way my Savior leads me
What have I to ask beside?
Can I doubt His tender mercy, who through life has been my Guide?
Heav'nly peace, divinest comfort, here by faith in Him to dwell!
For I know, whate'er befall me, Jesus doeth all things well.

Oh Lord, You are so patient and forgiving. Please forgive me for my unbelief and lack of trust in You.

Text: Psalm 78:45-49

[45] He sent among them swarms of flies,
   which fed on them,
   and frogs, which devastated them.
[46] He gave their crops to the caterpillar
  and the fruit of their labor to the locust.
[47] He killed their vines with hail
   and their sycamore fig trees with a flood.
[48] He handed over their livestock to hail
   and their cattle to lightning bolts.
[49] He sent his burning anger against them:
   fury, indignation, and calamity—a band of deadly messengers.

Truth: When the Israelites were in slavery in Egypt, as a result of their own sin and ignorance of God's direction, God still protected them. As they considered ways to become free from the bondage of Pharaoh's leadership, they turned to their leader, Moses, who, in turn, sought the face of God. Regardless of the lack of consistency in the faith of the Israelites, God's plan to bring His children out of bondage would not be disrupted. He brought a number of plagues in Egypt until Pharaoh finally released the Israelites from slavery.

Thought: Now is never a bad time to get right with God. You've never gone too far away, allowed too much to come into your life that God's hand cannot reach you. When God prompts your heart that a change is needed, that is the Holy Spirit calling. Follow that leadership.

Tune: Hide me now under Your wings
Cover me within Your mighty hand
When the oceans rise and thunders roar
I will soar with You above the storm
Father You are King over the flood
I will be still and know You are God

Holy Spirit, draw me near to You today, nearer than I've ever been.

Text: Psalm 78:50-55

50 He cleared a path for his anger.
He did not spare them from death but delivered their lives to the plague.
51 He struck all the firstborn in Egypt,
the first progeny of the tents of Ham.
52 He led his people out like sheep
and guided them like a flock in the wilderness.
53 He led them safely, and they were not afraid;
but the sea covered their enemies.
54 He brought them to his holy territory,
to the mountain his right hand acquired.
55 He drove out nations before them.
He apportioned their inheritance by lot
and settled the tribes of Israel in their tents.

Truth: God "cleared a path" for his anger, He "delivered their lives" to the plague. He "struck" every firstborn in Egypt. Those we might look at as consequences, but then there was His grace. He "led his people out like sheep", "guided them like a flock in the wilderness", "led them safely", "brought them to his holy territory", and much more.

Thought: God cared about the Israelites, just as he does for us today. He has sent us His son, making it possible for us to have forgiveness from our sins and salvation. Jesus has prepared a place for us and awaits us there. Even when the children of Israel were scared and didn't know what all was going on, God made a way for them and took care of them.

Tune: God will make a way where there seems to be no way
He works in ways we cannot see, He will make a way for me
He will be my guide, hold me closely to His side
With love and strength for each new day
He will make a way, He will make a way

Heavenly Father, thank you for always making a way in my life, when sometimes I feel there seems to be no way. I know you are with me.

Text: Psalm 78:56-61

56 But they rebelliously tested the Most High God,
   for they did not keep his decrees.
57 They treacherously turned away like their fathers;
   they became warped like a faulty bow.
58 They enraged him with their high places
   and provoked his jealousy with their carved images.
59 God heard and became furious;
   he completely rejected Israel.
60 He abandoned the tabernacle at Shiloh,
   the tent where he resided among mankind.
61 He gave up his strength to captivity
   and his splendor to the hand of a foe.

Truth: The Israelites rebelled, turned away and provoked God, time and time again throughout the Old Testament. God would sometimes leave His tent and the Israelites would be turned over to their enemies. They would forget about God, not keep his commands, and even turn to idols.

Thought: Do you ever wonder how they could forget about God? How could they rebel and turn away and provoke God to anger? We may think that we would never do that, but are we all totally obedient to God? We sin, don't we? We aren't above being sinful and sometimes even turn to our own idols. We are good at trying to justify our motives when we sin.

Tune: Spirit come and change the atmosphere
Convict and open hearts to hear
The anthems that the angels sing
The worship of the King of kings
For Jesus reigns over all He reigns
We exalt Your name high above the heavens
We exalt Your name all of creation sings praise
For Jesus reigns over all He reigns

Holy God, showme what areas I need to change in my life to exalt You.

Songs for Life – Day 180 - June 29

Text: Psalm 78:62-66

[62] He surrendered his people to the sword
    because he was enraged with his heritage.
[63] Fire consumed his chosen young men,
    and his young women had no wedding songs.
[64] His priests fell by the sword,
    and the widows could not lament.
[65] The Lord awoke as if from sleep,
    like a warrior from the effects of wine.
[66] He beat back his foes;
    he gave them lasting disgrace.

Truth: "Sword" and "fire" used in this passage refers to weapons of destruction in ancient warfare. There had been so much destruction that wedding songs and the wailing of widows had been silenced.

Thought: Most of us don't carry around a "sword" these days, but are we constantly under attack? Yes. Do we seek protection? Yes. Hebrews 4:12 says *"For the word of God is living and active. Sharper than any double-edged sword."* So, if you carry around your Bible, have its words hidden in your heart, you are not unprotected. You are never alone when you have God.

Tune: These are the days of Elijah
Declaring the Word of the Lord
And these are the days of Your servant Moses
Righteousness being restored
And though these are days of great trials
Of famine and darkness and sword
Still we are the voice
In the desert crying
Prepare ye the way of the Lord

Father, I ask you to give me the desire to ingest your Holy Word into my heart, mind and soul. When you are with me, I'm never alone!

Songs for Life – Day 181 - June 30

Text: Psalm 78:67-72

⁶⁷ He rejected the tent of Joseph
  and did not choose the tribe of Ephraim.
⁶⁸ He chose instead the tribe of Judah,
  Mount Zion, which he loved.
⁶⁹ He built his sanctuary like the heights,
  like the earth that he established forever.
⁷⁰ He chose David his servant
  and took him from the sheep pens;
⁷¹ he brought him from tending ewes
  to be shepherd over his people Jacob—over Israel, his inheritance.
⁷² He shepherded them with a pure heart
  and guided them with his skillful hands.

Truth: God chose to raise up David from the line of Judah to be the King of Israel. David had been a shepherd boy, and now God was using him to be a shepherd of God's chosen people. King David had his faults and failures just like the rest of us but was able to still be used by God to protect and lead the people.

Thought: All throughout the Bible we see evidence of men who made poor choices, sinned, traveled the wrong path at times, but were still used by God. With that thought in mind, even though you and I have made mistakes along the way, sinned against God, and traveled in the wrong direction, God is still with us and will forgive us, IF we just ask. Come back to God today and seek forgiveness and restore your relationship with our God in Heaven.

Tune: Come just as you are; Hear the Spirit call
Come just as you are
Come and see (come and see)
Come receive (come receive), Come and live (come and live) forever

Lord, I ask Your forgiveness on my sins and my wickedness. Please forgive me and fill me with Your presence and let people see You in me.

Songs for Life – Day 182 – July 1

Text: Psalm 79:1-7

¹ God, the nations have invaded your inheritance,
desecrated your holy temple, and turned Jerusalem into ruins.
² They gave the corpses of your servants to the birds of the sky for food,
the flesh of your faithful ones to the beasts of the earth.
³ They poured out their blood like water all around Jerusalem,
and there was no one to bury them.
⁴ We have become an object of reproach to our neighbors,
a source of mockery and ridicule to those around us.
⁵ How long, Lord? Will you be angry forever?
Will your jealousy keep burning like fire?
⁶ Pour out your wrath on the nations that don't acknowledge you,
on the kingdoms that don't call on your name,
⁷ for they have devoured Jacob and devastated his homeland.

Truth: The psalmist is pleading with the Lord to turn his wrath on those who are seeking to destroy the "inheritance", or "the church" (the Jews). They have shed innocent blood, mocked and derided the people, and the Jews are seeking God's hand to turn the wickedness onto their attackers.

Thought: "How long, Lord?" Is that a question you have asked? "How long do I have to endure this trial?" "How long will You wait before You send Jesus to end this world and take us home?" Rest assured, God is a jealous God and He will not allow this "marriage" relationship between He and the church to be disrupted long. If we trust God, we trust His timing.

Tune: Here's my heart Lord, Here's my heart Lord
Here's my heart Lord, speak what is true
'Cause I am found I am Yours, I am loved I'm made pure
I have life I can breathe, I am healed I am free
Here's my heart Lord, Here's my heart Lord
Here's my heart Lord, speak what is true

Father, though it is hard, I trust You, I trust Your hand, and I trust Your timing. Give me the peace to wait on You.

Text: Psalm 79:8-13

⁸ Do not hold past iniquities against us;
let your compassion come to us quickly,
for we have become very weak.
⁹ God of our salvation, help us—for the glory of your name.
Rescue us and atone for our sins, for your name's sake.
¹⁰ Why should the nations ask, "Where is their God?"
Before our eyes, let vengeance for the shed blood of your servants
be known among the nations.
¹¹ Let the groans of the prisoners reach you;
according to your great power,
preserve those condemned to die.
¹² Pay back sevenfold to our neighbors
the reproach they have hurled at you, Lord.
¹³ Then we, your people, the sheep of your pasture,
will thank you forever;
we will declare your praise to generation after generation.

Truth: This passage begins with an acknowledgement that part of the reason the Jews were being persecuted is because of their own sin. They have failed to put God first in everything. The psalmist's prayer is basically "forgive us, help us, and let the nations know about it!"

Thought: I cannot control how others act or what happens to them. I can only control how I respond to God's call on my life to be holy, righteous, and pure before Him. Take time to focus today, not on your enemies, but on the need for holiness, for forgiveness of sin, in your own life.

Tune: Sweetly Lord have we heard Thee calling, come follow Me
And we see where Thy footprints falling, lead us to Thee
Footprints of Jesus that make the pathway glow
We will follow the steps of Jesus where'er they go

O Lord, teach me to be holy. Reveal anything in my life that needs to be confessed so that I can have a right relationship with You.

<u>Songs for Life – Day 184 - July 3</u>

Text: Psalm 80:1-7

[1] Listen, Shepherd of Israel, who leads Joseph like a flock;
you who sit enthroned between the cherubim,
shine [2] on Ephraim, Benjamin, and Manasseh.
Rally your power and come to save us.
[3] Restore us, God;
make your face shine on us,
so that we may be saved.
[4] Lord God of Armies,
how long will you be angry with your people's prayers?
[5] You fed them the bread of tears
and gave them a full measure of tears to drink.
[6] You put us at odds with our neighbors;
our enemies mock us.
[7] Restore us, God of Armies;
make your face shine on us, so that we may be saved.

Truth: Twice in this brief passage, the psalmist asks the Lord to "Restore us, God; make your face shine on us, so that we may be saved" The only way for restoration, the only way to forgiveness, the only way for man to be turned to God wholly and completely is that God reveal Himself to us and we allow Him to do His work within us.

Thought: "I'm already a Christian. What do I need to be restored from?" Is God the priority with your time, your wallet, your family? Once we trust Jesus, we are in the refining process, the process of sanctification. Are there areas of your life that are not totally sold out to God?

Tune: Lead me to the cross, where Your love poured out
Bring me to my knees, Lord I lay me down
Rid me of myself, I belong to You
Oh lead me lead me to the cross

Heavenly Father, teach me to be more like You. Shape me, mold me, and refine me. Sanctify me by Your grace. I want to be like You, Lord.

Songs for Life – Day 185 – July 4

Text: Psalm 80:8-19

[8] You dug up a vine from Egypt; you drove out the nations and planted it.

[9] You cleared a place for it; it took root and filled the land.

[10] The mountains were covered by its shade,
and the mighty cedars with its branches.

[11] It sent out sprouts toward the Sea and shoots toward the River.

[12] Why have you broken down its walls
so that all who pass by pick its fruit?

[13] Boars from the forest tear at it and creatures of the field feed on it.

[14] Return, God of Armies.
Look down from heaven and see; take care of this vine,

[15] the root your right hand planted, the son that you made strong for yourself.

[16] It was cut down and burned; they perish at the rebuke of your countenance.

[17] Let your hand be with the man at your right hand,
with the son of man you have made strong for yourself.

[18] Then we will not turn away from you;
revive us, and we will call on your name.

[19] Restore us, Lord, God of Armies;
make your face shine on us, so that we may be saved.

Truth: The psalmist refers to he and his people as the "vine". A vine is only as good as its root system. If we are rooted in Christ, the vine can withstand anything that weather or circumstances bring its way.

Thought: How many times have you prayed the prayer like the psalmist, "God, if you'll fix me one more time . . . I'll never turn my back on you"? God never tires of hearing the cries of His children and is always ready to heal, restore and help the vine to grow again.

Tune: Mine eyes have seen the glory of the coming of the Lord
He is trampling out the vintage where the grapes of wrath are stored
He hath loosed the fateful lightning of His terrible swift sword
His truth is marching on

Lord, thank you for the freedom as Americans that we have, but most of all, thank you for our freedom in Christ, paid for by Jesus with His life.

Text: Psalm 81:1-7

¹ Sing for joy to God our strength;
shout in triumph to the God of Jacob.
² Lift up a song—play the tambourine,
the melodious lyre, and the harp.
³ Blow the horn on the day of our feasts
during the new moon and during the full moon.
⁴ For this is a statute for Israel,
an ordinance of the God of Jacob.
⁵ He set it up as a decree for Joseph
when he went throughout the land of Egypt.
I heard an unfamiliar language:
⁶ "I relieved his shoulder from the burden;
his hands were freed from carrying the basket.
⁷ You called out in distress, and I rescued you;
I answered you from the thundercloud.
I tested you at the Waters of Meribah. Selah

Truth: Sing for joy to God our strength! Shout in triumph to the God of Jacob! The Israelites were celebrating festivals and praising the Lord for His devotion to caring for them in the wilderness. While enslaved in Egypt, they had to carry baskets full of bricks, and now their baskets were empty because the Lord heard and rescued them.

Thought: How do you praise the Lord? Do you sing aloud? Shout? Jesus rescued us from being lost sinners by His death on the cross, just like God rescued the Israelites. Shouldn't we sing and shout and praise God too? Praise is the best response to God saving Grace!

Tune: I'm just a sinner saved by grace
When I stood condemned to death, He took my place
Now I grow and breathe in freedom with each breath of life I take
Loved and forgiven back with the living, I'm just a sinner saved by grace

Father, I am just a sinner saved by grace. You deserve all my praise!

Songs for Life – Day 187 - July 6

Text: Psalm 81:8-16

[8] Listen, my people, and I will admonish you.
Israel, if you would only listen to me!
[9] There must not be a strange god among you;
you must not bow down to a foreign god.
[10] I am the Lord your God, who brought you up from the land of Egypt.
Open your mouth wide, and I will fill it.
[11] "But my people did not listen to my voice; Israel did not obey me.
[12] So I gave them over to their stubborn hearts to follow their own plans.
[13] If only my people would listen to me and Israel would follow my ways,
[14] I would quickly subdue their enemies
and turn my hand against their foes."
[15] Those who hate the Lord would cower to him;
their doom would last forever.
[16] But he would feed Israel with the best wheat.
"I would satisfy you with honey from the rock."

Truth: You almost hear the desperation and regret in the voice saying, "but my people did not listen to my voice", and "If only my people would listen to me." So many blessings awaited their obedience, but instead the Israelites were turned over to their enemies and their stubborn hearts.

Thought: As a parent, many times I've said to my children, if you would just have obeyed what I said, this would not have happened. Why is it that we seem to learn things the hard way, even in our spiritual lives? God's Word gives us clear direction, so why do we choose to subject ourselves to the consequences of disobedience?

Tune: When we walk with the Lord; In the light of His Word
What a glory He sheds on our way; While we do His good will
He abides with us still; And with all who will trust and obey
Trust and obey; For there's no other way;
To be happy in Jesus; But to trust and obey

Father, please help me to Trust and Obey You, for there IS no other way!

Text: Psalm 82:1-8

[1] God stands in the divine assembly;
he pronounces judgment among the gods:
[2] "How long will you judge unjustly
and show partiality to the wicked? Selah
[3] Provide justice for the needy and the fatherless;
uphold the rights of the oppressed and the destitute.
[4] Rescue the poor and needy;
save them from the power of the wicked."
[5] They do not know or understand;
they wander in darkness.
All the foundations of the earth are shaken.
[6] I said, "You are gods; you are all sons of the Most High.
[7] However, you will die like humans and fall like any other ruler."
[8] Rise up, God, judge the earth, for all the nations belong to you.

Truth: "Provide justice for the needy and the fatherless" . . . the weak and needy are those who are powerless against those who would exploit or oppress them. Who else is weak and needy? Believers are weak and needy, for we need God's presence and power in every aspect of our lives

Thought: Traditional thought would tell us that the longer we serve God, the stronger we get. However, the truth is, the longer we serve God, the more we realize how weak and needy we really are. Acknowledging our weaknesses and needs before God empowers His work within us.

Tune: Rescue the perishing, care for the dying
Snatch them in pity, from sin and the grave
Weep o'er the erring one, lift up the fallen
Tell them of Jesus, the mighty to save
Rescue the perishing, care for the dying
Jesus is merciful, Jesus will save

Lord Jesus, in order to receive the fullness of Your presence in my life, I know that I must acknowledge that I am poor and needy before You.

Text: Psalm 83:1-8

¹ God, do not keep silent.
Do not be deaf, God; do not be quiet.
² See how your enemies make an uproar;
those who hate you have acted arrogantly.
³ They devise clever schemes against your people;
they conspire against your treasured ones.
⁴ They say, "Come, let us wipe them out as a nation
so that Israel's name will no longer be remembered."
⁵ For they have conspired with one mind;
they form an alliance against you—
⁶ the tents of Edom and the Ishmaelites,
Moab and the Hagrites,
⁷ Gebal, Ammon, and Amalek,
Philistia with the inhabitants of Tyre.
⁸ Even Assyria has joined them;
they lend support to the sons of Lot. Selah

Truth: The psalmist is seeking God's hand of protection against the enemy. The enemy wants to seek and destroy God's people, much like we see Satan's desire to distract and destroy God's people today.

Thought: "Speak, Lord, for Your servant is listening!" "Move, God, for I am ready to see Your hand at work!" These are prayers that reflect the appeal in verse 1. Are you ready to hear God's voice today? Are you ready to see God's hand at work, regardless of what He's calling you to?

Tune: *Lord I come I confess, bowing here I find my rest*
And without You I fall apart, You're the one that guides my heart
Lord I need You oh I need You, ev'ry hour I need You
My one defense my righteousness, oh God how I need You

Speak, Lord, for Your servant is listening! Move, God, for I am ready to see Your hand at work! I need to feel Your presence today, to know that You are there and working today.

Text: Psalm 83:9-18

[9] Deal with them as you did with Midian,
as you did with Sisera
and Jabin at the Kishon River.
[10] They were destroyed at En-dor;
they became manure for the ground.
[11] Make their nobles like Oreb and Zeeb,
and all their tribal leaders like Zebah and Zalmunna,
[12] who said, "Let us seize God's pastures for ourselves."
[13] Make them like tumbleweed, my God, like straw before the wind.
[14] As fire burns a forest, as a flame blazes through mountains,
[15] so pursue them with your tempest
and terrify them with your storm.
[16] Cover their faces with shame so that they will seek your name, Lord.
[17] Let them be put to shame and terrified forever;
let them perish in disgrace.
[18] May they know that you alone—whose name is the Lord—
are the Most High over the whole earth.

Truth: The psalmist here shows us how to pray for our enemies. "Pursue them with your tempest", "terrify them with your storm", and "cover their faces with shame so that they will seek your name, Lord"

Thought: Fire can be a destroyer, or it can be fuel. May our prayer today be that God would set our souls ablaze, that He stirs up the fires within us to worship Him, and even that His fire would touch those who oppose us, that they may receive the love of Christ.

Tune: Set my soul afire Lord set my soul afire
Make my life a witness, of Thy saving pow'r
Millions grope in darkness, waiting for Thy Word
Set my soul afire, Lord, set my soul afire

Jesus, let me be fueled by Your fire today. Burn away anything in my life that does not need to be there.

Songs for Life – Day 191 - July 10

Text: Psalm 84:1-7

¹ How lovely is your dwelling place, Lord of Armies.
² I long and yearn for the courts of the Lord;
my heart and flesh cry out for the living God.
³ Even a sparrow finds a home,
and a swallow, a nest for herself
where she places her young—
near your altars, Lord of Armies,
my King and my God.
⁴ How happy are those who reside in your house,
who praise you continually. Selah
⁵ Happy are the people whose strength is in you,
whose hearts are set on pilgrimage.
⁶ As they pass through the Valley of Baca,
they make it a source of spring water;
even the autumn rain will cover it with blessings.
⁷ They go from strength to strength;
each appears before God in Zion.

Truth: At certain times, the Israelites would travel to Jerusalem to worship God in the temple. The "house" (verse 4) would be a lovely and happy place because they desired to worship God.

Thought: Do you *desire* to worship God? Maybe you need to think and pray about the desires of your heart. *"God give me desire to worship"*.

Tune: Come into His presence; With thanksgiving in your heart
And give Him praise; And give Him praise
Come into His presence; With thanksgiving in your heart
Your voices raise; Your voices raise
Give glory and honor and power unto Him
Jesus the name above all names

Father God, I want to have the sincere desire to be in Your presence, and to worship You. Fill my weaknesses and shortcomings with desire.

Text: Psalm 84:8-12

[8] Lord God of Armies, hear my prayer;
listen, God of Jacob. Selah
[9] Consider our shield, God;
look on the face of your anointed one.
[10] Better a day in your courts
than a thousand anywhere else.
I would rather stand at the threshold of the house of my God
than live in the tents of wicked people.
[11] For the Lord God is a sun and shield.
The Lord grants favor and honor;
he does not withhold the good
from those who live with integrity.
[12] Happy is the person who trusts in you, Lord of Armies!

Truth: The psalmist is praying that God would bless His anointed, or set apart, King during their reign on earth. God is our "sun and shield," meaning our provision and protection. The psalmist knew that it was better to spend one day worshipping God in His house, then a thousand days elsewhere!

Thought: Do you realize how blessed we are to be able to freely worship God? Do you feel privileged to "get" to go to church? God is our source of light and energy. Do you want to be blessed, and then put your trust in God? Worship the one true God. Make that a priority in your life.

Tune: How lovely is Your dwelling place; O Lord almighty
For my soul longs and even faints for You; For here my heart is satisfied
Within Your presence; I sing beneath the shadow of Your wings
Better is one day in Your courts, Better is one day in Your house
Better is one day in Your courts, than thousands elsewhere
Than thousands elsewhere

Lord, thank you that I can freely worship you. Thank you for being my provider and protector. Today I give you my best, as You do for me.

Songs for Life – Day 193 - July 12

Text: Psalm 85:1-7

[1] Lord, you showed favor to your land; you restored the fortunes of Jacob.
[2] You forgave your people's guilt; you covered all their sin. Selah
[3] You withdrew all your fury; you turned from your burning anger.
[4] Return to us, God of our salvation,
and abandon your displeasure with us.
[5] Will you be angry with us forever?
Will you prolong your anger for all generations?
[6] Will you not revive us again
so that your people may rejoice in you?
[7] Show us your faithful love, Lord,
and give us your salvation.

Truth: The psalmist recalls the times in the past where God has blessed His people. He has been Forgiver and Provider. He withdrew His wrath. Because God has done this before, the psalmist can confidently pray "Will you not revive us again, so that your people may rejoice in you?"

Thought: Revival . . . People say all of the time "our country needs revival", or "our world needs revival", but the truth is, the only people that can receive revival are those who are in the church and who are true believers. One cannot be "re-vived" until they have once been "vived". It is not all of "those people" who need revival . . . but it is me, O Lord.

Tune: Coming now to Thee O Christ my Lord
Trusting only in Thy precious Word
Let my humble pray'r to Thee be heard
And send a great revival in my soul
Send a great revival in my soul (In my soul)
Send a great revival in my soul (In my soul)
Let the Holy Spirit come and take control
And send a great revival in my soul

Heavenly Father, revive me . . . take the pieces of my heart that I have held back from you and stir the fires of revival once again.

Text: Psalm 85:8-13

[8] I will listen to what God will say; surely the Lord will declare peace
to his people, his faithful ones, and not let them go back to foolish ways.
[9] His salvation is very near those who fear him,
so that glory may dwell in our land.
[10] Faithful love and truth will join together;
righteousness and peace will embrace.
[11] Truth will spring up from the earth,
and righteousness will look down from heaven.
[12] Also, the Lord will provide what is good, and our land will yield its crops.
[13] Righteousness will go before him to prepare the way for his steps.

Truth: The psalmist expresses His acknowledgement that God has
revived His people previously and has given his plea that God would do it
again. Then, His attention turns to getting ready for revival.

Thought: Revival starts with God but is reflected in a series of responses
by His people. We see it here in an openness to listen to God's voice (v8),
a confidence in God's message (v8), the ability of God to turn people from
their sins (v8), and that He is the source of salvation (v9). Are you ready
for revival or are you still holding back, waiting for some "holy moment"?
God is already calling His children to revival. Tell Him you are ready!

Tune: When the music fades all is stripped away, and I simply come
Longing just to bring something that's of worth that will bless Your heart
I'll bring You more than a song
For a song in itself is not what You have required
You search much deeper within, through the way things appear
You're looking into my heart
I'm coming back to the heart of worship
And it's all about You all about You Jesus
I'm sorry Lord for the thing I've made it
When it's all about You all about You Jesus

Father, I am listening. I trust Your Word. I confess my sin. I exalt You.

Text: Psalm 86:1-9

¹ Listen, Lord, and answer me, for I am poor and needy.

² Protect my life, for I am faithful.

You are my God; save your servant who trusts in you.

³ Be gracious to me, Lord, for I call to you all day long.

⁴ Bring joy to your servant's life, because I appeal to you, Lord.

⁵ For you, Lord, are kind and ready to forgive,

abounding in faithful love to all who call on you.

⁶ Lord, hear my prayer; listen to my plea for mercy.

⁷ I call on you in the day of my distress, for you will answer me.

⁸ Lord, there is no one like you among the gods,

and there are no works like yours.

⁹ All the nations you have made

will come and bow down before you, Lord, and will honor your name.

Truth: As God begins the process of revival, the believer begins to "go deeper" and realize his or her need for a greater dependence on God and a lesser dependence on self. This passage is a great illustration of that.

Thought: The visual of God inclining His ear toward us brings forth the image of a father bending down to hear every word that his child is speaking. The God who is "kind and ready to forgive" is interested in EVERY word that His children speak to Him.

Tune: These are the days of Elijah, declaring the Word of the Lord
And these are the days, of Your servant Moses
Righteousness being restored
And though these are days, of great trials
Of famine and darkness and sword
Still we are the voice in the desert crying prepare ye the way of the Lord
Behold He comes, riding on the clouds
Shining like the sun, at the trumpet call
So, lift your voice, it's the year of Jubilee
And out of Zion's hill salvation comes

Father, hear my heart today. Incline Your ear to me. I need You.

Text: Psalm 86:10-17

[10] For you are great and perform wonders;
you alone are God.
[11] Teach me your way, Lord, and I will live by your truth.
Give me an undivided mind to fear your name.
[12] I will praise you with all my heart, Lord my God,
and will honor your name forever.
[13] For your faithful love for me is great,
and you rescue my life from the depths of Sheol.
[14] God, arrogant people have attacked me;
a gang of ruthless men intends to kill me.
They do not let you guide them.
[15] But you, Lord, are a compassionate and gracious God,
slow to anger and abounding in faithful love and truth.
[16] Turn to me and be gracious to me.
Give your strength to your servant; save the son of your female servant.
[17] Show me a sign of your goodness;
my enemies will see and be put to shame
because you, Lord, have helped and comforted me.

Truth: The psalmist prays some of God's character back to Him. He acknowledges God as great, as One who does wondrous things, as merciful and gracious, as slow to anger, and as One who abounds in steadfast love. As his heart is full, he cannot help expressing praise.

Thought: Expressing praise to God opens up our heart. Once I express how great He is, I'm ready to look at my life how He sees it and realize that I need him to "teach me your way", so that "I will live by your truth". God never gets tired of hearing his children tell Him how great He is.

Tune: Amazing love, how can it be, that You my King would die for me
Amazing love, I know it's true
It's my joy to honor You, in all I do, I honor You

Father, I praise You with all that I have today. You are awesome!

Text: Psalm 87:1-7

[1] The city he founded is on the holy mountains.
[2] The Lord loves Zion's city gates
more than all the dwellings of Jacob.
[3] Glorious things are said about you,
city of God. Selah
[4] "I will make a record of those who know me:
Rahab, Babylon, Philistia, Tyre, and Cush—
each one was born there."
[5] And it will be said of Zion,
"This one and that one were born in her."
The Most High himself will establish her.
[6] When he registers the peoples,
the Lord will record,
"This one was born there." Selah
[7] Singers and dancers alike will say,
"My whole source of joy is in you."

Truth: Jerusalem, the chosen city of God; His founded city - also known as Zion, is where God met His people in praise and worship. The psalmist wants people of all nations to become fellow heirs in the Gospel.

Thought: Just like the Israelites from long ago, we also are called to spread the Word of the Lord to all nations. We are called to be a "Kingdom of Priests" and let everyone know the source of our joyful blessings. Our help and source come from our Lord and Savior Jesus Christ. Tell someone!!

Tune: Go tell it on the mountain
Over the hills and ev'rywhere
Go tell it on the mountain
That Jesus Christ is born

Father in Heaven, I love that you have freely given us Your written Word to help guide and direct our lives. Thank you for the gift of salvation.

Text: Psalm 88:1-10

[1] Lord, God of my salvation, I cry out before you day and night.

[2] May my prayer reach your presence; listen to my cry.

[3] For I have had enough troubles, and my life is near Sheol.

[4] I am counted among those going down to the Pit.
I am like a man without strength,

[5] abandoned among the dead. I am like the slain lying in the grave,
whom you no longer remember, and who are cut off from your care.

[6] You have put me in the lowest part of the Pit,
in the darkest places, in the depths.

[7] Your wrath weighs heavily on me;
you have overwhelmed me with all your waves. Selah

[8] You have distanced my friends from me;
you have made me repulsive to them. I am shut in and cannot go out.

[9] My eyes are worn out from crying.
Lord, I cry out to you all day long; I spread out my hands to you.

[10] Do you work wonders for the dead?
Do departed spirits rise up to praise you? Selah

Truth: The psalmist seems to express the heart of a troubled life, going from crisis to crisis, never seemingly being able to get ahead of the "stuff of life". Yet, even in the midst of a trial-ridden life, he expresses "I cry out before you day and night."

Thought: We cannot define the goodness of God by our circumstances. Every trial the Christian goes through is designed to work together for God's glory and for the good of those who love Him. God is working! His mercies are new every morning. He will reveal Himself in His perfect time.

Tune: To God be the glory, to God be the glory
To God be the glory, for the things He has done
With his blood He has saved me, with His power, He has raised me
To God be the glory, for the things He has done

Today, and every day, I call upon you, O Lord. I lift my hands to You.

Text: Psalm 88:11-18

[11] Will your faithful love be declared in the grave,
your faithfulness in Abaddon?
[12] Will your wonders be known in the darkness
or your righteousness in the land of oblivion?
[13] But I call to you for help, Lord; in the morning my prayer meets you.
[14] Lord, why do you reject me?
Why do you hide your face from me?
[15] From my youth, I have been suffering and near death.
I suffer your horrors; I am desperate.
[16] Your wrath sweeps over me; your terrors destroy me.
[17] They surround me like water all day long;
they close in on me from every side.
[18] You have distanced loved one and neighbor from me;
darkness is my only friend.

Truth: The child of God is not exempt from trials. Sometimes it seems that we go through more than our share. The psalmist gives an honest approach before God of how he is feeling.

Thought: The truth is, not everything we go through in life is good. People get sick, we lose loved ones, accidents and tragedies happen to believers and non-believers alike. Our faith is tested in these trials - where does our hope really lie? Do we just trust in God when things are good, or do we REALLY trust God?

Tune: In and out of situations, that tug-of-war at me
All day long I struggle, for answers that I need
Then I come into His presence, all my questions become clear
And for a sacred moment, no doubt can interfere
In the presence of Jehovah, God Almighty Prince of Peace
Troubles vanish hearts are mended, in the presence of the King

Father, I can handle whatever You choose for me to go through if I have Your presence with me always.

Text: Psalm 89:1-4

[1] I will sing about the Lord's faithful love forever;
I will proclaim your faithfulness to all generations with my mouth.
[2] For I will declare,
"Faithful love is built up forever;
you establish your faithfulness in the heavens."
[3] The Lord said,
"I have made a covenant with my chosen one;
I have sworn an oath to David my servant:
[4] 'I will establish your offspring forever
and build up your throne for all generations.'" Selah

Truth: One of the most fundamental character traits of God is His steadfast love. He is not fickle, He does not waver, He never loves us any less than completely, and His love will continue for generations to come. The psalmist is right to lift his voice and sing of this steadfast love, to declare it to the church and to the world.

Thought: Verse 3 mentions a covenant. A covenant is different than a contract. Contracts involve two parties and they can be broken. When God makes a covenant, it is unconditional. He initiates it, He carries it out, and it will never be broken. Thank God for His steadfast love today and for the fact that He will never, ever, ever love you any less than completely.

Tune: Lord I lift Your name on high
Lord I love to sing Your praises
I'm so glad You're in my life, I'm so glad You came to save us

You came from heaven to earth to show the way
From the earth to the cross my debt to pay
From the cross to the grave, from the grave to the sky
Lord I lift Your name on high

Father God, You initiated a relationship with me and I have responded.
Thank you for the promise that nothing can take that away from me.

<u>Songs for Life – Day 201 - July 20</u>

Text: Psalm 89:5-12

[5] Lord, the heavens praise your wonders—
your faithfulness also—in the assembly of the holy ones.
[6] For who in the skies can compare with the Lord?
Who among the heavenly beings is like the Lord?
[7] God is greatly feared in the council of the holy ones,
more awe-inspiring than all who surround him.
[8] Lord God of Armies, who is strong like you, Lord?
Your faithfulness surrounds you.
[9] You rule the raging sea; when its waves surge, you still them.
[10] You crushed Rahab like one who is slain;
you scattered your enemies with your powerful arm.
[11] The heavens are yours; the earth also is yours.
The world and everything in it—you founded them.
[12] North and south—you created them.
Tabor and Hermon shout for joy at your name.

Truth: Do the heavens really praise the wonders of God? Step outside early one morning, watch and listen. Hear the sound of the birds flying and singing. Take a look at the trees as they press toward the sky. Look at the grass and the flowers, how they look for nourishment by water and sunshine. All of those things underscore the fact that there is a Creator and He is good.

Thought: "The heavens are yours; the earth also is yours". God has allowed us to enjoy all of those things in nature, but they all belong to Him. He provides us with resources to live and to enjoy life, but they all belong to Him. Thank God today for all of the things He has allowed us to enjoy.

Tune: God of wonders beyond our galaxy, You are holy, holy
The universe declares Your majesty, You are holy, holy
Lord of heaven and earth, Lord of heaven and earth

Almighty God, Thank You for allowing me to see Your handiwork on a daily basis. May I never take it for granted.

Songs for Life – Day 202 - July 21

Text: Psalm 89:13-18

[13] You have a mighty arm;
your hand is powerful; your right hand is lifted high.
[14] Righteousness and justice are the foundation of your throne;
faithful love and truth go before you.
[15] Happy are the people who know the joyful shout;
Lord, they walk in the light from your face.
[16] They rejoice in your name all day long,
and they are exalted by your righteousness.
[17] For you are their magnificent strength; by your favor our horn is exalted.
[18] Surely our shield belongs to the Lord, our king to the Holy One of Israel.

Truth: God is mighty, and strong is His hand. Righteousness, steadfast love and faithfulness go before Him. He is our Shield. Whatever you need, God IS.

Thought: Verse 15 could be restated, "Blessed are the people who know the shout of victory by Your hand, the ones who are led by Your light and who live their lives in Your presence." How do we get to the place where we recognize God's hand, where we are living our lives in His presence? We stay in His Word, we pray without ceasing, we listen for His voice, and we look to see where He is working and join Him.

Tune: I am not skilled to understand
What God has willed what God has planned
I only know at His right hand, stands One who is my Savior
I take Him at His word and deed, Christ died to save me this I read
And in my heart I find a need, of Him to be my Savior
That He would leave His place on high, and come for sinful man to die
You count it strange so once did I, before I knew my Savior
My Savior loves my Savior lives, my Savior's always there for me
My God He was my God He is, my God is always gonna be

Father, I am not capable of living life on my own. I want to grow in that relationship with You every day. I know that whatever I need, You are.

Songs for Life – Day 203 - July 22

Text: Psalm 89:19-24

[19] You once spoke in a vision to your faithful ones
and said: "I have granted help to a warrior;
I have exalted one chosen from the people.
[20] I have found David my servant;
I have anointed him with my sacred oil.
[21] My hand will always be with him,
and my arm will strengthen him.
[22] The enemy will not oppress him;
the wicked will not afflict him.
[23] I will crush his foes before him
and strike those who hate him.
[24] My faithfulness and love will be with him,
and through my name his horn will be exalted.

Truth: David was called by God and anointed to succeed Saul as King of Israel. David was known as a "man after God's own heart". In giving this vision, God has assured that the one He calls to a task will be equipped by, and protected by, the mighty hand of God.

Thought: "If God calls you to it, He'll bring you through it". "The will of God will never take you where the grace of God will not protect you". Child of God, if He has called you to a task, position or role, He WILL equip you for it. Trust His Word, trust His hand, and bring Him your concerns.

Tune: This is amazing grace
This is unfailing love
That You would take my place
That You would bear my cross
You laid down Your life
That I would be set free
Oh Jesus I sing for all that You've done for me

Father God, I need Your grace for every step, every breath, every decision, every opportunity. Thank You for Your amazing grace.

Text: Psalm 89:25-29

[25] I will extend his power to the sea
and his right hand to the rivers.
[26] He will call to me, 'You are my Father,
my God, the rock of my salvation.'
[27] I will also make him my firstborn,
greatest of the kings of the earth.
[28] I will always preserve my faithful love for him,
and my covenant with him will endure.
[29] I will establish his line forever, his throne as long as heaven lasts.

Truth: The calling of David as King of Israel is one of the most significant events in Biblical history. The Messiah was to come from the family birth line of David. David's home place was Bethlehem, the birth place of Jesus Christ. What made David great was nothing of his own accord. What made David great was God's steadfast love and hand on him, as well as David's willingness to let God mold and shape his heart.

Thought: A carpenter can have the right tools, but if he doesn't know how to use them, they are, at best, toys, and at worst, instruments of destruction. God gives us the tools He desires us to have and will equip us to use them, as long as we acknowledge that they are His.

Tune: Giver of ev'ry breath I breathe, Author of all eternity
Giver of ev'ry perfect thing, to You be the glory
Maker of heaven and of earth, no one can comprehend Your worth
King over all the universe, to You be the glory
And I'm alive because I'm alive in You
(And) it's all because of Jesus I'm alive
It's all because the blood of Jesus Christ
That covers me and raised this dead man's life
It's all because of Jesus (I'm alive I'm alive I'm alive)

Dear Lord, show me how to use the tools You have given me. Give me a thirst for Your Word and the grace to be able to understand it.

Text: Psalm 89:30-37

[30] If his sons abandon my instruction and do not live by my ordinances,
[31] if they dishonor my statutes and do not keep my commands,
[32] then I will call their rebellion to account with the rod,
their iniquity with blows.
[33] But I will not withdraw my faithful love from him
or betray my faithfulness.
[34] I will not violate my covenant or change what my lips have said.
[35] Once and for all I have sworn an oath by my holiness;
I will not lie to David.
[36] His offspring will continue forever,
his throne like the sun before me,
[37] like the moon, established forever,
a faithful witness in the sky."Selah

Truth: The grace of God is not only what saves us, it is what sustains us. As children of God, when we disobey or get off-track, we can certainly open ourselves up to the rebuke and chastisement of God, but He never takes His hand from us.

Thought: "I'm not sure God even listens to me anymore". "Why would God bless me after the way I have ignored Him?" If you've ever thought something like this or are thinking it now, you are not alone. As humans, it is so easy to get off of the straight and narrow path, but God never fails to hear the humble cries of His children for forgiveness and restoration.

Tune: Amazing grace how sweet the sound
That saved a wretch like me
I once was lost but now am found
Was blind but now I see

Father God, You are the Author of grace, and it really is amazing! Help me not to be ashamed to return to You anytime I turn aside.

Text: Psalm 89:38-45

[38] But you have spurned and rejected him;
you have become enraged with your anointed.
[39] You have repudiated the covenant with your servant;
you have completely dishonored his crown.
[40] You have broken down all his walls;
you have reduced his fortified cities to ruins.
[41] All who pass by plunder him;
he has become an object of ridicule to his neighbors.
[42] You have lifted high the right hand of his foes;
you have made all his enemies rejoice.
[43] You have also turned back his sharp sword
and have not let him stand in battle.
[44] You have made his splendor cease and have overturned his throne.
[45] You have shortened the days of his youth;
you have covered him with shame. Selah

Truth: David's son, as successor, was facing an incredibly challenging circumstance. It seems that God is removing His hand of protection. However, in allowing the enemies to rise against him, God is not abandoning him, but instead giving him grace for an opportunity to repent.

Thought: God uses circumstances, at times, to bring us to a place of humility. Sometimes our vision gets clouded and all we see is the fact that we are being attacked. God allows these things to bring Himself glory. Surrender your situation to Him and wait for victory.

Tune: Here I am, humbled by Your majesty
Covered by Your grace so free
Here I am, knowing I'm a sinful man
Covered by the blood of the Lamb
Now I've found the greatest love of all is mine
Since You laid down Your life, the greatest sacrifice
Majesty majesty, Your grace has found me just as I am
Empty-handed but alive in Your hands

Oh Lord, help me not to see my circumstances, but to see only You.

Text: Psalm 89:46-48

46 How long, Lord? Will you hide forever?
Will your anger keep burning like fire?
47 Remember how short my life is.
Have you created everyone for nothing?
48 What courageous person can live and never see death?
Who can save himself from the power of Sheol? Selah

Truth: The psalmist has come to the place where he is expressing his true feelings. He feels that God is not working in his life, that he may be feeling like the wrath of God is upon him. He seems to be expressing that life is pointless if he's going to have to go through all of this "stuff".

Thought: Whenever God is moving, or whenever it seems God is not moving, there is always a greater purpose. There is never a time when God is NOT working. When it seems God is far away, we should do some soul-searching, asking God to reveal to us anything in our heart or life that is hindering our spiritual life. As we grow in our faith, the standard of our spiritual life is raised. God may bring conviction in your life for something that He does not convict another person about.

Tune: Before the day before the light
Before the world revolved around the sun
God on high stepped down into time
And wrote the story of His love for everyone
He has filled our hearts with wonder
So that we always remember
You and I are made to worship; You and I are called to love
You and I are forgiven and free
When you and I embrace surrender, when you and I choose to believe
Then you and I will see who we were meant to be

Holy Spirit, I confess that I cannot always see Your greater purpose. Sometimes I wonder if You are even there at all. But, You created me to worship You and I trust that You are always with me.

Text: Psalm 89:49-52

49 Lord, where are the former acts of your faithful love
that you swore to David in your faithfulness?
50 Remember, Lord, the ridicule against your servants—
in my heart I carry abuse from all the peoples—
51 how your enemies have ridiculed, Lord,
how they have ridiculed every step of your anointed.
52 Blessed be the Lord forever.
Amen and amen.

Truth: Even in the psalmist's low point, even as he has expressed his deep dissatisfaction, even as he has confessed impatience with God's lack of visible activity, he still knows that he is God's child and that he is blessed. "Blessed be the Lord forever. Amen and Amen."

Thought: When you are close with someone, you can be very honest about your feelings and know that you can negotiate the highs and lows of your relationship, because the love is very strong. God understands that we get frustrated, just as parents understand that their children get frustrated. However, He ALWAYS knows what is best for us. Can you ever remember a time when you got so impatient for God to move, but later realized why He was waiting? He's good like that!

Tune: I will bless the Lord forever
I will trust Him at all times
He has delivered me from all fear
He has set my feet upon a rock
And I will not be moved
And I'll say of the Lord

You are my shield my strength, my portion Deliverer
My shelter strong tower, my very present help in time of need

Heavenly Father, forgive my frustration. I know You have a plan and I just get impatient. I know Your timing is always best.

Text: Psalm 90:1-8

[1] Lord, you have been our refuge in every generation.
[2] Before the mountains were born,
before you gave birth to the earth and the world,
from eternity to eternity, you are God.
[3] You return mankind to the dust,
saying, "Return, descendants of Adam."
[4] For in your sight a thousand years
are like yesterday that passes by,
like a few hours of the night.
[5] You end their lives; they sleep.
They are like grass that grows in the morning—
[6] in the morning it sprouts and grows;
by evening it withers and dries up.
[7] For we are consumed by your anger; we are terrified by your wrath.
[8] You have set our iniquities before you,
our secret sins in the light of your presence.

Truth: Moses is praying for God's blessing on the wandering Israelites. He acknowledges the eternal existence of God; He, who was there before the earth and brought the universe into existence. Man's life is frail, and the body will return to dust, but God is not subject to time. God knows all, IS all, and is everlasting. You can't hide anything from God.

Thought: It is hard to wrap our finite minds around God's time, and how He's all knowing and omnipresent. Verse 8 says He knows our secret sin. Sin is sin. There is no level of sin. We serve a Holy God who knows us.

Tune: He knows, He knows; Every hurt and every sting
He has walked the suffering; He knows, He Knows
Let your burdens come undone; Lift your eye up to the One
Who knows; He knows

Holy God, help me to identify the sin hidden in my heart and confess it to you. Cleanse my heart, O God.

Songs for Life – Day 210 - July 29

Text: Psalm 90:9-17

[9] For all our days ebb away under your wrath;
we end our years like a sigh.
[10] Our lives last seventy years or, if we are strong, eighty years.
Even the best of them are struggle and sorrow;
indeed, they pass quickly and we fly away.
[11] Who understands the power of your anger?
Your wrath matches the fear that is due you.
[12] Teach us to number our days carefully
so that we may develop wisdom in our hearts.
[13] Lord—how long? Turn and have compassion on your servants.
[14] Satisfy us in the morning with your faithful love
so that we may shout with joy and be glad all our days.
[15] Make us rejoice for as many days as you have humbled us,
for as many years as we have seen adversity.
[16] Let your work be seen by your servants,
and your splendor by their children.
[17] Let the favor of the Lord our God be on us;
establish for us the work of our hands— establish the work of our hands!

Truth: Our days are numbered, and soon they will pass away. We need to make the most of our time here and pass on the power and knowledge of God to our children.

Thought: Life is short. It's too short to live with anger, resentment and un-forgiveness. Those things eat away at you like rust on metal. Pray for those that caused your anger and be forgiving, just as God forgives us. Our children are watching us and learning.

Tune: Show me how to love the unlovable;
Show me how to reach the unreachable
Help me now to do the impossible; Forgiveness I want to finally set it free
Show me how to see what Your mercy sees;
Help me now to give what You gave to me, forgiveness, oh forgiveness

Lord, thank you for redemption and forgiveness that you extend to us.

<u>Songs for Life – Day 211 - July 30</u>

Text: Psalm 91:1-8

[1] The one who lives under the protection of the Most High
dwells in the shadow of the Almighty.
[2] I will say concerning the Lord, who is my refuge and my fortress,
my God in whom I trust:
[3] He himself will rescue you from the bird trap,
from the destructive plague.
[4] He will cover you with his feathers; you will take refuge under his wings.
His faithfulness will be a protective shield.
[5] You will not fear the terror of the night, the arrow that flies by day,
[6] the plague that stalks in darkness, or the pestilence that ravages at noon.
[7] Though a thousand fall at your side
and ten thousand at your right hand, the pestilence will not reach you.
[8] You will only see it with your eyes
and witness the punishment of the wicked.

Truth: With the protection that God provides and promises, comes protection from the schemes of those who would seek to destroy, from diseases intended for those who are unfaithful. The image given is that of a very protective bird, allowing us to be protected in his "shadow".

Thought: No matter the circumstance, no matter the challenge, there is always refuge in the shadow of His wings, as we are sheltered by the "Most High". Stay close to God today and allow Him to take care of whatever you feel is attacking you.

Tune: From the ends of the earth, From the depths of the sea
From the heights of the heavens, Your name be praised
From the hearts of the weak, From the shouts of the strong
From the lips of all people, this song we raise Lord
Throughout the endless ages, You will be crowned with praises
Lord Most High
Exalted in every nation, Sovereign of all creation
Lord Most High, be magnified

Lord, I dwell in Your shelter. You are the Most High God. Protect me!

Songs for Life – Day 212 - July 31

Text: Psalm 91:9-16

[9] Because you have made the Lord—my refuge,
the Most High—your dwelling place,
[10] no harm will come to you;
no plague will come near your tent.
[11] For he will give his angels orders concerning you,
to protect you in all your ways.
[12] They will support you with their hands
so that you will not strike your foot against a stone.
[13] You will tread on the lion and the cobra;
you will trample the young lion and the serpent.
[14] Because he has his heart set on me, I will deliver him;
I will protect him because he knows my name.
[15] When he calls out to me, I will answer him;
I will be with him in trouble. I will rescue him and give him honor.
[16] I will satisfy him with a long life
and show him my salvation.

Truth: God is the speaker in this section of Scripture. He is describing the blessing He gives to those who know and love Him. Holding fast to Him in love means a "deep longing" for God or a "clinging" to God.

Thought: God desires an intimate love relationship with His children. He intends for that relationship to be both real and personal. Too many people live their lives without having a real and personal relationship with Christ. Ask Him to reveal Himself in a real and personal way today.

Tune: I am resolved no longer to linger, charmed by the world's delight
Things that are higher, things that are nobler
These have allured my sight
I will hasten to Him, hasten so glad and free
Jesus greatest highest, I will come to Thee

Lord, draw me into Your presence, Your shelter, Your refuge today. I want to have a closer relationship than we have ever had before.

Text: Psalm 92:1-9

[1] It is good to give thanks to the Lord, to sing praise to your name, Most High,

[2] to declare your faithful love in the morning and your faithfulness at night,

[3] with a ten-stringed harp and the music of a lyre.

[4] For you have made me rejoice, Lord, by what you have done;
    I will shout for joy because of the works of your hands.

[5] How magnificent are your works, Lord,
    how profound your thoughts!

[6] A stupid person does not know, a fool does not understand this:

[7] though the wicked sprout like grass and all evildoers flourish,
    they will be eternally destroyed.

[8] But you, Lord, are exalted forever.

[9] For indeed, Lord, your enemies—
    indeed, your enemies will perish; all evildoers will be scattered.

Truth: While others around him may be giving thanks to Baal or some other false God, the psalmist is giving thanks and singing praises to the Lord Most High. It is the Lord Most High whose works are great, whose thoughts are deep and who makes us glad and joyous by His works.

Thought: If you start each day with the Lord, you'll never have to be concerned that you will live a day without Him. The psalmist speaks of declaring God's steadfast love in the morning and his faithfulness at night, which seems to imply walking all day with The Lord.

Tune: Thank You for the cross Lord, Thank You for the price You paid
Bearing all my sin and shame, in love You came and gave amazing grace
Thank You for this love Lord, Thank You for the nail-pierced hands
Washed me in Your cleansing flow,
Now all I know Your forgiveness and embrace
Worthy is the Lamb seated on the throne
Crown You now with many crowns, You reign victorious
High and lifted up Jesus Son of God
The Darling of heaven crucified, Worthy is the Lamb, Worthy is the Lamb

Father, help me to walk with You, every moment today.

Text: Psalm 92:10-15

¹⁰ You have lifted up my horn
  like that of a wild ox;
  I have been anointed with the finest oil.
¹¹ My eyes look at my enemies;
  when evildoers rise against me,
  my ears hear them.
¹² The righteous thrive like a palm tree
  and grow like a cedar tree in Lebanon.
¹³ Planted in the house of the Lord,
  they thrive in the courts of our God.
¹⁴ They will still bear fruit in old age,
  healthy and green,
¹⁵ to declare: "The Lord is just;
  he is my rock,
  and there is no unrighteousness in him."

Truth: The reference to the finest oil in verse 10 is a reference to banquet guests. In that day, banquet guests were usually anointed with oil, which refreshed their skin and imparted a pleasing scent.

Thought: Are you in need of some of the "finest oil" today? Have the circumstances of life made your heart hurt and your shoulders ache? Seek the Lord, praise His name, take the focus off of your circumstances for a few moments and declare that the Lord is your rock and fortress. Trust Him, love Him, and worship Him today.

Tune: Spirit of the Living God, fall fresh on me
Spirit of the Living God, fall fresh on me
Melt me mold me, fill me use me
Spirit of the Living God
Fall fresh on me

Holy Spirit, fall fresh on me like fresh anointing oil. I need to be refreshed by Your Spirit today and filled to capacity, even to overflowing.

Text: Psalm 93:1-5

[1] The Lord reigns! He is robed in majesty;
 the Lord is robed, enveloped in strength.
 The world is firmly established;
 it cannot be shaken.
[2] Your throne has been established
 from the beginning;
 you are from eternity.
[3] The floods have lifted up, Lord,
 the floods have lifted up their voice;
 the floods lift up their pounding waves.
[4] Greater than the roar of a huge torrent—
 the mighty breakers of the sea—
 the Lord on high is majestic.
[5] Lord, your testimonies are completely reliable;
 holiness adorns your house
 for all the days to come.

Truth: "*The LORD reigns*" - He has always reigned! God established the world, His throne and His control, and it remains in His hands. Notice the word "flood" or "floods" is used 3 times. Floods are ancient symbols of chaos and evil, the worst thing they could imagine. Guess What??? GOD IS MIGHTIER THAN ANY FLOOD!

Thought: Think about your worst fear, struggle, pain or hurt. God IS mightier than that! It's no surprise to God. He is there for us and He is trustworthy.

Tune: Jesus Messiah; Name above all names;
Blessed Redeemer; Emmanuel
The rescue for sinners; the ransom from Heaven;
Jesus Messiah, LORD of All.

Heavenly Father, I have many fears and struggles, but today I will rest in knowing that you are mightier than any of my fears and struggles.

Text: Psalm 94:1-7

[1] Lord, God of vengeance—
   God of vengeance, shine!
[2] Rise up, Judge of the earth;
   repay the proud what they deserve.
[3] Lord, how long will the wicked—
   how long will the wicked celebrate?
[4] They pour out arrogant words;
   all the evildoers boast.
[5] Lord, they crush your people;
   they oppress your heritage.
[6] They kill the widow and the resident alien
   and murder the fatherless.
[7] They say, "The Lord doesn't see it.
   The God of Jacob doesn't pay attention."

Truth: The psalmist is calling on the Lord as Judge to bring justice to arrogant evildoers, to those who disobey Him. Not only do the wicked defy God's laws, they mock God's ability to punish them. When we have a personal relationship with God, we also have a personal relationship with His people. We hurt when we see the righteous oppressed.

Thought: Recent changes in our world have led many in the Christian community to strike back in force, resulting in the use of God's Word as a weapon. God did not call us to change the world, only to make disciples. Sometimes our reactions destroy our witness. Nothing has caught God by surprise, and He is more than capable of defending Himself. Trust God for the outcome – seek His grace and direction for leaders.

Tune: Turn your eyes upon Jesus, look full in His wonderful face
And the things of earth will grow strangely dim
In the light of His glory and grace

*Lord, I know that You have this world in the palm of your mighty hand.
Remove my fears and help me to trust You.*

Text: Psalm 94:8-15

8 Pay attention, you stupid people!
   Fools, when will you be wise?
9 Can the one who shaped the ear not hear,
   the one who formed the eye not see?
10 The one who instructs nations,
   the one who teaches mankind knowledge—does he not discipline?
11 The Lord knows the thoughts of mankind;
   they are futile.
12 Lord, how happy is anyone you discipline
   and teach from your law
13 to give him relief from troubled times
   until a pit is dug for the wicked.
14 The Lord will not leave his people
   or abandon his heritage,
15 for the administration of justice will again be righteous,
   and all the upright in heart will follow it.

Truth: God knows the hearts of each man better than his closest friend or brother ever could. If He created the ear, He hears all. If He created the eye, He sees all. If He allowed sin into the world, He knows how to deal with it. The Lord will not forsake his people.

Thought: When we accept Jesus Christ as our Lord and Savior we are grafted into the vine. We become part of the royal bloodline. As a loving Father provides for and protects His children, so God will never abandon His heritage. You have a Father who loves you!

Tune: O the blood, crimson love, Price of life's demand
Shameful sin, placed on Him, the Hope of ev'ry man
O the blood of Jesus washes me, O the blood of Jesus shed for me
What a sacrifice that saved my life, Yes, the blood it is my victory

Father, I am thankful for the blood of Your Son, Jesus Christ, who gave His life and shed His blood so that I could be grafted into the vine.

Text: Psalm 94:16-23

¹⁶ Who stands up for me against the wicked?
   Who takes a stand for me against evildoers?
¹⁷ If the Lord had not been my helper,
   I would soon rest in the silence of death.
¹⁸ If I say, "My foot is slipping,"
   your faithful love will support me, Lord.
¹⁹ When I am filled with cares,
   your comfort brings me joy.
²⁰ Can a corrupt throne be your ally,
   a throne that makes evil laws?
²¹ They band together against the life of the righteous
   and condemn the innocent to death.
²² But the Lord is my refuge;
   my God is the rock of my protection.
²³ He will pay them back for their sins
   and destroy them for their evil.
   The Lord our God will destroy them.

Truth: The terms refuge and rock of my protection here are metaphors for God's protection. The psalmist combines terms to emphasize God's strength against the wicked.

Thought: When we go through trials and tribulations, sometimes we say "why???" The truth is, if we had no trials, we wouldn't understand how good God is, or how needy we really are. Thank God for what He teaches you today in the trials, and for being your stronghold and rock of refuge.

Tune: Your Name is a strong and mighty tower
Your Name is a shelter like no other
Your Name let the nations sing it louder
'Cause nothing has the power to save but Your Name

Father, Your name is what I can run to when I am afraid, when I am in need and when I have made mistakes and need forgiveness.

Text: Psalm 95:1-5

¹ Come, let us shout joyfully to the Lord,
    shout triumphantly to the rock of our salvation!
² Let us enter his presence with thanksgiving;
    let us shout triumphantly to him in song.
³ For the Lord is a great God,
    a great King above all gods.
⁴ The depths of the earth are in his hand,
    and the mountain peaks are his.
⁵ The sea is his; he made it.
    His hands formed the dry land.

Truth: The psalmist is calling on the children of God to sing to the Lord, to honor Him, to exalt Him, and to worship Him. God has the highest of mountains and the depths of the earth in His hand, as well as everything in between.

Thought: Singing to the Lord is not reserved simply for those who have "a good singing voice". When the psalmist says, "let us sing", he is speaking to the church, to the people of God. Singing His praises involves our heart, our mind, our voice, and really our body. Spend a few moments singing a song or hymn of praise to God today and bask in His presence.

Tune: Sing to the King Who is coming to reign
Glory to Jesus the Lamb that was slain
Life and salvation His Empire shall bring
And joy to the nations when Jesus is King

Come let us sing a song, a song declaring that we belong to Jesus
He is all we need
Lift up a heart of praise, sing now with voices raised to Jesus
Sing to the King

Lord Jesus, I lift my voice to sing Your praises today. I give you my heart, my mind and my soul. I belong to YOU, Jesus!

Text: Psalm 95:6-11

[6] Come, let us worship and bow down;
   let us kneel before the Lord our Maker.
[7] For he is our God, and we are the people of his pasture,
   the sheep under his care. Today, if you hear his voice:
[8] Do not harden your hearts as at Meribah,
   as on that day at Massah in the wilderness
[9] where your fathers tested me;
   they tried me, though they had seen what I did.
[10] For forty years I was disgusted with that generation;
   I said, "They are a people whose hearts go astray;
   they do not know my ways."
[11] So I swore in my anger, "They will not enter my rest."

Truth: Worship . . . bow down . . . kneel . . . these are words of instruction that demand submission to a higher authority. We are instructed to worship because He is Lord. We are called to bow down because we are low, and He is high and lifted up. He is our God and we are His people.

Thought: I can remember going to my grandmother's house when I was a child and hearing her requests for the grandchildren to perform. Sing, dance, play an instrument, give a speech . . . it didn't matter whether it was any good or not. God loves to hear His children sing. When His praises are sung, it glorifies Him and invites His presence. Worship and bow down before Him today.

Tune: Come let us worship and bow down
Let us kneel before the Lord our God our Maker
Come let us worship and bow down
Let us kneel before the Lord our God our Maker
For He is our God, and we are the people of His pasture
And the sheep of His hand, just the sheep of His hand

Holy God, I kneel before you today, worshipping your Holy Name and giving you all of the glory, I can give You. You are awesome, God!

Text: Psalm 96:1-6

[1] Sing a new song to the Lord;
   let the whole earth sing to the Lord.
[2] Sing to the Lord, bless his name;
   proclaim his salvation from day to day.
[3] Declare his glory among the nations,
   his wondrous works among all peoples.
[4] For the Lord is great and is highly praised;
   he is feared above all gods.
[5] For all the gods of the peoples are idols,
   but the Lord made the heavens.
[6] Splendor and majesty are before him;
   strength and beauty are in his sanctuary.

Truth: The phrase "*Sing to the Lord*" is mentioned 3 times. Repetition means it's very important and that we should to pay attention. We are to praise God for ALL His works. He has given us so much! All creation was made by God. There are many recorded events in our Bible and in our lives to praise Him for - especially His Son that was sacrificed for our sins, our salvation, and our eternal life! So... sing to the Lord - for He is great!

Thought: When I read these verses, the phrase "day to day" just jumps out at me. Reflect on singing to the Lord - day to day. Not only on Sunday mornings, or Wednesday nights, but day to day - as in everyday! God is here for us every day. Shouldn't we give Him our attention daily as we await His return?

Tune: While I'm waiting I will serve You
While I'm waiting I will worship, while I'm waiting I will not faint
I'll be running the race even while I wait
I'm waiting, I'm waiting on You Lord
And I am peaceful, I'm waiting on You Lord
Though it's not easy no, but faithfully I will wait, yes, I will wait

Lord, fill me and mold me and increase my desire to seek You, each day.

Text: Psalm 96:7-13

[7] Ascribe to the Lord, you families of the peoples,
  ascribe to the Lord glory and strength.
[8] Ascribe to the Lord the glory of his name;
  bring an offering and enter his courts.
[9] Worship the Lord in the splendor of his holiness;
  let the whole earth tremble before him.
[10] Say among the nations: "The Lord reigns.
  The world is firmly established; it cannot be shaken.
  He judges the peoples fairly."
[11] Let the heavens be glad and the earth rejoice;
  let the sea and all that fills it resound.
[12] Let the fields and everything in them celebrate.
  Then all the trees of the forest will shout for joy
[13] before the Lord, for he is coming—for he is coming to judge the earth.
  He will judge the world with righteousness
  and the peoples with his faithfulness.

Truth: Similar to yesterday's verses, we have the words "*ascribe to the Lord*" written 3 times. Ascribe means to credit, assign or attribute. We are to credit the Lord's glory and strength that is due Him. Our God reigns now and forever. One day, everything, people, trees, the whole earth and everything in it will rejoice to the Lord!

Thought: Do you feel that your finite mind just can't fathom the Glory and Splendor of the Lord? I do. It seems incomprehensible. Verse 13 ends with "*He will judge the world righteousness, and the peoples with his faithfulness.*" Jesus is coming…Are you ready?

Tune: You shall go out with joy, and be led forth with peace
The mountains and the hills will break forth before you
There'll be shouts of joy, and all the trees of the field
Will clap will clap their hands

Lord, I want to be faithful to give you credit for everything in my life.

Text: Psalm 97:1-7

[1] The Lord reigns! Let the earth rejoice;
   let the many coasts and islands be glad.
[2] Clouds and total darkness surround him;
   righteousness and justice are the foundation of his throne.
[3] Fire goes before him
   and burns up his foes on every side.
[4] His lightning lights up the world;
   the earth sees and trembles.
[5] The mountains melt like wax at the presence of the Lord—
   at the presence of the Lord of the whole earth.
[6] The heavens proclaim his righteousness; all the peoples see his glory.
[7] All who serve carved images,
   those who boast in idols, will be put to shame.
   All the gods must worship him.

Truth: All people were created by God to worship. Many choose to worship things other than Jehovah God, whether it be another "god", or something less idyllic, like attention, money, or self. One only needs to look into the sky and examine nature all around us to see that God is real.

Thought: Though we worship God, we still struggle with worship of "worthless idols". Anything we put before God is an idol, whether that be our smart phones or other technology, pleasure, work, food, or a personal relationship. Ask God to reveal the "worthless idols" in your life.

Tune: Over all the earth You reign on high
Every mountain stream every sunset sky
But my one request Lord my only aim
Is that You'd reign in me again
Lord reign in me, reign in Your pow'r
Over all my dreams, in my darkest hour
You are the Lord of all I am, so, won't You reign in me again

Lord, reveal any idols in my life that are keeping me from seeing You.

Text: Psalm 97:8-12

[8] Zion hears and is glad,
 Judah's villages rejoice
 because of your judgments, Lord.
[9] For you, Lord,
 are the Most High over the whole earth;
 you are exalted above all the gods.
[10] You who love the Lord, hate evil!
 He protects the lives of his faithful ones;
 he rescues them from the power of the wicked.
[11] Light dawns for the righteous,
 gladness for the upright in heart.
[12] Be glad in the Lord, you righteous ones,
 and give thanks to his holy name.

Truth: The psalmist is calling for God's people to remain loyal to Him and trust in his future help and blessings. This loyalty is demonstrated in outward acts of worship and service, as well as an inward allegiance.

Thought: The believer receives the benefits of gladness, preservation, deliverance, light, and joy. We demonstrate our appreciation for those things by allowing God to control our heart and by obeying Him. What is the condition of your heart today? Do you need to ask God to take control once again? How is your obedience? What areas do you need His direction in today?

Tune: What a fellowship what a joy divine
Leaning on the everlasting arms
What a blessedness what a peace is mine
Leaning on the everlasting arms
Leaning, leaning, safe and secure from all alarms
Leaning, leaning, leaning on the everlasting arms

Heavenly Father, I declare my faithfulness to You today. You have always been faithful to me and continue to love me.

Text: Psalm 98

¹ Sing a new song to the Lord, for he has performed wonders;
   his right hand and holy arm have won him victory.
² The Lord has made his victory known;
   he has revealed his righteousness in the sight of the nations.
³ He has remembered his love
   and faithfulness to the house of Israel;
   all the ends of the earth have seen our God's victory.
⁴ Let the whole earth shout to the Lord;
   be jubilant, shout for joy, and sing.
⁵ Sing to the Lord with the lyre,
   with the lyre and melodious song.
⁶ With trumpets and the blast of the ram's horn shout triumphantly
   in the presence of the Lord, our King.
⁷ Let the sea and all that fills it, the world and those who live in it, resound.
⁸ Let the rivers clap their hands; let the mountains shout together for joy
⁹ before the Lord, for he is coming to judge the earth.
   He will judge the world righteously and the peoples fairly.

Truth: The psalmist is calling for action in giving praise and thanks to the Lord. We are to sing a new song, make a joyful noise, and sound the trumpets and horns. Even the rivers clap their hands and the hills sing for joy. All of God's creation sings His praises.

Thought: You can make a joyful noise in singing, but also in giving testimony with your voice or with your life about the goodness of God in your life. Share your testimony of God's goodness with someone today.

Tune: There's within my heart a melody, Jesus whispers sweet and low
Fear not I am with thee peace be still, in all of life's ebb and flow
Jesus Jesus Jesus, Sweetest name I know
Fills my ev'ry longing, Keeps me singing as I go

Father, empower me today to give You praise, not only in singing Your praises, but in telling others of Your goodness and how You have blessed.

Songs for Life – Day 226 - August 14

Text: Psalm 99

[1] The Lord reigns! Let the peoples tremble.

He is enthroned between the cherubim. Let the earth quake.

[2] The Lord is great in Zion; he is exalted above all the peoples.

[3] Let them praise your great and awe-inspiring name. He is holy.

[4] The mighty King loves justice. You have established fairness;

you have administered justice and righteousness in Jacob.

[5] Exalt the Lord our God; bow in worship at his footstool. He is holy.

[6] Moses and Aaron were among his priests;

Samuel also was among those calling on his name.

They called to the Lord and he answered them.

[7] He spoke to them in a pillar of cloud;

they kept his decrees and the statutes he gave them.

[8] Lord our God, you answered them. You were a forgiving God to them,

but an avenger of their sinful actions.

[9] Exalt the Lord our God;

bow in worship at his holy mountain, for the Lord our God is holy.

Truth: *"The LORD reigns", "the LORD is great", "he is exalted", "awe-inspiring" ...you can pray these phrases to God about Him. We can, and should, tell God how great He is.*

Thought: Read the last line, "*...the LORD our God is holy!*" These words are really a summarization of the whole Psalm. Break it down: **The** - none other; **LORD** - KING; **Our** - mine, yours; **God** - creator; **Holy** - perfect, righteous. It's personal, my friends!

Tune: Lost are saved find their way at the sound of your great name
All condemned feel no shame at the sound of your great name
Every fear has no place at the sound of your great name
The enemy—he has to leave at the sound of your great name
Worthy is the Lamb; that was slain for us; Son of God and Man
You are high and lifted up and all the world will praise your great name

Father God, You are Holy! You are high and lifted up! Praise Your Name!

Songs for Life – Day 227 - August 15

Text: Psalm 100

[1] Let the whole earth shout triumphantly to God!

[2] Serve the Lord with gladness;
   come before him with joyful songs.

[3] Acknowledge that the Lord is God.
   He made us, and we are his—
   his people, the sheep of his pasture.

[4] Enter his gates with thanksgiving
   and his courts with praise.
   Give thanks to him and bless his name.

[5] For the Lord is good, and his faithful love endures forever;
   his faithfulness, through all generations.

Truth: The call goes out to the entire world to sing the praises of Jehovah God. He is their God, whether they acknowledge Him in this life or not. One day, every knee will bow, and every tongue will confess that Jesus is Lord to the glory of God the Father.

Thought: Praise is contagious. When God's people begin to worship Him in a worship service, something special happens. Some may lift their hands, some may weep, some may shout, others close their eyes, others are singing from the bottom of their lungs. It's joyous and contagious. Give some praise to God today and see how it affects others around you.

Tune: I will worship, with all of my heart
I will praise You, with all of my strength
I will seek You, All of my days
I will follow, all of Your ways

I will give You all my worship, I will give You all my praise
You alone I long to worship
You alone are worthy of my praise

Father, You alone are worthy of praise. You are the only wise God. You are Jehovah. You are mighty, You are Truth and You are Lord.

Text: Psalm 101

¹ I will sing of faithful love and justice;
    I will sing praise to you, Lord.
² I will pay attention to the way of integrity. When will you come to me?
    I will live with a heart of integrity in my house.
³ I will not let anything worthless guide me.
    I hate the practice of transgression; it will not cling to me.
⁴ A devious heart will be far from me;
    I will not be involved with evil.
⁵ I will destroy anyone who secretly slanders his neighbor;
    I cannot tolerate anyone with haughty eyes or an arrogant heart.
⁶ My eyes favor the faithful of the land so that they may sit down with me.
    The one who follows the way of integrity may serve me.
⁷ No one who acts deceitfully will live in my palace;
    the one who tells lies will not be retained here to guide me.
⁸ Every morning I will destroy
    all the wicked of the land,
    wiping out all evildoers from the Lord's city.

Truth: The psalmist gives testimony as well as a declaration of his loyalty to God. He testifies that he will separate himself from anything evil and any attitude that is contrary to the character of God.

Thought: "I will" … a declaration, a pointed statement, an assertion of great intention and promise. The psalmist says "I will" no less than eight times. When it comes to your relationship to God, what will you say "I will" to today?

Tune: Wherever He leads I'll go, wherever He leads I'll go
I'll follow my Christ who loves me so
Wherever He leads I'll go

Father, I will follow You today. I will trust You. I will sing Your praises. I will give You glory. I will testify of Your goodness in my life. I will, in response to whatever You ask.

Text: Psalm 102:1-7

[1] Lord, hear my prayer;
   let my cry for help come before you.
[2] Do not hide your face from me in my day of trouble.
   Listen closely to me;
   answer me quickly when I call.
[3] For my days vanish like smoke,
   and my bones burn like a furnace.
[4] My heart is suffering, withered like grass;
   I even forget to eat my food.
[5] Because of the sound of my groaning,
   my flesh sticks to my bones.
[6] I am like an eagle owl,
   like a little owl among the ruins.
[7] I stay awake;
   I am like a solitary bird on a roof.

Truth: The Psalmist is crying out for God's attention. He was in physical turmoil and realized that he needed God in his lonely distress.

Thought: *"Hear my prayer"* – seemingly a call of desperation. Do you ever feel like no one listens to you or perhaps they listen, but are not really "hearing" what you are saying? Sometimes you want to have someone to listen to you and hear your heart and not be judgmental or full of opinions while you're trying to express your thoughts. We do have someone - God.

Tune: My help comes from You; You're right here, pulling me through
You carry my weakness, my sickness,
my brokenness all on Your shoulders; Your shoulders
My help comes from You, You are my rest, my rescue
I don't have to see to believe
that You're lifting me up on Your shoulders, Your shoulders

Father, today I give you my brokenness, I pour out my heart to You, because I know you are there and you hear me.

Text: Psalm 102:8-14

[8] My enemies taunt me all day long;
   they ridicule and use my name as a curse.
[9] I eat ashes like bread
   and mingle my drinks with tears
[10] because of your indignation and wrath;
   for you have picked me up and thrown me aside.
[11] My days are like a lengthening shadow,
   and I wither away like grass.
[12] But you, Lord, are enthroned forever;
   your fame endures to all generations.
[13] You will rise up and have compassion on Zion,
   for it is time to show favor to her—
   the appointed time has come.
[14] For your servants take delight in its stones
   and favor its dust.

Truth: Once again our Psalmist is full of misery and sadness. He is suffering because of God's *"indignation and wrath,"* (Vs 10). He knows the sun is setting on his time here and takes comfort in the knowledge that God will be *"enthroned forever,"* (Vs 12).

Thought: "Enthroned forever" – What does that mean? Enthroned: on a throne, to invest with sovereign authority, to exalt, revered, sacred. Forever: without ever ending, for always, permanently. God will have sovereign authority on His throne permanently, without end. Our life is finite here on Earth. But we can look to God for our eternity!

Tune: (Oh) I'm running to Your arms, I'm running to Your arms
The riches of Your love will always be enough
Nothing compares to Your embrace, light of the world forever reign

Father in Heaven, please examine my heart and reveal to me things that need to be cleansed. My desire is to be a true and faithful servant and to worship You!

Text: Psalm 102:15-23

¹⁵ Then the nations will fear the name of the Lord,
 and all the kings of the earth your glory,
¹⁶ for the Lord will rebuild Zion;
 he will appear in his glory.
¹⁷ He will pay attention to the prayer of the destitute
 and will not despise their prayer.
¹⁸ This will be written for a later generation,
 and a people who have not yet been created will praise the Lord:
¹⁹ He looked down from his holy heights—
 the Lord gazed out from heaven to earth—
²⁰ to hear a prisoner's groaning,
 to set free those condemned to die,
²¹ so that they might declare
 the name of the Lord in Zion and his praise in Jerusalem,
²² when peoples and kingdoms are assembled to serve the Lord.
²³ He has broken my strength in midcourse; he has shortened my days.

Truth: "*This will be written for a later generation*" - In other words, write all this down for those not even born yet; that they may come to know God, our Lord. Our Bible is a record to us of ALL God's promises.

Thought: Verse 22 - "*when peoples and kingdoms are assembled to serve the LORD*"...The Bible is very clear in Philippians 2:10 "*...so that at the name of Jesus every knee should bow, in heaven and on earth and under the earth and every tongue confess that Jesus Christ is Lord...*" One day, all the earth will bow and know that Jesus Christ is Lord!

Tune: One day every tongue; Will confess You are God
One day every knee will bow; Still the greatest treasure remains
For those who gladly choose You now; Come now is the time to worship
Come now is the time to give your heart; Come just as you are to worship
Come just as you are before your God; Come

Father God, thank you for your Word. It teaches me about You daily.

Text: Psalm 102:24-28

²⁴ I say: "My God, do not take me in the middle of my life!
   Your years continue through all generations.
²⁵ Long ago you established the earth,
   and the heavens are the work of your hands.
²⁶ They will perish, but you will endure;
   all of them will wear out like clothing.
   You will change them like a garment, and they will pass away.
²⁷ But you are the same, and your years will never end.
²⁸ Your servants' children will dwell securely,
   and their offspring will be established before you."

Truth: The psalmist is asking for more time on earth but knows that his earthly life is nothing compared to eternity with God. He also acknowledges that God existed before creation and will exist after creation has perished. Verse 27, "*you are the same*".... God never changes! He will remain a constant.

Thought: What do the words "God never changes" mean to you? Malachi 3:6 says, "*For I the Lord do not change...*" For you and me, that is a promise that we can take to heart. Our God, who was, and is, and is to come, will always be the same, yesterday, today and tomorrow!

Tune: O Lord my God, when I in awesome wonder
Consider all the worlds Thy hands have made
I see the stars, I hear the rolling thunder
Thy pow'r thru'out the universe displayed

Then sings my soul, My Savior God to Thee
How great Thou art, how great Thou art
Then sings my soul, My Savior God to Thee
How great Thou art, how great Thou art

Almighty God, I thank you for your promises that You never change. I can rest in the safety of that knowledge and Your Grace and Your Love.

Text: Psalm 103:1-5

[1] My soul, bless the Lord,
   and all that is within me, bless his holy name.
[2] My soul, bless the Lord,
   and do not forget all his benefits.
[3] He forgives all your iniquity;
   he heals all your diseases.
[4] He redeems your life from the Pit;
   he crowns you with faithful love and compassion.
[5] He satisfies you with good things;
   your youth is renewed like the eagle.

Truth: The psalmist reminds us of some of the wonderful benefits of knowing the Lord: forgiveness of sin, healing, redemption, love, compassion, and so much more. He brings those things as a renewal like the strength and speed of the eagle.

Thought: Have you ever felt like you were taken for granted? Probably all of us have at one time or another. God has done so much for us that it can be easy to take Him for granted. Take some time to let all that is within you bless the holy name of the Lord today! Every breath we breathe, every step we take is because of the grace & mercy of the Lord.

Tune: Every move I make I make in You, You make me move Jesus
Every breath I take I breathe in You
Every step I take I take in You, You are my way Jesus
Every breath I take I breathe in You

Waves of mercy waves of grace,
everywhere I look I see Your face
Your love has captured me,
Oh my God this love how can it be

Father, I never want to be guilty of taking You for granted, but I know that I have. Thank you for providing everything I need and so much more.

Text: Psalm 103:6-14

[6] The Lord executes acts of righteousness
  and justice for all the oppressed.
[7] He revealed his ways to Moses,
  his deeds to the people of Israel.
[8] The Lord is compassionate and gracious,
  slow to anger and abounding in faithful love.
[9] He will not always accuse us or be angry forever.
[10] He has not dealt with us as our sins deserve
  or repaid us according to our iniquities.
[11] For as high as the heavens are above the earth,
  so great is his faithful love toward those who fear him.
[12] As far as the east is from the west,
  so far has he removed our transgressions from us.
[13] As a father has compassion on his children,
  so the Lord has compassion on those who fear him.
[14] For he knows what we are made of,
  remembering that we are dust.

Truth: This passage deals with the character of God. Because of His loving nature, God acts on behalf of His children. He is merciful. He is gracious. He abounds in steadfast love.

Thought: We serve a compassionate God! If He were not, our consequences for our sin would be swift and drastic.

Tune: You are beautiful beyond description, Too marvelous for words
Too wonderful for comprehension, Like nothing ever seen or heard
Who can grasp Your infinite wisdom,
Who can fathom the depth of Your love
You are beautiful beyond description, Majesty enthroned above
And I stand I stand in awe of You, I stand I stand in awe of You
Holy God to whom all praise is due, I stand in awe of You

God, today I reflect on Your love. It is amazing, and I don't deserve it.

Text: Psalm 103:15-22

¹⁵ As for man, his days are like grass—he blooms like a flower of the field;
¹⁶ when the wind passes over it, it vanishes,
   and its place is no longer known.
¹⁷ But from eternity to eternity
   the Lord's faithful love is toward those who fear him,
   and his righteousness toward the grandchildren
¹⁸ of those who keep his covenant,
   who remember to observe his precepts.
¹⁹ The Lord has established his throne in heaven,
   and his kingdom rules over all.
²⁰ Bless the Lord, all his angels of great strength,
   who do his word, obedient to his command.
²¹ Bless the Lord, all his armies, his servants who do his will.
²² Bless the Lord, all his works in all the places where he rules.
   My soul, bless the Lord!

Truth: "The Lord's faithful love is toward those who fear him." This is a relationship of response. God first loves us and then we love Him in return. The way we demonstrate that love is by living lives of obedience.

Thought: Like a flower that blooms in season and then can be gone, man's life can seem brief. God's love does not change with the seasons, nor does it ever lose any intensity. It is from everlasting to everlasting.

Tune: Lord I come to You, Let my heart be changed renewed
Flowing from the grace that I found in You
And Lord I've come to know the weaknesses I see in me
Will be stripped away, by the pow'r of Your love
Hold me close, Let Your love surround me
Bring me near, Draw me to Your side
And as I wait, I'll rise up like the eagle
And I will soar with You, Your Spirit leads me on, In the pow'r of Your love

Dear Lord, let Your love surround me today. Your love is power!

Text: Psalm 104:1-9

[1] My soul, bless the Lord! Lord my God, you are very great;
    you are clothed with majesty and splendor.
[2] He wraps himself in light as if it were a robe,
    spreading out the sky like a canopy,
[3] laying the beams of his palace on the waters above,
    making the clouds his chariot, walking on the wings of the wind,
[4] and making the winds his messengers,
    flames of fire his servants.
[5] He established the earth on its foundations;
    it will never be shaken.
[6] You covered it with the deep as if it were a garment;
    the water stood above the mountains.
[7] At your rebuke the water fled;
    at the sound of your thunder they hurried away—
[8] mountains rose and valleys sank—to the place you established for them.
[9] You set a boundary they cannot cross;
    they will never cover the earth again.

Truth: The psalmist begins by praising God for His majesty and splendor, then describes God's work in creation. Beginning with verse 5, there are references here that correspond to Day 3 of Creation.

Thought: In verse 4, there is reference to a flaming fire. Fire has several purposes. It provides heat and energy. It can give fuel. It also can burn away things that are unnecessary. Where do you need the Creator to bring fire in your life today? Are you needing fuel for the journey? Are there things in your life that need to be burned away? God can do both!

Tune: Shine Jesus shine, Fill this land with the Father's glory
Blaze Spirit blaze, set our hearts on fire
Flow river flow, flood the nations with grace and mercy
Send forth Your word Lord, and let there be light

Father God, fill me with Your fire. Burn away what is not needed in my life.

Text: Psalm 104:10-13

[10] He causes the springs to gush into the valleys;
   they flow between the mountains.
[11] They supply water for every wild beast;
   the wild donkeys quench their thirst.
[12] The birds of the sky live beside the springs;
   they make their voices heard among the foliage.
[13] He waters the mountains from his palace;
   the earth is satisfied by the fruit of your labor.

Truth: When God created the heavens and the earth, the animals of the land, sea and sky, He created them with the intention of providing for them. He has indeed provided for them from the time of creation. Whenever water sources get low, God brings the rain which provides the water for nourishment. How much more does our loving God provide for the crown of His creation, man! He knows each need that we have.

Thought: Water . . . a cool drink can bring refreshment on hot day or after working or exercising. Without it for an extended period, life ceases to exist. In the same way that God provides water for nourishment, He provides living water to nourish our souls. Water is at its most effective state when it is moving. Ask God for a fresh touch of living water today to nourish your soul. Let it wash over you like a healing stream.

Tune: I come to the garden alone
While the dew is still on the roses
And the voice I hear falling on my ear
The Son of God discloses

And He walks with me, and He talks with me
And He tells me I am His own
And the joy we share as we tarry there, none other has ever known

Oh Lord, I need a fresh drink of water from Your fountain. My spirit is dry and thirsty. Cleanse me and fill me today, O Lord.

Text: Psalm 104:14-18

[14] He causes grass to grow for the livestock
   and provides crops for man to cultivate, producing food from the earth,
[15] wine that makes human hearts glad—
   making his face shine with oil—
   and bread that sustains human hearts.
[16] The trees of the Lord flourish,
   the cedars of Lebanon that he planted.
[17] There the birds make their nests;
   storks make their homes in the pine trees.
[18] The high mountains are for the wild goats;
   the cliffs are a refuge for hyraxes.

Truth: God's kindness is exhibited in His provisions for daily life. For centuries God has brought rain from the skies to nourish the earth. While each part of creation has been created to give glory to God, God has created some with the purpose of aiding mankind and others simply to draw attention to His glory.

Thought: If God did not have a purpose for your life, He wouldn't continue to provide for your needs. He's given grass to feed the livestock so that man could be fed with it. He's created plants that provide fruit and vegetables for man's nourishment. God has literally provided for every need. Reflect today on how God has provided for your every need and give Him thanks. Every provision has been led by His hand.

Tune: Wonderful merciful Savior, Precious Redeemer and Friend
Who would have thought that a Lamb could rescue the souls of men?
Oh, You rescue the souls of men
You are the One that we praise, You are the One we adore
You give the healing and grace, our hearts always hunger for
Oh, our hearts always hunger for

Father God, I confess that sometimes I wonder what my purpose is in this life. You rescued me from sin, so I know You have purpose for me.

Text: Psalm 104:19-23

[19] He made the moon to mark the festivals;
  the sun knows when to set.
[20] You bring darkness, and it becomes night,
  when all the forest animals stir.
[21] The young lions roar for their prey
  and seek their food from God.
[22] The sun rises; they go back
  and lie down in their dens.
[23] Man goes out to his work
  and to his labor until evening.

Truth: The psalmists moves here from elements of the third day of creation to elements of the fourth day of creation: the sun and moon, light and darkness. Even the young lions roaring for their prey is part of the providence of God. God created this world to allow for all of His creatures to survive.

Thought: Everything in the world has its place . . . including you. God created you so that you might bring glory and honor to Him. He has a plan especially for you. It may not be exactly like the plan He has for anyone else. If He created you, He will provide for you. What is He saying to you today? Is He leading you into a new area? Is He preparing to equip you for a new ministry? Is He calling you to be more active in the church?

Tune: I have a song I love to sing since I have been redeemed
Of my Redeemer Savior King
Since I have been redeemed

Since I have been redeemed
Since I have been redeemed, I will glory in His name
Since I have been redeemed, I will glory in my Savior's name

Father, show me where You're working and where I should join You today.

Text: Psalm 104:24-29

[24] How countless are your works, Lord!
   In wisdom you have made them all; the earth is full of your creatures.
[25] Here is the sea, vast and wide,
   teeming with creatures beyond number—
   living things both large and small.
[26] There the ships move about,
   and Leviathan, which you formed to play there.
[27] All of them wait for you
   to give them their food at the right time.
[28] When you give it to them, they gather it;
   when you open your hand they are satisfied with good things.
[29] When you hide your face, they are terrified;
   when you take away their breath,
   they die and return to the dust.

Truth: Everything in creation is dependent on the hand and provision of God. The psalmist continues the journey through the days of Creation here by referring to the sea creatures – the fifth day. We see the reference to Leviathan, a legendary sea monster. Perhaps this is a reference to Satan and the disruption he gives in our "waters" of life. Even Satan is part of God's creation and has a purpose which ultimately brings God glory.

Thought: Sometimes we wonder why God allows Satan to have influence in our lives. We think that our lives would be so much easier without temptation, without distraction, without the influence of evil. However, the appearance of evil serves to bring glory to the goodness of God. We learn more through our struggles than in our mountaintop experiences.

Tune: I need Thee every hour, most gracious Lord
No tender voice like Thine can peace afford
I need Thee O I need Thee, every hour I need Thee
O bless me now my Savior, I come to Thee

Holy God, give me the discernment & wisdom, to resist the enemy today.

Text: Psalm 104:30-35

[30] When you send your breath, they are created,
and you renew the surface of the ground.
[31] May the glory of the Lord endure forever;
may the Lord rejoice in his works.
[32] He looks at the earth, and it trembles;
he touches the mountains, and they pour out smoke.
[33] I will sing to the Lord all my life;
I will sing praise to my God while I live.
[34] May my meditation be pleasing to him;
I will rejoice in the Lord.
[35] May sinners vanish from the earth
and wicked people be no more.
My soul, bless the Lord! Hallelujah!

Truth: This passage is reflective of the sixth day of creation, the crowning day of creation. It was on this day that man was created. Notice the reference to the Holy Spirit in verse 30. Without the Holy Spirit, man is powerless. Without the Holy Spirit, man is rudderless. Without the daily empowerment of the Holy Spirit, we can easily be controlled by the flesh.

Thought: The psalmist said, "I will sing to the Lord all my life". In our moments of victory, that is easy to say. What about in your valleys? Are you still declaring that you will sing to the Lord? What enables us to do that, when our strength is weak? It's the power of the Holy Spirit within us.

Tune: I will sing of my Redeemer and His wondrous love to me
On the cruel cross He suffered, from the curse to set me free

Sing O sing of my Redeemer, with His blood He purchased me
On the cross He sealed my pardon
Paid the debt and made me free

O Lord I will sing Your praises as long as I live. I will sing of my salvation, which You purchased for me. You paid my debt and set me free!

Text: Psalm 105:1-6

¹ Give thanks to the Lord, call on his name;
   proclaim his deeds among the peoples.
² Sing to him, sing praise to him;
   tell about all his wondrous works!
³ Honor his holy name;
   let the hearts of those who seek the Lord rejoice.
⁴ Seek the Lord and his strength;
   seek his face always.
⁵ Remember the wondrous works he has done,
   his wonders, and the judgments he has pronounced,
⁶ you offspring of Abraham his servant,
   Jacob's descendants—his chosen ones.

Truth: This passage is filled with so many directives: give thanks, call, proclaim, sing, tell, seek and remember. We are called to celebrate the Lord's goodness and share it with others. Look back, or remember, what all God has done for you, so you will be encouraged to go on ahead, because you know He has been and always will be faithful.

Thought: We use the Bible, God's Holy Word, to read about how God took care of his people. He saved them time and time again. They weren't perfect, nor did God use perfect people to lead his children. When you are down and out, seek God, His strength, His presence... continually! His strength is perfect.

Tune: His strength is perfect when our strength is gone
He'll carry us when we can't carry on
Raised in His power
The weak become strong
His strength is perfect
His strength is perfect

Lord, I come before You, acknowledging that I have weaknesses, troubles and trials. I seek You and Your strength to carry me through.

Text: Psalm 105:7-11

[7] He is the Lord our God;
 his judgments govern the whole earth.
[8] He remembers his covenant forever,
 the promise he ordained
 for a thousand generations—
[9] the covenant he made with Abraham,
 swore to Isaac,
[10] and confirmed to Jacob as a decree
 and to Israel as a permanent covenant:
[11] "I will give the land of Canaan to you
 as your inherited portion."

Truth: Once again, this psalm is recounting some of the Old Testament covenants made to some of the most well-known Bible men listed in Israel's history. Verse 8, *"He remembers his covenant forever,"* tells us that God will keep and never forget his covenants for all eternity. He is the LORD, our God.... He means what he says and says what He means.

Thought: HE IS THE LORD OUR GOD... meaning, there is no other, no one... OUR God... yours and mine.......God issued everlasting covenants.... meaning, never ending commitments. He is the everlasting God whose authority is all over the earth and nothing is beyond his reach.

Tune: 'Cause I hear a voice
and he calls me redeemed
When others say I'll never be enough
And greater is the One living inside of me
than he who is living in the world
In the world, in the world
greater is the One living inside of me
than he who is living in the world

Holy God. My desire is to have a close and personal relationship with you. Be Lord over my life.

Songs for Life – Day 244 – September 1

Text: Psalm 105:12-19

[12] When they were few in number, very few indeed,
and resident aliens in Canaan,
[13] wandering from nation to nation
and from one kingdom to another,
[14] he allowed no one to oppress them;
he rebuked kings on their behalf:
[15] "Do not touch my anointed ones,
or harm my prophets."
[16] He called down famine against the land
and destroyed the entire food supply.
[17] He had sent a man ahead of them—
Joseph, who was sold as a slave.
[18] They hurt his feet with shackles; his neck was put in an iron collar.
[19] Until the time his prediction came true, the word of the Lord tested him.

Truth: Some Old Testament events are referenced here including the story of Joseph and his time in Egypt. That included slavery, prison, dream interpretations, and the famine that was coming. *"Do not touch my anointed ones"*, says the Lord. He chose the "prophets" or those who represented Him and protected them.

Thought: God will reveal Himself to his prophets when the time is right. Like Joseph - he didn't know why he was sold into slavery, but what his brothers did for evil, God meant it for good. If not for Joseph gaining knowledge and trusting in God, then he would not have been ready for the assignment God had for him.

Tune: In His time in His time
He makes all things beautiful; In His time
Lord please show me ev'ry day; As You're teaching me Your way
That You do just what You say; In Your time

Father, help me to understand that things happen in Your time. Help me to be ready and willing and able, when You call.

Songs for Life – Day 245 – September 2

Text: Psalm 105:20-25

[20] The king sent for him and released him;
the ruler of peoples set him free.
[21] He made him master of his household,
ruler over all his possessions—
[22] binding his officials at will and instructing his elders.
[23] Then Israel went to Egypt;
Jacob lived as an alien in the land of Ham.
[24] The Lord made his people very fruitful;
he made them more numerous than their foes,
[25] whose hearts he turned to hate his people
and to deal deceptively with his servants.

Truth: This begins with Joseph being set free from prison and being made a ruler over the Pharaoh's possessions. Then Jacob, also known as Israel, comes to Egypt to save his family from famine and be reunited with Joseph. Eventually they would become slaves to the Egyptians.

Thought: Do you wonder how over time they became slaves; where once they were free? Have you become a "slave" to someone or something? Once you were free in worship to God, but maybe something happened? Tragedy? Sinful nature? What's keeping you down - or holding you back from faithful service to God?

Tune: Through You the blind will see
Through You the mute will sing, through You the dead will rise
Through You all hearts will praise, through You the darkness flees
Through You my heart screams I am free
I am free to run (I am free to run)
I am free to dance (I am free to dance)
I am free to live for You (I am free to live for You)
I am free I am free (Yeah I am free I am free)

Heavenly Father, You are God Almighty! I praise Your name! Help me to be free from things that hinder my worship to You! I Love You, God!

Songs for Life – Day 246 – September 3

Text: Psalm 105:26-36

²⁶ He sent Moses, his servant, and Aaron, whom he had chosen.

²⁷ They performed his signs among them and miracles in the land of Ham.

²⁸ He sent darkness, and made the land dark;
   they did not rebel against his words.

²⁹ He turned their waters into blood and caused their fish to die.

³⁰ Their land swarmed with frogs,
   even in the chambers of their kings.

³¹ He spoke, and there came swarms of flies,
   and gnats throughout their country.

³² He gave them hail for rain,
   and fiery lightning bolts through their land.

³³ He struck down their vines and fig trees,
   and shattered the trees of their country.

³⁴ He spoke, and the locusts came,
   young locusts without number,

³⁵ which devoured all the vegetation in their land
   and ate up the fruit of their ground.

³⁶ He struck down all the firstborn in their land,
   the firstfruits of all their strength.

Truth: Here we have the 10 plagues that God set over Pharaoh when Moses and Aaron went to rescue the Israelites. Pharaoh's heart was so hardened that they had to suffer through 10 plagues.

Thought: Those plagues served not only to soften Pharaoh's heart, but to increase the dependence of the Israelites on the Lord. Is your heart hardened about someone or something? Ask God to help you let go.

Tune: I know that I've held on too long; to everything keeping me from learning to let go; Learning to let you…
Move me closer to a heart that's open
I'm learning to let go; I'm learning to let go

Almighty God, Help soften my heart, to be open to You!

Text: Psalm 105:37-42

[37] Then he brought Israel out with silver and gold,
and no one among his tribes stumbled.
[38] Egypt was glad when they left,
for the dread of Israel had fallen on them.
[39] He spread a cloud as a covering and gave a fire to light up the night.
[40] They asked, and he brought quail
and satisfied them with bread from heaven.
[41] He opened a rock, and water gushed out;
it flowed like a stream in the desert.
[42] For he remembered his holy promise to Abraham his servant.

Truth: Once again, this highlights the Israelites' leaving of Egypt and their slavery to Pharaoh. Verse 39 shows how the Lord manifested himself while leading them. In Verse 40-41 we see God's wonderful provisions to meet the need of His people. Last, we see that God remembered His promise to Abraham to establish the Israelites in the promised land.

Thought: God will always fulfill His Word and complete His work. Numbers 23:19 *"God is not man, that He should lie, or a son of man, that he should change His mind. Has he said, and will he not do it? Or has he spoken, and will he not fulfill it?"*

Tune: You're the God of this city; You're the King of these people
You're the Lord of this nation; You are
You're the light in this darkness; You're the hope to the hopeless
You're the peace to the restless; You are

Greater things have yet to come;
And greater things have still to be done in this city
Greater things have yet to come;
And greater things have still to be done here

Lord, You are God of ALL. You are the ultimate provider. Thank you for all you have done for me. I know You will be faithful to Your Word.

Songs for Life – Day 248 – September 5

Text: Psalm 105:43-45

⁴³ He brought his people out with rejoicing,
his chosen ones with shouts of joy.
⁴⁴ He gave them the lands of the nations,
and they inherited
what other peoples had worked for.
⁴⁵ All this happened
so that they might keep his statutes
and obey his instructions.
Hallelujah!

Truth: This is the final culmination of God's plan for His people at this time. They were out of Egypt and into the Promised Land. God intended that his people would live out their lives in obedience to Him and observe his laws. In their time of trial, they learned about faithfulness. They also learned about the sovereignty of Almighty God. He IS faithful.

Thought: "Praise the LORD!" Think about when you prayed for something over and over and eventually it came to pass. Perhaps there was a time that you prayed for a child, a certain job, passing a certification test or maybe getting good medical test results. Afterwards, you just sat back and relaxed and said, "Praise the LORD!" Isn't that an awesome feeling? God was with you the entire time and answered your prayers in His time, for His glory.   There is always more going on than we can see in the moment.

Tune: Oh, happy day, happy day
You washed my sin away
Oh, happy day, happy day
I'll never be the same
Forever I am changed

Father, Thank You for hearing my cries and for saving me from my sins by the power of Your Son, Jesus Christ. Thank You for the times that You have caused me to wait so You could reveal Your greater glory.

Text: Psalm 106:1-5

106 [1] Hallelujah!
Give thanks to the Lord, for he is good;
his faithful love endures forever.
[2] Who can declare the Lord's mighty acts
or proclaim all the praise due him?
[3] How happy are those who uphold justice,
who practice righteousness at all times.
[4] Remember me, Lord,
when you show favor to your people.
Come to me with your salvation
[5] so that I may enjoy the prosperity of your chosen ones,
rejoice in the joy of your nation, and boast about your heritage.

Truth: This historical psalm recites a series of events from Israel's history to illustrate God's steadfast love in the face of Israel's rebellion and unfaithfulness. The people of God are called on to give thanks.

Thought: God made a covenant with Israel and gave the expectation that they would live righteous lives as a result of the grace of God. The truth is, the way we live our lives is a direct result of the work of God within us.

Tune: Beautiful Lord wonderful Savior
I know for sure all of my days are held in Your hand
Crafted into Your perfect plan
You gently call me into Your presence, guiding me by Your Holy Spirit
Teach me dear Lord to live all of my life through Your eyes
I'm captured by Your holy calling
Set me apart I know You're drawing me to Yourself
Lead me Lord I pray
Take me mold me, Use me fill me, I give my life to the Potter's hand
Call me guide me, Lead me walk beside me
I give my life, to the Potter's hand

Father, You are the Potter, I am the clay. Mold me as You see fit.

Text: Psalm 106:6-12

6 Both we and our fathers have sinned;
we have done wrong and have acted wickedly.
7 Our fathers in Egypt did not grasp
the significance of your wondrous works
or remember your many acts of faithful love;
instead, they rebelled by the sea—the Red Sea.
8 Yet he saved them for his name's sake,
to make his power known.
9 He rebuked the Red Sea, and it dried up;
he led them through the depths as through a desert.
10 He saved them from the power of the adversary;
he redeemed them from the power of the enemy.
11 Water covered their foes;
not one of them remained.
12 Then they believed his promises
and sang his praise.

Truth: The story of the children of Israel at the Red Sea is one of the most incredible stories of God's deliverance in the face of man's lack of faith. The people were glad to follow Moses when they thought they were free, but when they encountered the Red See before them with Pharaoh's army behind them, they lost heart, lacked faith and trust.

Thought: We are no different than the children of Israel. How many times can you look back at your life and see where God has parted stormy waters for you and allowed you to pass through on dry ground?

Tune: Grace grace God's grace,
grace that will pardon and cleanse within
Grace grace God's grace,
grace that is greater than all our sin

Lord Jesus, thank You for your marvelous grace that You grant me each day. Without Your grace, I am nothing.

Songs for Life – Day 251 – September 8

Text: Psalm 106:13-18

[13] They soon forgot his works and would not wait for his counsel.
[14] They were seized with craving in the wilderness
and tested God in the desert.
[15] He gave them what they asked for,
but sent a wasting disease among them.
[16] In the camp they were envious of Moses
and of Aaron, the Lord's holy one.
[17] The earth opened up and swallowed Dathan;
it covered the assembly of Abiram.
[18] Fire blazed throughout their assembly; flames consumed the wicked.

Truth: The children of Israel had been in slavery to Pharaoh for so long that they had come to accept it as normal. They remembered the fact that at least while enslaved in Egypt they had water to drink and food to eat. They were willing to be satisfied with the things they could see rather than trust God to provide what they could not see.

Thought: Perhaps, you have recently faced, or are facing now, a situation that seems hopeless. There is a wall of water in front of you and an army closing in behind you. This is your crisis of belief, an opportunity for you to trust God. Trust God with the situation and the results.

Tune: Seated above enthroned in the Father's love
Destined to die poured out for all mankind
God's only Son perfect and spotless One
He never sinned but suffered as if He did
All authority, every victory is Yours, all authority, every victory is Yours
Savior worthy of honor and glory, worthy of all our praise
For You overcame
Jesus awesome in power forever, awesome and great is Your Name
For You overcame

Holy God, when I'm faced with obstacles on each side, I know You have the power to overcome. I trust You to rescue me, God.

Songs for Life – Day 252 – September 9

Text: Psalm 106:19-23

[19] At Horeb they made a calf and worshiped the cast metal image.
[20] They exchanged their glory for the image of a grass-eating ox.
[21] They forgot God their Savior, who did great things in Egypt,
[22] wondrous works in the land of Ham,
awe-inspiring acts at the Red Sea.
[23] So he said he would have destroyed them—
if Moses his chosen one
had not stood before him in the breach
to turn his wrath away from destroying them.

Truth: This section remembers when the nation convinced Aaron to make a golden calf for idol worship while Moses was on the mountain receiving the commandments of God. Moses interceded on behalf of the people and saved them from the wrath of God. In this, he foreshadowed the work of Jesus Christ, who not only prayed for His people but died to save them.

Thought: It seems ridiculous that the people turned to a calf made of gold to have something to worship while Moses was on the mountain meeting with God. Because they could not see God at work with their physical eyes, they turned to something else for comfort. How often do we, even the children of God, turn to something to escape? People use all kinds of things for an escape: alcohol, drugs, computers, smart phones, television, books, etc. All the while, they are not escaping but just drowning out the noise that will still be there when the temporary escape wears off. The answer is not to escape but to stand still and trust God.

Tune: We fall down
We lay our crowns, at the feet of Jesus
The greatness of mercy and love, at the feet of Jesus
And we cry holy, holy, holy, And we cry holy, holy, holy
And we cry holy, holy, holy is the Lamb

Lord, though I don't mean to, I confess that I use other things as an escape from life's trials when I should turn to You first. Forgive me.

Text: Psalm 106:24-31

[24] They despised the pleasant land and did not believe his promise.
[25] They grumbled in their tents and did not listen to the Lord.
[26] So he raised his hand against them with an oath
that he would make them fall in the desert
[27] and would disperse their descendants among the nations,
scattering them throughout the lands.
[28] They aligned themselves with Baal of Peor
and ate sacrifices offered to lifeless gods.
[29] They angered the Lord with their deeds,
and a plague broke out against them.
[30] But Phinehas stood up and intervened,
and the plague was stopped.
[31] It was credited to him as righteousness
throughout all generations to come.

Truth: The children of Israel no longer believed that God would lead them to the Promised Land. They offered sacrifices to the dead and provoked the Lord to anger.

Thought: Phineas was a priest who impaled a couple for ritually defiling the tabernacle sanctuary. It was the prayer of this righteous man, who stood in the gap for the Israelites that caused God to stop the intended plague. Perhaps there is someone in your life that has been spiritually blinded to the point that their choices indicate they have lost trust in God. Can you stand in the gap for someone before the Lord today?

Tune: I bring an offering of worship to my King
No one on earth deserves the praises that I sing
Jesus may You receive the honor that You're due
O Lord I bring an offering to You
(I bring an offering to You)

Lord, bring to my heart today the names of those I can stand in the gap for. Let me not judge their lives but ask You to impart grace on them.

Text: Psalm 106:32-39

[32] They angered the Lord at the Waters of Meribah,
and Moses suffered because of them;
[33] for they embittered his spirit, and he spoke rashly with his lips.
[34] They did not destroy the peoples as the Lord had commanded them
[35] but mingled with the nations
and adopted their ways.
[36] They served their idols,
which became a snare to them.
[37] They sacrificed their sons and daughters to demons.
[38] They shed innocent blood—the blood of their sons and daughters
whom they sacrificed to the idols of Canaan;
so the land became polluted with blood.
[39] They defiled themselves by their actions
and prostituted themselves by their deeds.

Truth: The people complained at Meribah about a lack of water. Though Moses, through God's hand, was able to provide water by striking the rock, Moses allowed the bitterness of the people to get the best of him and he ultimately spoke back to them in anger.

Thought: Circumstances should not dictate our level of trust in Almighty God. Are there circumstances in your life that you are allowing to steal your joy? God is bigger than your circumstances.

Tune: Lost are saved find their way, at the sound of Your great Name
All condemned feel no shame, at the sound of Your great Name
Ev'ry fear has no place, at the sound of Your great Name
The enemy he has to leave at the sound of Your great Name
Jesus worthy is the Lamb that was slain for us
The Son of God and man, You are high and lifted up
And all the world will praise, Your great Name

Lord, let my trust in You not be controlled by my circumstances.

Songs for Life – Day 255 – September 12

Text: Psalm 106:40-43

40 Therefore the Lord's anger burned against his people,
and he abhorred his own inheritance.
41 He handed them over to the nations;
those who hated them ruled over them.
42 Their enemies oppressed them,
and they were subdued under their power.
43 He rescued them many times,
but they continued to rebel deliberately
and were beaten down by their iniquity.

Truth: From the time of the judges until the Assyrian and Babylonian exiles, God used the hand of His enemies to discipline Israel for their sin. The psalmist depicts how God punished Israel for its disobedience and unfaithfulness.

Thought: The children of Israel went repeatedly through a cycle of trusting God, then letting their guard down, then getting frustrated, then worshiping idols, then coming to the end of their rope, then trusting God again. Is your spiritual life a continual cycle of ups and downs or are you on a steady move forward with The Lord? Ask God to open your eyes to see where He is working and then adjust your life to Him, focusing less on your circumstances.

Tune: There's a peace I've come to know
Though my heart and flesh may fail
There's an anchor for my soul, I can say it is well
Jesus has overcome, and the grave is overwhelmed
The victory is won, He is risen from the dead
I will rise when He calls my name, no more sorrow no more pain
I will rise on eagle's wings
Before my God fall on my knees and rise I will rise (I will rise)

Heavenly Father, thank you for being my Peace, my Anchor. Open my eyes today, that I may see where You are working. I will join You.

Text: Psalm 106:44-48

[44] When he heard their cry, he took note of their distress,
[45] remembered his covenant with them,
and relented according to the abundance of his faithful love.
[46] He caused them to be pitied before all their captors.
[47] Save us, Lord our God,
and gather us from the nations,
so that we may give thanks to your holy name
and rejoice in your praise.
[48] Blessed be the Lord God of Israel,
from everlasting to everlasting.
Let all the people say, "Amen!"
Hallelujah!

Truth: *"When he heard their cry, he took note of their distress."* Though it seemed at times the children of Israel did not learn from their mistakes, God was there every time they fell to bring them comfort and to restore them when they cried to Him.

Thought: You may think that your sin is too bad for God to forgive. You may feel that your past is too bad for God to use you. You may think that you've wasted too many years and others are just too far ahead of you for God to do a mighty work in your life. Do not believe those lies!

Tune: You choose the humble and raise them high
You choose the weak and make them strong
You heal our brokenness inside, and give us life
The same love that set the captives free
The same love that opened eyes to see
Is calling us all by name, You are calling us all by name
The same God that spread the heavens wide
The same God that was crucified
Is calling us all by name, You are calling us all by name

Father, I trust the blood of Your Son today to cover my past forever.

Songs for Life – Day 257 – September 14

Text: Psalm 107:1-3

¹ Give thanks to the Lord, for he is good;
his faithful love endures forever.
² Let the redeemed of the Lord proclaim
that he has redeemed them from the power of the foe
³ and has gathered them from the lands—
from the east and the west,
from the north and the south.

Truth: The sin of the Israelites had brought them consequences which resulted in them losing their homeland and being scattered in all four directions. But God brought them back, redeemed them, and treated them as if they had never left.

Thought: *"Give thanks to the Lord, for he is good; his faithful love endures forever."* You can say that over and over, either out loud or in your mind, and experience a change of focus as you focus on the goodness of God. Then spend some in response to verse 2, *"Let the redeemed of the Lord proclaim"* by thanking God for His redemption plan, declaring *"I . . . AM . . . REDEEMED!"* Rejoice, child of God! You've been REDEEMED by the blood of the Lamb of God!

Tune: Seems like all I could see was the struggle
Haunted by ghosts that lived in my past
Bound up in shackles of all my failures
Wond'ring how long is this gonna last
Then You look at this pris'ner and say to me
Son stop fighting a fight that's already been won

I am redeemed You set me free
So I'll shake off these heavy chains, and wipe away ev'ry stain
'Cause I'm not who I used to be, I am redeemed

Father God, I am REDEEEMED! I give you thanks today and every day for the fact that I can say I am REDEEMED!

Songs for Life – Day 258 – September 15

Text: Psalm 107:4-9

[4] Some wandered in the desolate wilderness,
finding no way to a city where they could live.
[5] They were hungry and thirsty;
their spirits failed within them.
[6] Then they cried out to the Lord in their trouble;
he rescued them from their distress.
[7] He led them by the right path
to go to a city where they could live.
[8] Let them give thanks to the Lord
for his faithful love
and his wondrous works for all humanity.
[9] For he has satisfied the thirsty
and filled the hungry with good things.

Truth: This is the first group of those who were banished from the land as a result of the exile. Some of the exiles wandered in the desert, finding no way to a city to dwell in. Their proper home was the Promised Land, but God had sent them away. When they cried to the LORD, God delivered them, bringing them to a city to dwell in. The proper response is for them to thank the LORD for his steadfast love.

Thought: There is only one way for the soul to be satisfied, else it remains in turmoil. The love of God is the only balm, the only satisfaction, the only redemption for the soul. His love is steadfast, continuous, and satisfies every longing of the soul. Thank God for His love and let it fill your soul.

Tune: Love came down and rescued me
Love came down and set me free, and I am Yours I am forever Yours
Mountain high or valley low, I sing out remind my soul
That I am Yours I am forever Yours

Father, Your love is all I really need. It is Your love that drew me to a love relationship with You through salvation and shows me how to live life.

Text: Psalm 107:10-16

10 Others sat in darkness and gloom—
prisoners in cruel chains—
11 because they rebelled against God's commands
and despised the counsel of the Most High.
12 He broke their spirits with hard labor;
they stumbled, and there was no one to help.
13 Then they cried out to the Lord in their trouble;
he saved them from their distress.
14 He brought them out of darkness and gloom
and broke their chains apart.
15 Let them give thanks to the Lord for his faithful love
and his wondrous works for all humanity.
16 For he has broken down the bronze gates
and cut through the iron bars.

Truth: The next group of exiles sat in darkness and in the shadow of death. The word prisoners is an indicator that these people suffered as captives and forced laborers because they had rebelled against the words of God. But even though they rejected God's covenant by their rebellion, God still heard them when they cried to the LORD in their trouble and brought them out of darkness and the shadow of death.

Thought: Choosing not to trust God caused a bit of temporary blindness to the Israelites. The same thing happens to us when we make choices based on our desires versus what God's desires are. Ask God to remove the blinders and to help you to look at your life as He sees it, to make whatever changes are necessary to line up with His plan for your life.

Tune: My chains are gone I've been set free
My God my Savior has ransomed me
And like a flood His mercy rains, unending love amazing grace

Father, help me to see my life today as You see it. Remove the blinders that are on my life because of my choices.

Text: Psalm 107:17-22

[17] Fools suffered affliction
because of their rebellious ways and their iniquities.
[18] They loathed all food
and came near the gates of death.
[19] Then they cried out to the Lord in their trouble;
he saved them from their distress.
[20] He sent his word and healed them; he rescued them from the Pit.
[21] Let them give thanks to the Lord for his faithful love
and his wondrous works for all humanity.
[22] Let them offer sacrifices of thanksgiving
and announce his works with shouts of joy.

Truth: Some of the exiles were fools through their sinful ways. Their own stupidity brought on their affliction, so that they despised any kind of food. Nevertheless, God heard and relieved them when they cried to the Lord in their trouble. In context, healed them is not simply the relief of bodily ailments but also their return to the Promised Land. These people should thank the LORD, specifically with sacrifices of thanksgiving, using songs of joy in their worship to tell of God's deeds.

Thought: *"Then they cried out to the Lord in their trouble: he saved them from their distress."* God always hears the cries of His children. Sometimes He allows our circumstances to take us into the valley in order to bring us back to Himself. There is freedom in repentance, freedom in forgiveness and freedom in redemption. Have you gotten away from Him in an area of your life? Confess, repent and receive redemption today.

Tune: There is a fountain filled with blood drawn from Immanuel's veins
And sinners plunged beneath that flood lose all their guilty stains
Lose all their guilty stains, lose all their guilty stains
And sinners plunged beneath that flood lose all their guilty stains

Father, reveal to me today any way in my life that is not pleasing to You. I want to confess, repent and be free.

Text: Psalm 107:23-32

²³ Others went to sea in ships, conducting trade on the vast water.

²⁴ They saw the Lord's works, his wondrous works in the deep.

²⁵ He spoke and raised a stormy wind that stirred up the waves of the sea.

²⁶ Rising up to the sky, sinking down to the depths,

their courage melting away in anguish,

²⁷ they reeled and staggered like a drunkard,

and all their skill was useless.

²⁸ Then they cried out to the Lord in their trouble,

and he brought them out of their distress.

²⁹ He stilled the storm to a whisper,

and the waves of the sea were hushed.

³⁰ They rejoiced when the waves grew quiet.

Then he guided them to the harbor they longed for.

³¹ Let them give thanks to the Lord for his faithful love

and his wondrous works for all humanity.

³² Let them exalt him in the assembly of the people

and praise him in the council of the elders.

Truth: As the storm increased in its fury, they cried to the LORD in their trouble. God made the storm be still. These people should thank the LORD for his steadfast love. They have returned to the Promised Land, where they can give thanks to God in the congregation.

Thought: *"Let them give thanks to the Lord for his faithful love"* . . . God intended us to worship "in the assembly", as the body of believers together. There is nothing like God's people praising Him together! How is your worship "in the assembly"? Do you look forward to exalting Him with other believers or are you going through the motions?

Tune: Jesus Lamb of God, Worthy is Your name
Jesus Lamb of God, Worthy is Your name

Father in Heaven, I lift up your Holy name today. You are God, you are love, you are power, and you are strength. You are worthy of all praise!

Text: Psalm 107:33-38

33 He turns rivers into desert,
springs into thirsty ground,
34 and fruitful land into salty wasteland,
because of the wickedness of its inhabitants.
35 He turns a desert into a pool,
dry land into springs.
36 He causes the hungry to settle there,
and they establish a city where they can live.
37 They sow fields and plant vineyards
that yield a fruitful harvest.
38 He blesses them, and they multiply greatly;
he does not let their livestock decrease.

Truth: God may take a pleasant and prosperous land and turn it into a waste if the evil of its inhabitants calls for it, and he may reverse this judgment and make the land fruitful and pleasant again, in his mercy to the hungry.

Thought: God's hand moves wherever there is a need, and He brings about situations for His glory. When we are dry, He can turn our parched heart into a spring of living water. When we turn aside from Him, He can allow our hearts to become as dry as dust. Where is your heart today? Are you dry, in need of a shower of grace? If God is moving in your life, take some time to tell Him about it and thank Him.

Tune: I will sing of my Redeemer and His wondrous love to me
On the cruel cross He suffered, from the curse to set me free
Sing O sing of my Redeemer
With His blood He purchased me
On the cross He sealed my pardon
Paid the debt and made me free

Father God, you are my Redeemer. Today I ask You to reveal Yourself to me in a powerful way, which I might see where You are working.

Songs for Life – Day 263 – September 20

Text: Psalm 107:39-43

[39] When they are diminished and are humbled
by cruel oppression and sorrow,
[40] he pours contempt on nobles
and makes them wander in a trackless wasteland.
[41] But he lifts the needy out of their suffering
and makes their families multiply like flocks.
[42] The upright see it and rejoice, and all injustice shuts its mouth.
[43] Let whoever is wise pay attention to these things
and consider the Lord's acts of faithful love.

Truth: The final verse closes by inviting whoever is wise, those who genuinely seek to live godly lives, to focus on the things of God, to meditate on them. Recall the works of God. Celebrate His goodness and grace to His children through the stories in the Word of God. Learn from their mistakes. Most of all, meditate on the steadfast love of the Lord.

Thought: Life moves fast. It is like a vapor that you can't hold but soon goes away. With distractions readily available, it is very easy not to take time and meditate on the things of God. You may have to get up 30 minutes earlier, make different plans for your lunch break, or take some time to "pull away". Be still before the Lord and meditate on His love, His works, His grace and His mercy today.

Tune: A thousand times I've failed, still Your mercy remains
And should I stumble again, still I'm caught in Your grace
Everlasting, Your light will shine when all else fades
Never-ending, Your glory goes beyond all fame
In my heart in my soul, Lord I give You control
Consume me from the inside out Lord
Let justice and praise, become my embrace
To love You from the inside out

Almighty God, I sing Your praises today and then I sit and wait to hear Your voice. Let me not clutter my life so that I do not hear You today.

Text: Psalm 108:1-6

[1] My heart is confident, God;
I will sing; I will sing praises with the whole of my being.
[2] Wake up, harp and lyre! I will wake up the dawn.
[3] I will praise you, Lord, among the peoples;
I will sing praises to you among the nations.
[4] For your faithful love is higher than the heavens,
and your faithfulness reaches to the clouds.
[5] God, be exalted above the heavens,
and let your glory be over the whole earth.
[6] Save with your right hand and answer me
so that those you love may be rescued.

Truth: This psalm is more of David personally giving thanks and exalting God. He is praising God for His steadfast love and asking that God's Glory would be over all the earth.

Thought: Verse 3 *"I praise you, Lord, among the peoples;"* - what does that say to you? To me, I think we are being reminded about telling others about Jesus in our lives today. Do you publicly acknowledge that God was faithful in your life to help you deal with a certain situation? God is the God of the good times and the tough times. Perhaps today, you could thank God for all He has done for you and share it with someone as an encouragement.

Tune: Who am I without Your grace, another smile another face
Another breath a grain of sand passing quickly through Your hand
I give my life an offering take it all take everything
Let them see You in me let them hear You when I speak
Let them feel You when I sing
Let them see You, just let them see You in me

Father God, I ask that You allow others to see You in me. Help me to be more willing to share Your love and faithfulness with others. Thank you for that You have done for me.

<u>Songs for Life – Day 265 – September 22</u>

Text: Psalm 108:7-13

[7] God has spoken in his sanctuary:
"I will celebrate! I will divide up Shechem.
I will apportion the Valley of Succoth.
[8] Gilead is mine, Manasseh is mine, and Ephraim is my helmet;
Judah is my scepter.
[9] Moab is my washbasin;
I throw my sandal on Edom.
I shout in triumph over Philistia."
[10] Who will bring me to the fortified city?
Who will lead me to Edom?
[11] God, haven't you rejected us?
God, you do not march out with our armies.
[12] Give us aid against the foe,
for human help is worthless.
[13] With God we will perform valiantly;
he will trample our foes.

Truth: David is expressing his personal confidence in God and then pleading and praying for God's help against his enemies. Even David knew that without God's help, it would be pointless to fight.

Thought: *"With God we will gain the victory"* - Verse 13 (NIV). This is only 'WITH GOD'. Matthew 19:26 says, *"But Jesus looked at them and said, "With man this is impossible, but with God all things are possible."* For you and me, today, it would be pointless for us to carry on our lives without God. Put your personal confidence in God, today! Don't wait!

Tune: Are you walking daily by the Savior's side
Are you washed in the blood of the Lamb
Do you rest each moment in the Crucified
Are you washed in the blood of the Lamb

Father God, I desire to walk daily with You and have a personal and saving relationship with You. With You alone, I can face tomorrow.

<u>Songs for Life – Day 266 – September 23</u>

Text: Psalm 109:1-5

[1] God of my praise, do not be silent.
[2] For wicked and deceitful mouths open against me;
they speak against me with lying tongues.
[3] They surround me with hateful words
and attack me without cause.
[4] In return for my love they accuse me,
but I continue to pray.
[5] They repay me evil for good,
and hatred for my love.

Truth: The opening section describes the situation. People attack the singer without cause. They accuse him in return for his love. The singer has shown the accusers love and good, which they repay with evil and hatred. The psalm offers the right response: I give myself to prayer, both prayers for his enemies in the past and now in prayer for God's help in the present.

Thought: What is the right response when we feel attacked? Prayer. What is the right response when we are overwhelmed? Prayer. What is the right response when we are filled with joy? Prayer. Prayer is the question as well as the answer for the believers. Spend some extra time in prayer today, both sharing with God and listening for His response.

Tune: What a friend we have in Jesus
All our sins and griefs to bear
What a privilege to carry
Everything to God in prayer
O what peace we often forfeit
O what needless pain we bear
All because we do not carry
Everything to God in prayer

Dear Lord, I have no greater friend than You. Today I commit to a continual mode of prayer, listening for Your voice.

Songs for Life – Day 267 – September 24

Text: Psalm 109:6-15

[6] Set a wicked person over him; let an accuser stand at his right hand.

[7] When he is judged, let him be found guilty,
and let his prayer be counted as sin.

[8] Let his days be few; let another take over his position.

[9] Let his children be fatherless and his wife a widow.

[10] Let his children wander as beggars,
searching for food far from their demolished homes.

[11] Let a creditor seize all he has;
let strangers plunder what he has worked for.

[12] Let no one show him kindness,
and let no one be gracious to his fatherless children.

[13] Let the line of his descendants be cut off;
let their name be blotted out in the next generation.

[14] Let the iniquity of his fathers
be remembered before the Lord,
and do not let his mother's sin be blotted out.

[15] Let their sins always remain before the Lord,
and let him remove all memory of them from the earth.

Truth: The psalmist curses his adversaries. He wants his enemies to be exterminated and their families to be destroyed as well.

Thought: Verse 8 of this Psalm is commonly quoted when people are disappointed in how an election turns out. It's understandable, but it's not always God's plan to remove someone from office. Rather than praying leaders out, we pray the Holy Spirit in.

Tune: Have faith in God, He's on His throne
Have faith in God, He watches o'er His own
He cannot fail He must prevail
Have faith in God, Have faith in God

Father God, I lift up the leaders of our nation, our state, our county, and our city. I pray that Your grace and love would penetrate each heart today.

Text: Psalm 109:16-20

[16] For he did not think to show kindness,
but pursued the suffering, needy, and brokenhearted
in order to put them to death.
[17] He loved cursing—let it fall on him;
he took no delight in blessing—let it be far from him.
[18] He wore cursing like his coat—
let it enter his body like water and go into his bones like oil.
[19] Let it be like a robe he wraps around himself,
like a belt he always wears.
[20] Let this be the Lord's payment to my accusers,
to those who speak evil against me.

Truth: Covenant faithfulness is most clearly seen in showing kindness to the most vulnerable, for example the poor and needy and the brokenhearted. This is especially those among one's fellow members of God's people. The psalmist is calling for curses upon the person who has rejected kindness and generosity.

Thought*:* The world will only know that we are Christians by our love and actions. We also have a great responsibility to those already in the church to help meet needs. Are there needs that God is laying on your heart today for members of the body of believers? Is God reminding you to show kindness to others outside the body? You might be who God uses to bring them into the Kingdom.

Tune: There's a call comes ringing, o'er the restless wave
Send the light send the light
There are souls to rescue, there are souls to save
Send the light send the light

Send the light, the blessed gospel light, let it shine, from shore to shore
Send the light, the blessed gospel light, let it shine, forevermore

Father, help me to send Your light through my life to the world today.

Text: Psalm 109:21-25

²¹ But you, Lord, my Lord,
deal kindly with me for your name's sake;
because your faithful love is good, rescue me.
²² For I am suffering and needy;
my heart is wounded within me.
²³ I fade away like a lengthening shadow;
I am shaken off like a locust.
²⁴ My knees are weak from fasting,
and my body is emaciated.
²⁵ I have become an object of ridicule to my accusers;
when they see me, they shake their heads in scorn.

Truth: David petitioned the court for justice by asking for deliverance for the judge's sake and then for his own sake (vv. 22–25). Afterwards, he requested that his enemies be rightfully punished (vv. 26–29).

Thought: *"But you, Lord, my Lord, deal kindley with me for your name's sake"*. What a prayer of submission by the psalmist! We were created for God's glory, we exist for God's glory, and our responsibility is to reflect God's glory. Ask God to help you put aside selfish desires today, that your life may reflect God's glory in every aspect.

Tune: Your love is amazing, steady and unchanging
Your love is a mountain, firm beneath my feet
Your love is a myst'ry, how You gently lift me
When I am surrounded, Your love carries me

Hallelujah hallelujah hallelujah
Your love makes me sing
Hallelujah hallelujah hallelujah
Your love makes me sing

Father God, glorify Yourself in my life today, whatever the circumstances.

Songs for Life – Day 270 – September 27

Text: Psalm 109:26-31

[26] Help me, Lord my God;
save me according to your faithful love
[27] so they may know that this is your hand
and that you, Lord, have done it.
[28] Though they curse, you will bless.
When they rise up, they will be put to shame,
but your servant will rejoice.
[29] My accusers will be clothed with disgrace;
they will wear their shame like a cloak.
[30] I will fervently thank the Lord with my mouth;
I will praise him in the presence of many.
[31] For he stands at the right hand of the needy
to save him from those who would condemn him.

Truth: The psalm closes with hope. The singer is confident that he will give great thanks to the LORD in public worship (so that all the faithful can join in the praise). He will be found in the midst of the throng in worship, rather than fall prey to those who condemn his soul to death.

Thought: *"I will fervently thank the Lord with my mouth"*. Sing the praises of God Almighty today! Stand in the congregation and honor the Lord with songs of praise! Lift up your voice right where you are today.

Tune: Holy holy holy, Lord God Almighty
Early in the morning, our song shall rise to Thee
Holy holy holy, merciful and mighty
God in three persons, blessed Trinity
Holy holy holy, Lord God Almighty
All Thy works shall praise Thy name in earth and sky and sea
Holy holy holy, merciful and mighty
God in three persons, blessed Trinity

Heavenly Father, I lift my voice to sing Your praises today. Thank You for putting a song in my heart, for giving us great songs to sing to You.

Text: Psalm 110:1-7

[1] This is the declaration of the Lord to my Lord:
"Sit at my right hand until I make your enemies your footstool."
[2] The Lord will extend your mighty scepter from Zion.
Rule over your surrounding enemies.
[3] Your people will volunteer on your day of battle.
In holy splendor, from the womb of the dawn,
the dew of your youth belongs to you.
[4] The Lord has sworn an oath and will not take it back:
"You are a priest forever
according to the pattern of Melchizedek."
[5] The Lord is at your right hand;
he will crush kings on the day of his anger.
[6] He will judge the nations, heaping up corpses;
he will crush leaders over the entire world.
[7] He will drink from the brook by the road;
therefore, he will lift up his head.

Truth: Jesus sits at the right hand of the Father, and one day all of the enemies will be subdued and will be His footstool.

Thought: Waiting is one of the hardest things for people to do, especially when we are waiting for God to act. Many times, we cannot see the reason for God's timing until after the fact. What are you waiting on God to do today? His timing is perfect. Wait, trust the Lord, be patient.

Tune: The Savior is waiting to enter your heart
Why don't you let Him come in
There's nothing in this world to keep you apart
What is your answer to Him
Time after time He has waited before, and now He is waiting again
To see if you're willing, to open the door
O how He wants to come in

Holy God, help me to wait on You today. I know Your timing is perfect.

Text: Psalm 111:1-5

111 Praise the LORD!

[1] Hallelujah!
I will praise the Lord with all my heart
in the assembly of the upright and in the congregation.
[2] The Lord's works are great,
studied by all who delight in them.
[3] All that he does is splendid and majestic;
his righteousness endures forever.
[4] He has caused his wondrous works to be remembered.
The Lord is gracious and compassionate.
[5] He has provided food for those who fear him;
he remembers his covenant forever.

Truth: Hallelujah! Praise the LORD! Give thanks and praise to God with your whole heart. These words are really the summary of these verses. He is telling us to remember all the great works of God and how He provided protection and even things such as food for their basic needs.

Thought: Do you notice the word "works" is mentioned 2 times in these 5 verses? It is referring to God's works. The splendor, majesty, wondrous and great works of the Lord are to be remembered and praised. I am guilty of just asking God for things, such as blessing for someone, or to heal someone. I forget that God created the sunrise, or a beautiful rainbow, or pretty trees and flowers. God has already done and given so much for us. God remembers his promises and covenants, as we should daily remember God.

Tune: Give thanks to the Lord our God and King, His love endures forever
For He is good, He is above all things, His love endures forever
Sing praise, sing praise

O Lord, I am in awesome wonder of all You have done and all You continue to do for me. Thank You for all you have created and given me. I praise Your Holy Name!

Text: Psalm 111:6-10

[6] He has shown his people the power of his works
by giving them the inheritance of the nations.
[7] The works of his hands are truth and justice;
all his instructions are trustworthy.
[8] They are established forever and ever,
enacted in truth and in uprightness.
[9] He has sent redemption to his people.
He has ordained his covenant forever.
His name is holy and awe-inspiring.
[10] The fear of the Lord is the beginning of wisdom;
all who follow his instructions have good insight.
His praise endures forever.

Truth: God's works are faithful, just, trustworthy and forever. The Message says is like this - *"All His products are guaranteed to last - never out of date, never obsolete, rust proof."*

Thought: We are known as a disposable society, where things are just tossed and never repaired. Isn't it great to know there is one thing that will never ever expire, break, or go out on you? That's the WORD OF OUR GOD! He's always there, no matter what time of day or night... ready for you. He's got this!

Tune: But the voice of truth tells me a different story
The voice of truth says, "Do not be afraid!"
The voice of truth says, "This is for My glory"
Out of all the voices calling out to me (Calling out to me)
I will choose to listen and believe the voice of truth

Lord, I choose to hear Your voice today. To seek You, and Your face. I know You will always be there for me.

Songs for Life – Day 274 – October 1

Text: Psalm 112:1-5

[1] Hallelujah!
Happy is the person who fears the Lord,
taking great delight in his commands.
[2] His descendants will be powerful in the land;
the generation of the upright will be blessed.
[3] Wealth and riches are in his house,
and his righteousness endures forever.
[4] Light shines in the darkness for the upright.
He is gracious, compassionate, and righteous.
[5] Good will come to the one who lends generously
and conducts his business fairly.

Truth: This passage is like Psalm 1, in that it contrasts the path of the righteous with the path of the wicked. The psalmist describes the character of the righteous, then recalls the blessings that come to them.

Thought: If the psalmist calls someone happy who fears the Lord - that must be a good thing, right? We don't normally think of fear as being a good thing. We think of fear as being something that comes over us when we are anticipating something bad ahead. However, fear of the Lord is not that at all. It is honoring the Lord with your life, understanding that God owns all and knows all, while loving His children with an everlasting love.

Tune: Some through the waters, some through the flood
Some through the fire, but all thro' the blood
Some through great sorrow, but God gives a song
In the night season, and all the day long
In shady green pastures, so rich and so sweet
God leads His dear children along
Where the water's cool flow, bathes the weary one's feet
God leads His dear children along

Father, I don't fear You in the way that I'm afraid of you. Help me to live in a way that reflects the Godly fear that keeps me focused on You.

Text: Psalm 112:6-10

[6] He will never be shaken.
The righteous one will be remembered forever.
[7] He will not fear bad news;
his heart is confident, trusting in the Lord.
[8] His heart is assured; he will not fear.
In the end he will look in triumph on his foes.
[9] He distributes freely to the poor;
his righteousness endures forever.
His horn will be exalted in honor.
[10] The wicked one will see it and be angry;
he will gnash his teeth in despair.
The desire of the wicked leads to ruin.

Truth: The psalmist continues the description of what the righteous man is by adding what he does. The righteous man is a man of faith and trust, one who gives freely, and one who helps minister to those in need.

Thought: For the righteous, those who have entrusted our lives to Christ, circumstances should not determine our level of faith in God on a particular day. God is still good, whether we are having a bad day, or whether our situation looks bleak. Though you may not understand it, God does, and these tests of faith can help sharpen our focus. Look for the hand of God - on the mountains as well as in the valleys.

Tune: Jesus You're my firm foundation
I know I can stand secure
Jesus You're my firm foundation
I put my hope in Your holy Word, I put my hope in Your holy Word

I have a living hope, I have a future
God has a plan for me , of this I'm sure of this I'm sure

Heavenly Father, You are my firm foundation. No matter what circumstances come my way today, my trust is in You.

Text: Psalm 113:1-9

[1] Hallelujah!
Give praise, servants of the Lord; praise the name of the Lord.
[2] Let the name of the Lord be blessed both now and forever.
[3] From the rising of the sun to its setting,
let the name of the Lord be praised.
[4] The Lord is exalted above all the nations, his glory above the heavens.
[5] Who is like the Lord our God—
the one enthroned on high,
[6] who stoops down to look
on the heavens and the earth?
[7] He raises the poor from the dust
and lifts the needy from the trash heap
[8] in order to seat them with nobles—
with the nobles of his people.
[9] He gives the childless woman a household,
making her the joyful mother of children.
Hallelujah!

Truth: This short hymn of praise celebrates the way in which the great and majestic God who rules over all takes notice of the lowly. Such a God is indeed worthy to be praised by all mankind.

Thought: Praise the Lord! We say that phrase often in response to something that God has done or prevented from happening to us. However, Praise the Lord is, at its core, giving God glory just for being who He is. Focus praise on who He is today, not just what He does.

Tune: We bring the sacrifice of praise into the house of the Lord
We bring the sacrifice of praise into the house of the Lord
And we offer up to You the sacrifices of thanksgiving
And we offer up to You the sacrifices of joy

Almighty God, Giver of Life, Wonderful Counselor. You are great, You are awesome and worthy of all of the praise I could ever give and much more.

Text: Psalm 114:1-8

[1] When Israel came out of Egypt—
the house of Jacob from a people
who spoke a foreign language—
[2] Judah became his sanctuary,
Israel, his dominion.
[3] The sea looked and fled;
the Jordan turned back.
[4] The mountains skipped like rams,
the hills, like lambs.
[5] Why was it, sea, that you fled?
Jordan, that you turned back?
[6] Mountains, that you skipped like rams?
Hills, like lambs?
[7] Tremble, earth, at the presence of the Lord,
at the presence of the God of Jacob,
[8] who turned the rock into a pool, the flint into a spring.

Truth: This short chapter is referring to events in the Exodus like the parting of the Red Sea and the Jordan River. Notice the use of word imagery here comparing mountains and hills to rams and lambs. Even the earth trembles at God's omnipotence and presence.

Thought: *"Mountains skipped like rams?"* I think of mountains as being huge, un-movable objects. What does that tell us about the power of the Lord if some of the strongest forces in nature can't resist God's Power? God is unlimited, unimaginable, un-definable and uncontainable.

Tune: I can only imagine; What it will be like
When I walk by Your side;
I can only imagine, what my eyes will see
When Your face is before me, I can only imagine

Lord, I humbly bow before You, acknowledging that You are the all-powerful God. You are mighty, and worthy of praise.

Text: Psalm 115:1-8

[1] Not to us, Lord, not to us, but to your name give glory
because of your faithful love, because of your truth.
[2] Why should the nations say,
"Where is their God?"
[3] Our God is in heaven and does whatever he pleases.
[4] Their idols are silver and gold, made by human hands.
[5] They have mouths but cannot speak, eyes, but cannot see.
[6] They have ears but cannot hear,
noses, but cannot smell.
[7] They have hands but cannot feel,
feet, but cannot walk.
They cannot make a sound with their throats.
[8] Those who make them are just like them,
as are all who trust in them.

Truth: This is a hymn urging God's people to trust and worship the Lord alone. It reminds them that He alone is worthy of their deepest loyalty.

Thought: *"Not to us, Lord, not to us, but to your name give glory"*. The psalmist said "not to us" twice, not because it wasn't understood, but because he was emphasizing that we live in order to give God glory.

Tune: Not to us, but to Your name be the glory
Not to us, but to Your name be the glory
The cross before me the world behind
No turning back raise the banner high
It's not for me it's all for You
Let the heavens shake and split the sky
Let the people clap their hands and cry
It's not for us it's all for You

Father, help me to take my focus off of anything that I can do and place it on glorifying you and allowing you to work in and through me.

Text: Psalm 115:9-18

[9] Israel, trust in the Lord! He is their help and shield.

[10] House of Aaron, trust in the Lord!
He is their help and shield.

[11] You who fear the Lord, trust in the Lord!
He is their help and shield.

[12] The Lord remembers us and will bless us.
He will bless the house of Israel;
he will bless the house of Aaron;

[13] he will bless those who fear the Lord—
small and great alike.

[14] May the Lord add to your numbers,
both yours and your children's.

[15] May you be blessed by the Lord,
the Maker of heaven and earth.

[16] The heavens are the Lord's,
but the earth he has given to the human race.

[17] It is not the dead who praise the Lord,
nor any of those descending into the silence of death.

[18] But we will bless the Lord, both now and forever. Hallelujah!

Truth: In response to the warning in verse 8, this section calls all the members of God's people to trust in the LORD.

Thought: God is our help and our shield. He gives us strength to take the next step, and He protects us. Often it is in our times of desperation that we can experience the peace of God most powerfully. When you are weary, when you are desperate, seek His hand rather than an answer.

Tune: O worship the King all glorious above
And gratefully sing His wonderful love
Our Shield and Defender, the Ancient of Days
Pavilioned in splendor and girded with praise

Father, if You've brought me to it, You'll bring me through it. I trust You.

Songs for Life – Day 280 – October 7

Text: Psalm 116:1-9

[1] I love the Lord because he has heard
my appeal for mercy.
[2] Because he has turned his ear to me,
I will call out to him as long as I live.
[3] The ropes of death were wrapped around me,
and the torments of Sheol overcame me;
I encountered trouble and sorrow.
[4] Then I called on the name of the Lord: "Lord, save me!"
[5] The Lord is gracious and righteous;
our God is compassionate.
[6] The Lord guards the inexperienced;
I was helpless, and he saved me.
[7] Return to your rest, my soul,
for the Lord has been good to you.
[8] For you, Lord, rescued me from death,
my eyes from tears, my feet from stumbling.
[9] I will walk before the Lord in the land of the living.

Truth: The psalm opens with a straightforward statement of its overall theme: I love the LORD, because he has heard my voice and my pleas for mercy. The people of Israel are urged to love the Lord.

Thought: In verse 2 we see the key to the psalmist's resolve in the phrase "because he inclined his ear to me". The picture here is of a loving father or grandfather bending down or drawing close to his child or grandchild to not only hear every word they say, but make sure that they know that they are the most important person in the world at that moment.

Tune: I know He heard my prayer, He knows my every care,
He gives to me the blessed victory,
Oh yes! I feel Him now, My loyalty I vow,
I know the Savior heard my plea.

Lord, thank You that You listen to me as a loving father listens to his child.

Text: Psalm 116:10-19

[10] I believed, even when I said, "I am severely oppressed."

[11] In my alarm I said, "Everyone is a liar."

[12] How can I repay the Lord
for all the good he has done for me?

[13] I will take the cup of salvation
and call on the name of the Lord.

[14] I will fulfill my vows to the Lord
in the presence of all his people.

[15] The death of his faithful ones
is valuable in the Lord's sight.

[16] Lord, I am indeed your servant;
I am your servant, the son of your female servant.
You have loosened my bonds.

[17] I will offer you a sacrifice of thanksgiving
and call on the name of the Lord.

[18] I will fulfill my vows to the Lord
in the presence of all his people,

[19] in the courts of the Lord's house—
within you, Jerusalem. Hallelujah!

Truth: *"How can I repay the Lord for all the good he has done for me?"*
The answer is, with acts of public worship, as the following phrases show:
the cup of salvation; call on the name of the LORD; fulfill my vows in the
presence of all his people; and in the courts of the Lord's house.

Thought: Perhaps you've heard verse 15 at a funeral service or when
talking about a believing loved one who has passed away. God's loving
care does not stop once this life's journey is complete. It's just beginning.
He has your today in His hand, as well as all of your tomorrows.

Tune: Jesus paid it all, all to Him I owe
Sin had left a crimson stain, He washed it white as snow

Holy God, my life is in Your hands. Help me to walk as You lead today.

Text: Psalm 117:1-2

[1] Praise the Lord, all nations!
Glorify him, all peoples!
[2] For his faithful love to us is great;
the Lord's faithfulness endures forever.
Hallelujah!

Truth: *"Praise the LORD, all nations!"* - ALL NATIONS. That means beyond Israel, beyond Jews, to us! That includes You and me, the Gentiles. From the very beginning God showed His never-ending love to us. He sent His Son to give us all eternal life with Him and to redeem us. Jews and Gentiles alike, will all come together to worship our one true God.

Thought: This is the shortest Psalm, the shortest chapter, and it's placed as the middle chapter in our Bible. Read it again...... What is the main focus? Praising the LORD and how great God's never-ending love is for us. This is very plain and simple - the Christian Perspective. Because of God's greatness, we react in praise.

Tune: Think about His love
Think about His goodness
Think about His grace
That's brought us through
For as high as the heaven's above
So great is the measure
Of our Father's love
Great is the measure
Of our Father's love

Almighty Father, You are great and greatly to be praised. Your love, grace and mercy are never ending. I know I don't always give You the praise You deserve, so please forgive me Father. Raise my awareness to acknowledge You, each and every day.

Songs for Life – Day 283 – October 10

Text: Psalm 118:1-7

[1] Give thanks to the Lord, for he is good;
his faithful love endures forever.
[2] Let Israel say,
"His faithful love endures forever."
[3] Let the house of Aaron say,
"His faithful love endures forever."
[4] Let those who fear the Lord say,
"His faithful love endures forever."
[5] I called to the Lord in distress;
the Lord answered me
and put me in a spacious place.
[6] The Lord is for me; I will not be afraid.
What can a mere mortal do to me?
[7] The Lord is my helper,
Therefore, I will look in triumph on those who hate me.

Truth: The opening section calls on the congregation to give thanks to the LORD, for he is good. Each group among the people (Israel, the house of Aaron, and those who fear the LORD) should recite this marvelous truth. The "personal testimony" part of the psalm begins by recounting an instance in which the psalmist called on the LORD, the LORD answered him and set him free.

Thought: *"Oh give thanks to the Lord, for he is good"* . . . There is a difference in "being good" and "doing good things". God IS good. Focus today on the fact that God IS good, all the time.

Tune: God is good all the time
He put a song of praise in this heart of mine
God is good all the time
Through the darkest night His light will shine
God is good God is good all the time

Lord, I give thanks to You, for Your steadfast love endures forever!

Songs for Life – Day 284 – October 11

Text: Psalm 118:8-16

[8] It is better to take refuge in the Lord
than to trust in humanity.
[9] It is better to take refuge in the Lord
than to trust in nobles.
[10] All the nations surrounded me;
in the name of the Lord I destroyed them.
[11] They surrounded me, yes, they surrounded me;
in the name of the Lord I destroyed them.
[12] They surrounded me like bees;
they were extinguished like a fire among thorns;
in the name of the Lord I destroyed them.
[13] They pushed me hard to make me fall, but the Lord helped me.
[14] The Lord is my strength and my song;
he has become my salvation.
[15] There are shouts of joy and victory in the tents of the righteous:
"The Lord's right hand performs valiantly!
[16] The Lord's right hand is raised.
The Lord's right hand performs valiantly!"

Truth: The experiences of God's help show that it is better to take refuge in the LORD than to trust in man. God is the only sure, the only completely safe refuge.

Thought: When do I need to take refuge in the Lord? Have you ever been hurt? Been unsure? Lacked confidence? Needed faith? Felt attacked? Felt like nobody understood your situation? Take refuge, find rest.

Tune: Precious name O how sweet, hope of earth and joy of heaven
Precious name O how sweet, hope of earth and joy of heaven
Take the name of Jesus with you, child of sorrow and of woe
It will joy and comfort give you, take it then where'er you go

*Lord, You are my refuge and strength. I trust You in times of trouble.
There is none like You. You are my hiding place.*

Songs for Life – Day 285 – October 12

Text: Psalm 118:17-24

[17] I will not die, but I will live and proclaim what the Lord has done.
[18] The Lord disciplined me severely but did not give me over to death.
[19] Open the gates of righteousness for me;
I will enter through them and give thanks to the Lord.
[20] This is the Lord's gate;
the righteous will enter through it.
[21] I will give thanks to you
because you have answered me
and have become my salvation.
[22] The stone that the builders rejected
has become the cornerstone.
[23] This came from the Lord;
it is wondrous in our sight.
[24] This is the day the Lord has made;
let us rejoice and be glad in it.

Truth: The experience of deliverance, and the security that the faithful have in God, lead to the reflection - I will not die, but I will live. The next line also clarifies for each member of the congregation why God would extend life: that I might recount the deeds of the LORD. The situations of danger were aiming to bring the psalmist to see more clearly that in him the singer is secure. God disciplines us to reveal Himself to us.

Thought: As a child, we typically thought of discipline as a negative. As we mature, we begin to understand that discipline is what shapes us in to what we need to be. God only disciplines those who He loves. We should embrace the discipline of God as refining us like gold

Tune: We believe in God the Father, we believe in Jesus Christ
We believe in the Holy Spirit, and He's given us new life
We believe in the crucifixion, we believe that He conquered death
We believe in the resurrection, and He's coming back again

Heavenly Father, mold me and shape me like the Potter shapes the clay.

Text: Psalm 118:25-29

25 Lord, save us!
Lord, please grant us success!
26 He who comes in the name of the Lord is blessed.
From the house of the Lord we bless you.
27 The Lord is God and has given us light.
Bind the festival sacrifice with cords
to the horns of the altar.
28 You are my God, and I will give you thanks.
You are my God; I will exalt you.
29 Give thanks to the Lord, for he is good;
his faithful love endures forever.

Truth: *Lord, save us. . .* Transliterated from Hebrew, this becomes "Hosanna" in the New Testament. These words were shouted by the crowd to Christ at the time of His triumphal entry to Jerusalem. Days later they rejected Him because He did not provide political deliverance.

Thought: The psalm ends as it began, urging us to give thanks to the Lord, for he is good; for his faithful love endures forever! Once we allow all of our thoughts to come between expressions of thanksgiving, then our cries of "give us success!" become focused on success on God's terms. Success is not measured in more money, more responsibility, more notoriety, but in in obedience and God's work through us.

Tune: Blessed be Your name, in the land that is plentiful
Where Your streams of abundance flow, blessed be Your name
Blessed be Your name, when I'm found in the desert place
Though I walk through the wilderness, blessed be Your name
Ev'ry blessing You pour out I'll turn back to praise
When the darkness closes in Lord, still I will say
Blessed be the name of the Lord, blessed be Your name
Blessed be the name of the Lord, blessed be Your glorious name

Father, today I come in the name of the Lord, exalting You, thanking You!

Text: Psalm 119:1-8

¹ How happy are those whose way is blameless,
who walk according to the Lord's instruction!
² Happy are those who keep his decrees
and seek him with all their heart.
³ They do nothing wrong;
they walk in his ways.
⁴ You have commanded that your precepts
be diligently kept.
⁵ If only my ways were committed
to keeping your statutes!
⁶ Then I would not be ashamed
when I think about all your commands.
⁷ I will praise you with an upright heart
when I learn your righteous judgments.
⁸ I will keep your statutes; never abandon me.

Truth: Happy are those who walk according to the Lord's instruction, who keep his decrees, who obey his commands, who keep his statues, and who obey what the righteous Judge has ruled to be right.

Thought: Following the will of God is a matter of obedience. Obedience comes as a result of the work of God within us. The work of God within us is deepened and developed through the Word of God. Until your growth in the Word of God starts to move forward, your Christian walk will not.

Tune: Ev'ry promise we can make, ev'ry prayer and step of faith
Ev'ry diff'rence we will make, is only by His grace
Ev'ry mountain we will climb, ev'ry ray of hope we shine
Ev'ry blessing left behind, is only by His grace
Grace alone which God supplies, strength unknown He will provide
Christ in us our Cornerstone, we will go forth in grace alone

Father God, I need Your grace today so that I may obey You fully. Give me a great desire for Your Word.

Songs for Life – Day 288 – October 15

Text: Psalm 119:9-16

[9] How can a young man keep his way pure?
By keeping your word.
[10] I have sought you with all my heart;
don't let me wander from your commands.
[11] I have treasured your word in my heart
so that I may not sin against you.
[12] Lord, may you be blessed;
teach me your statutes.
[13] With my lips I proclaim
all the judgments from your mouth.
[14] I rejoice in the way revealed by your decrees
as much as in all riches.
[15] I will meditate on your precepts and think about your ways.
[16] I will delight in your statutes; I will not forget your word.

Truth: The psalmist seeks to keep his way pure by keeping God's Word. God does not hide from us what pleases Him. He states it clearly in His Word. There is a deep connection between striving after moral perfection and the realization that the quest is itself impossible without God's help. God's law demands careful reflection.

Thought: *"I have treasured your word in my heart"* . . . "But I don't like to read!" The truth is, the only path to Godliness is growth in His Word, period. Read it, listen to it being read, study it, and discuss it. Ask God to give you an increasing thirst for His Word today.

Tune: Standing on the promises of Christ my King
Through eternal ages let His praises ring
Glory in the highest I will shout and sing
Standing on the promises of God
Standing, standing, standing on the promises of God my Savior
Standing, standing, I'm standing on the promises of God

Father, give me a thirst for Your Word today. Help me to be faithful to it.

Text: Psalm 119:17-24

[17] Deal generously with your servant
so that I might live;
then I will keep your word.
[18] Open my eyes so that I may contemplate
wondrous things from your instruction.
[19] I am a resident alien on earth;
do not hide your commands from me.
[20] I am continually overcome
with longing for your judgments.
[21] You rebuke the arrogant,
the ones under a curse,
who wander from your commands.
[22] Take insult and contempt away from me,
for I have kept your decrees.
[23] Though princes sit together speaking against me,
your servant will think about your statutes;
[24] your decrees are my delight and my counselors.

Truth: The psalmist's life depends on God's grace. We need God's grace to illuminate His Word. He must guide our understanding. The psalmist needs God's help in order to understand His Word.

Thought: *"Open my eyes, that I may contemplate wondrous things from your instruction"*. There are no shortcuts to understanding God's Word, but He has promised that the Holy Spirit will teach us all things.

Tune: Remember me
In a Bible cracked and faded by the years
Remember me, in a sanctuary filled with silent prayer
And age to age, and heart to heart, bound by grace and peace
Child of wonder, child of God
I've remembered you, Remember me

Father, open my eyes today, that I may see the truths from Your Word.

Text: Psalm 119:25-32

25 My life is down in the dust;
give me life through your word.
26 I told you about my life, and you answered me;
teach me your statutes.
27 Help me understand the meaning of your precepts
so that I can meditate on your wonders.
28 I am weary from grief;
strengthen me through your word.
29 Keep me from the way of deceit
and graciously give me your instruction.
30 I have chosen the way of truth;
I have set your ordinances before me.
31 I cling to your decrees;
Lord, do not put me to shame.
32 I pursue the way of your commands,
for you broaden my understanding.

Truth: The psalmist sees that, if left to himself, he would be walking in ways contrary to God's law. He determines to run on the path of obedience rather than merely avoiding the wrong paths

Thought: Understanding God's Word and His ways are not merely a matter of diving in and trying to understand. God must direct our path, open our eyes and give us understanding. Like the psalmist, you can pray *"Help me understand the meaning of your precepts"*.

Tune: Take time to be holy, peak oft with thy Lord
Abide in Him always, and feed on His Word
Make friends with God's children, Help those who are weak
Forgetting in nothing, His blessing to seek

Father, I want Your Word to come alive in me. Direct my eyes to the passage You have for me and open my heart to understanding.

Songs for Life – Day 291 – October 18

Text: Psalm 119:33-40

33 Teach me, Lord, the meaning of your statutes,
and I will always keep them.
34 Help me understand your instruction,
and I will obey it and follow it with all my heart.
35 Help me stay on the path of your commands, for I take pleasure in it.
36 Turn my heart to your decrees
and not to dishonest profit.
37 Turn my eyes from looking at what is worthless;
give me life in your ways.
38 Confirm what you said to your servant,
for it produces reverence for you.
39 Turn away the disgrace I dread;
indeed, your judgments are good.
40 How I long for your precepts!
Give me life through your righteousness.

Truth: The psalmist knows that God must supply the deepest motivation. He also realizes that his love for the Lord has its source in God Himself. In addition to running to God, He asks God to help him run away from things that are contrary to God's character. We must do both.

Thought: "Teach me", "help me understand", "turn my heart", "turn my eyes", "confirm", "turn away" – these are pleas from the psalmist. Even the most committed of believers need God's help every step of the way.

Tune: Tell me the story of Jesus, write on my heart every word
Tell me the story most precious, sweetest that ever was heard
Tell how the angels in chorus sang as they welcomed His birth
Glory to God in the highest, peace and good tidings to earth
Tell me the story of Jesus, write on my heart every word
Tell me the story most precious, sweetest that ever was heard

Father in Heaven, let me keep the childlike faith that I had when I first heard the stories from The Word, but not the same level of understanding.

Songs for Life – Day 292 – October 19

Text: Psalm 119:41-48

[41] Let your faithful love come to me, Lord,
your salvation, as you promised.
[42] Then I can answer the one who taunts me,
for I trust in your word.
[43] Never take the word of truth from my mouth,
for I hope in your judgments.
[44] I will always obey your instruction,
forever and ever.
[45] I will walk freely in an open place
because I study your precepts.
[46] I will speak of your decrees before kings
and not be ashamed.
[47] I delight in your commands,
which I love.
[48] I will lift up my hands to your commands,
which I love,
and will meditate on your statutes.

Truth: It is the genuine experience of God's grace and mercy that drives the faithful to seek his moral guidance. By keeping God's laws, the psalmist will be liberated from slavery to sin.

Thought: The psalmist seeks for love and salvation from God. Are there any greater blessings? Without love and salvation, our life is an empty shell with a terrible ending. Thank God for love and salvation!

Tune: I've found a Friend who is all to me, His love is ever true
I love to tell how He lifted me, and what His grace can do for you
Saved by His pow'r divine, saved to new life sublime
Life now is sweet, and my joy is complete
For I'm saved, saved, saved

Lord Jesus I am so thankful for salvation! I know that You are continuing to work out salvation in me. Continue Your work of transformation in me.

Text: Psalm 119:49-56

[49] Remember your word to your servant;
you have given me hope through it.
[50] This is my comfort in my affliction:
Your promise has given me life.
[51] The arrogant constantly ridicule me,
but I do not turn away from your instruction.
[52] Lord, I remember your judgments from long ago and find comfort.
[53] Rage seizes me because of the wicked who reject your instruction.
[54] Your statutes are the theme of my song during my earthly life.
[55] Lord, I remember your name in the night, and I obey your instruction.
[56] This is my practice: I obey your precepts.

Truth: The psalmist is grieving for those in "the church", the Israelites, who are living lives contrary to God's law. Rather than lashing out at them, he is exalting the Word of God, for he realizes that except for the Word, he could be in the same situation as those he is grieved over.

Thought: When God's Word becomes implanted within us, it comes out in our lives. We sing His songs, we meditate on His Word, our thoughts come into submission, we are convicted when we begin to stray, and the things that come from our mouth sound better. It all goes back to the implanted Word within us.

Tune: Redeemed how I love to proclaim it
Redeemed by the blood of the Lamb
Redeemed thro' His infinite mercy
His child and forever I am

Redeemed, redeemed, redeemed by the blood of the Lamb
Redeemed, redeemed, His child and forever I am

Father, You have saved me! You have redeemed me! I declare it today!

Text: Psalm 119:57-64

[57] The Lord is my portion;
I have promised to keep your words.
[58] I have sought your favor with all my heart;
be gracious to me according to your promise.
[59] I thought about my ways
and turned my steps back to your decrees.
[60] I hurried, not hesitating to keep your commands.
[61] Though the ropes of the wicked
were wrapped around me,
I did not forget your instruction.
[62] I rise at midnight to thank you
for your righteous judgments.
[63] I am a friend to all who fear you, to those who keep your precepts.
[64] Lord, the earth is filled with your faithful love; teach me your statutes.

Truth: The psalmist, as a believer, considers his own character and conduct, in order to bring those into greater submission to God's commandments. Obedience to the Lord happens in submission to Him.

Thought: None of us were intended to live life on an island, apart from others. We were created for community. Even if you live alone, you are never alone. The psalmist gives a living testimony of reflecting on his own ways, which causes him to turn his feet to the Lord's testimonies.

Tune: Serve the Lord with gladness in our works and ways
Come before His presence with our songs of praise
Unto Him our Maker, we would pledge anew
Life's supreme devotion to service true
Serve Him with gladness, Enter His courts with song
To our Creator true praises belong
Great is His mercy, wonderful is His name
We gladly serve Him, His great love proclaim

Father God, give me joy to serve You in the church You've placed me in.

Text: Psalm 119:65-72

[65] Lord, you have treated your servant well, just as you promised.

[66] Teach me good judgment and discernment,
for I rely on your commands.

[67] Before I was afflicted I went astray, but now I keep your word.

[68] You are good, and you do what is good;
teach me your statutes.

[69] The arrogant have smeared me with lies,
but I obey your precepts with all my heart.

[70] Their hearts are hard and insensitive,
but I delight in your instruction.

[71] It was good for me to be afflicted
so that I could learn your statutes.

[72] Instruction from your lips is better for me
than thousands of gold and silver pieces.

Truth: The psalmist found that affliction brought him back from wandering away from God. God uses distress and suffering in our lives to bring us back to him. In retrospect, the psalmist is thankful for his suffering because it has led to a new intimacy with the Lord.

Thought: *"Before I was afflicted I went astray, but now I keep your word"*. What situations in your past has God used to draw you back to Him? Are there situations in your life right now that God may be using to try and get your attention?

Tune: Water You turned into wine, opened the eyes of the blind
There's no one like You, none like You
Into the darkness You shine, out of the ashes we rise
There's no one like You, none like You
Our God is greater, our God is stronger
God You are higher than any other
Our God is healer, Awesome in power our God our God

Father God, I will trust in and obey Your Word today. Keep me close.

Text: Psalm 119:73-80

[73] Your hands made me and formed me;
give me understanding
so that I can learn your commands.
[74] Those who fear you will see me and rejoice,
for I put my hope in your word.
[75] I know, Lord, that your judgments are just
and that you have afflicted me fairly.
[76] May your faithful love comfort me
as you promised your servant.
[77] May your compassion come to me
so that I may live,
for your instruction is my delight.
[78] Let the arrogant be put to shame for slandering me with lies;
I will meditate on your precepts.
[79] Let those who fear you,
those who know your decrees, turn to me.
[80] May my heart be blameless regarding your statutes
so that I will not be put to shame.

Truth: As others who share the psalmist's deep commitment to the Lord see his happiness, they will be encouraged. He still is a work in progress, however. Submission to His Lordship is key to transformation.

Thought: Without mercy, the psalmist has no life. Without God's Word, there would be no testimony that others can see. When there is real transformation in our lives, we don't have to shout about it, people recognize it. God will use your transformation to draw others to Himself.

Tune: I believe in the Son, I believe in the Risen One
I believe I overcome, by the power of His blood
Amen amen, I'm alive I'm alive because He lives
Amen amen, Let my song join the one that never end (Because He lives)

Dear Lord, because You live, I can face today and tomorrow. Amen!

Text: Psalm 119:81-88

[81] I long for your salvation;
I put my hope in your word.
[82] My eyes grow weary
looking for what you have promised;
I ask, "When will you comfort me?"
[83] Though I have become like a wineskin dried by smoke,
I do not forget your statutes.
[84] How many days must your servant wait?
When will you execute judgment on my persecutors?
[85] The arrogant have dug pits for me;
they violate your instruction.
[86] All your commands are true;
people persecute me with lies—help me!
[87] They almost ended my life on earth,
but I did not abandon your precepts.
[88] Give me life in accordance with your faithful love,
and I will obey the decree you have spoken.

Truth: This passage focuses on the psalmist's sense of longing and desperation. He emphasizes that he has not stopped following God's directions even though he is suffering.

Thought: "When will you comfort me?" "How many days must your servant wait?" "When will you execute judgment on my persecutors?" Even the most committed of Biblical saints experienced trials. Trials are how we grow. Focus on what God is trying to teach you.

Tune: Jesus Jesus Jesus, there's just something about that name
Master Savior Jesus, like a fragrance after the rain
Jesus Jesus Jesus, let all heaven and earth proclaim
Kings and kingdoms may all pass away
But there's something about that name

Jesus, there IS something about Your name. Jesus…Jesus…Jesus...

Songs for Life – Day 298 – October 25

Text: Psalm 119:89-96

[89] Lord, your word is forever;
it is firmly fixed in heaven.
[90] Your faithfulness is for all generations;
you established the earth, and it stands firm.
[91] Your judgments stand firm today,
for all things are your servants.
[92] If your instruction had not been my delight,
I would have died in my affliction.
[93] I will never forget your precepts,
for you have given me life through them.
[94] I am yours; save me,
for I have studied your precepts.
[95] The wicked hope to destroy me,
but I contemplate your decrees.
[96] I have seen a limit to all perfection,
but your command is without limit.

Truth: As God is eternal, so is His word. It is forever valid. It speaks to all people and for all time.

Thought*:* The psalmist is clear . . . God's Word has saved his life. Can anyone join me in saying that God's Word has saved your life? It has certainly saved mine. What would life be like without *"For God so loved the world"* and *"the gift of God is eternal life in Christ Jesus"?*

Tune: I must needs go home by the way of the cross
There's no other way but this
I shall ne'er get sight of the gates of light
If the way of the cross I miss
The way of the cross leads home, the way of the cross leads home
It is sweet to know as I onward go, the way of the cross leads home

Father, Your Word has saved my life. It has taught me that my sin leads to death, that You have provided a way of redemption and an eternal home.

Text: Psalm 119:97-104

[97] How I love your instruction!
It is my meditation all day long.
[98] Your commands make me wiser than my enemies,
for they are always with me.
[99] I have more insight than all my teachers
because your decrees are my meditation.
[100] I understand more than the elders
because I obey your precepts.
[101] I have kept my feet from every evil path
to follow your word.
[102] I have not turned from your judgments,
for you yourself have instructed me.
[103] How sweet your word is to my taste—
sweeter than honey in my mouth.
[104] I gain understanding from your precepts;
therefore I hate every false way.

Truth: The psalmist loves the law because it comes from his God and Savior. The psalmist does not mean this as a boast but as an emphatic expression of his devotion to God's law.

Thought: *"How sweet your word is to my taste, sweeter than honey in my mouth!"* The Word of God is not only sharper than any two-edged sword, but it is also the balm that heals. It tastes sweeter than honey because it is pure, it is right, and it is truth.

Tune: I will sing the wondrous story, of the Christ who died for me
How He left His home in glory, for the cross of Calvary

Yes, I'll sing the wondrous story, of the Christ who died for me
Sing it with the saints in glory
Gathered by the crystal sea

Father God, Your Word is the balm for my soul, and strength in the valley.

Songs for Life – Day 300 – October 27

Text: Psalm 119:105-112

[105] Your word is a lamp for my feet and a light on my path.

[106] I have solemnly sworn to keep your righteous judgments.

[107] I am severely afflicted;
Lord, give me life according to your word.

[108] Lord, please accept my freewill offerings of praise,
and teach me your judgments.

[109] My life is constantly in danger,
yet I do not forget your instruction.

[110] The wicked have set a trap for me,
but I have not wandered from your precepts.

[111] I have your decrees as a heritage forever;
indeed, they are the joy of my heart.

[112] I am resolved to obey your statutes to the very end.

Truth: God's revelation provides the insight to guide His servant. He will not trip in the darkness. However, his obedience is not risk-free, for it exposes him to the wiles of his enemies. He could wish to be free of the danger, but is more concerned to live a godly life in spite of it.

Thought: *"Your word is a lamp for my feet and a light on my path."* This is one of the most commonly quoted passages in the Word in regard to God's Word. It's often quoted because it rings true. The Word does light our path, allow our feet to escape darkness and show us the way of righteousness. Ask God to draw you to the light of His Word today.

Tune: Thy Word is a lamp unto my feet, and a light unto my path
Thy Word is a lamp unto my feet, and a light unto my path
When I feel afraid, and I think I've lost my way
Still You're there right beside me
Nothing will I fear, as long as You are near
Please be near me to the end

Heavenly Father, guide my steps today with the light of Your Word.

Text: Psalm 119:113-120

[113] I hate those who are double-minded,
but I love your instruction.
[114] You are my shelter and my shield;
I put my hope in your word.
[115] Depart from me, you evil ones,
so that I may obey my God's commands.
[116] Sustain me as you promised, and I will live;
do not let me be ashamed of my hope.
[117] Sustain me so that I can be safe
and always be concerned about your statutes.
[118] You reject all who stray from your statutes,
for their deceit is a lie.
[119] You remove all the wicked on earth
as if they were dross from metal;
therefore, I love your decrees.
[120] I tremble in awe of you;
I fear your judgments.

Truth: This passage contrasts the psalmist's love of God's directions with his hatred of the "double-minded". However, he does not take pleasure in the destruction of the wicked, but instead dreads their fate. The psalmist emphasizes that those who are loyal to God's directions will be preserved.

Thought: Sometimes we just want to hide from the world, the distractions, the people, and the information that bombards us each day. The only true hiding place is found in The Lord. He is our hiding place and shield.

Tune: Jesus keep me near the cross, there a precious fountain
Free to all a healing stream, flows from Calv'ry's mountain
In the cross in the cross, be my glory ever
Till my raptured soul shall find, rest beyond the river

Holy God, I need You to be my shelter from the storms of life today. I need rest, I need refuge and I need a clear heart and mind.

Text: Psalm 119:121-124

121 I have done what is just and right;
do not leave me to my oppressors.
122 Guarantee your servant's well-being;
do not let the arrogant oppress me.
123 My eyes grow weary looking for your salvation
and for your righteous promise.
124 Deal with your servant based on your faithful love;
teach me your statutes.

Truth: Faithful love is the devotion that God shows toward His covenant people, demonstrating His mercy and compassion. He trusts in the love of God to be just, right, and to teach him the ways of God.

Thought: *"My eyes grow weary looking for your salvation and for your righteous promise".* One day, our salvation will become complete. Jesus will return, God's children will be called home, and we will get to enter into our permanent rest. Until then, the process of salvation is ongoing. God is calling us to a deeper walk as long as He gives us breath to breathe.

Tune: What a wonderful change in my life has been wrought
Since Jesus came into my heart
I have light in my soul for which long I had sought
Since Jesus came into my heart

Since Jesus came into my heart
Since Jesus came into my heart
Floods of joy o'er my soul
Like the sea billows roll
Since Jesus came into my heart

O Lord, You are calling me to a deeper walk. I will gladly walk that path, with You guiding me. You are my only hope and salvation.

Text: Psalm 119:125-128

125 I am your servant; give me understanding
so that I may know your decrees.
126 It is time for the Lord to act,
for they have violated your instruction.
127 Since I love your commands
more than gold, even the purest gold,
128 I carefully follow all your precepts
and hate every false way.

Truth: In this passage, the psalmist emphasizes his loyalty to God's directions with his anticipation of God's action. He still wants to know more of God's directions. He boldly calls on God. While he waits, he proclaims his loyalty to God's directions and his pleasure in keeping them.

Thought: The psalmist values the commandments of God as worth more than purest gold. They are precious, even priceless. Can you reflect back to a time when a particular verse or passage made a significant impact on your life? What was that? What did God do that impacted you?

Tune: Lord You are
More precious than silver
Lord You are
More costly than gold
Lord You are
More beautiful than diamonds
And nothing I desire
Compares with You

Lord, there is nothing more precious than Your commandments, Your promises, Your truths, and Your revelation. I desire that You would open my eyes, my ears and my heart today to hear Your Word. Implant it in my heart and tune my heart to hear only Your voice.

Text: Psalm 119:129-136

[129] Your decrees are wondrous;
therefore I obey them.
[130] The revelation of your words brings light
and gives understanding to the inexperienced.
[131] I open my mouth and pant
because I long for your commands.
[132] Turn to me and be gracious to me,
as is your practice toward those who love your name.
[133] Make my steps steady through your promise;
don't let any sin dominate me.
[134] Redeem me from human oppression,
and I will keep your precepts.
[135] Make your face shine on your servant,
and teach me your statutes.
[136] My eyes pour out streams of tears
because people do not follow your instruction.

Truth: The psalmist wants the Lord to guide him through life. He realizes that one is within the will of God while seeking to obey His revealed word. He also knows that obedience is impossible unless God supplies grace.

Thought: As we draw closer to God through His Word, He deepens our love and concern for others who are struggling. Ask God to give you a burden today for someone who needs to experience a move of God in their lives and increase their dependence on Him. Pray for them.

Tune: Days are filled with sorrow and care
Hearts are lonely and drear
Burdens are lifted at Calvary, Jesus is very near

Burdens are lifted at Calvary, Calvary, Calvary
Burdens are lifted at Calvary, Jesus is very near

Lord, I bring You the needs of others today, knowing You have answers.

Text: Psalm 119:137-140

[137] You are righteous, Lord,
and your judgments are just.
[138] The decrees you issue are righteous
and altogether trustworthy.
[139] My anger overwhelms me
because my foes forget your words.
[140] Your word is completely pure,
and your servant loves it.

Truth: God is both righteous and just. His decrees are righteous and trustworthy. The psalmist is focusing on the character of God rather than His directions. Following God is about allowing His character shape us, rather than letting our behavior attempt to change our character, which is futile.

Thought: When Jesus was on the cross, our sins were imputed, or placed upon Him. Then, and only then, could God impute His righteousness on us. It is not something we wear as clothing, but something that has been placed upon us as if it is ours. Don't focus today on doing the right "things" but in allowing God's righteousness, His character, guide your life.

Tune: What can wash away my sin
Nothing but the blood of Jesus
What can make me whole again
Nothing but the blood of Jesus

O precious is the flow
That makes me white as snow
No other fount I know
Nothing but the blood of Jesus

Father, I need you to clothe me in Your righteousness, but not just on the outside. I need You to transform me from the inside out, so that everything I say, everything I do reflects Your righteousness.

Text: Psalm 119:141-144

[141] I am insignificant and despised,
but I do not forget your precepts.
[142] Your righteousness is an everlasting righteousness,
and your instruction is true.
[143] Trouble and distress have overtaken me,
but your commands are my delight.
[144] Your decrees are righteous forever.
Give me understanding, and I will live.

Truth: Though the psalmist experiences "trouble and distress", he still finds pleasure in God's directions. Since God's directions will remain "righteous forever", the psalmist pleads for more insight into them so that he might continue to live a faithful life.

Thought: There are some things that are eternal in this world: God's Word, God's faithfulness, and God's righteousness are among them. The more of those good eternal things we focus on, the more we will reflect the character of God. Today is about one choice: will you walk in the righteousness of God?

Tune: We will glorify the King of kings, We will glorify the Lamb
We will glorify the Lord of lords
Who is the great I Am

Lord Jehovah reigns in majesty, We will bow before His throne
We will worship Him in righteousness
We will worship Him alone

Hallelujah to the King of kings, Hallelujah to the Lamb
Hallelujah to the Lord of lords
Who is the great I Am

Heavenly Father, I will seek to glorify You today in all that I say and do!

Text: Psalm 119:145-148

145 I call with all my heart; answer me, Lord.
I will obey your statutes.
146 I call to you; save me,
and I will keep your decrees.
147 I rise before dawn and cry out for help;
I put my hope in your word.
148 I am awake through each watch of the night
to meditate on your promise.

Truth: The Jews divided the night into 3 watches of 4 hours each, beginning at 6pm. The Romans taught them to divide the night into 4 watches of 3 hours each. It would seem the psalmist is awake, meditating on God's Word, at the beginning of each watch.

Thought: Have you ever had one of those sleepless nights, where you never could seem to get settled? Perhaps you had a time where you were sleeping soundly and suddenly you woke up hours before your intended time to get up and you couldn't go back to sleep. Sometimes God brings those times about in order to get our attention away from the distractions and noise of the day. Maybe you could set aside some time today to just meditate on God's Word, listen for His voice and just enjoy His presence.

Tune: Your blood speaks a better word
Than all the empty claims I've heard upon this earth
Speaks righteousness for me, and stands in my defense
Jesus it's Your blood
What can wash away our sins, what can make us whole again
Nothing but the blood, nothing but the blood of Jesus
What can wash us pure as snow
Welcomed as the friends of God
Nothing but Your blood, nothing but Your blood, King Jesus

Almighty God, Your blood stands as my defense. Your blood allows me to come to You with all of my "stuff" and lay it at Your feet.

Text: Psalm 119:149-152

149 In keeping with your faithful love, hear my voice.
Lord, give me life in keeping with your justice.
150 Those who pursue evil plans come near;
they are far from your instruction.
151 You are near, Lord,
and all your commands are true.
152 Long ago I learned from your decrees
that you have established them forever.

Truth: The psalmist describes two that "come near": those who pursue evil and attack, and the Lord. When both attack, who wins? The Lord's covenantal presence nullifies the negative effects of the presence of the enemy. The Lord's commandments are true, and His testimonies endure forever.

Thought: When God is near, His Word, His commandments are also near. It is impossible to separate His presence from His Word. When you read God's Word, you are inviting His presence. When you meditate on His Word, you are allowing his righteousness to fill you up and clothe you. If you feel God is far away, simply take verse 151 and read it over and over again until you feel the presence of God inhabit where you are.

Tune: I love to tell the story of unseen things above
Of Jesus and His glory, of Jesus and His love
I love to tell the story
Because I know 'tis true
It satisfies my longings as nothing else can do

I love to tell the story
'Twill be my theme in glory
To tell the old old story
Of Jesus and His love

Lord, you are near, and all your commandments are true.

Songs for Life - Day 309 - November 5

Text: Psalm 119:153-156

153 Consider my affliction and rescue me,
for I have not forgotten your instruction.
154 Champion my cause and redeem me;
give me life as you promised.
155 Salvation is far from the wicked
because they do not study your statutes.
156 Your compassions are many, Lord;
give me life according to your judgments.

Truth: The psalmist contrasts the distance of the wicked from any rescue to the greatness of God's mercy for those who follow His directions. He calls on God to "champion" his cause, and is calling on God as Righteous Defender to deliver, redeem and provide mercy.

Thought: Salvation is far from the wicked because they do not seek God and His Word. They cannot understand concepts like deliverance, redemption and mercy. Those are God's and reserved for His children. Do not hesitate to call on God today to deliver, to redeem, and to show you His mercy. The lessons you learn in the midst of the trial will help deepen your walk when God does deliver and redeem you by His mercy. *"Your compassions are many, Lord".*

Tune: The greatest day in history
Death is beaten You have rescued me
Sing it out Jesus is alive
The empty cross the empty grave
Life eternal You have won the day
Shout it out Jesus is alive, He's alive
And oh happy day happy day, You washed my sin away
Oh happy day happy day, I'll never be the same
Forever I am changed

Father, what a glorious day it was when you saved me from my sins! I am still very much in need of Your refuge, Your deliverance, and Your love.

Songs for Life - Day 310 - November 6

Text: Psalm 119:157-160

[157] My persecutors and foes are many.
I have not turned from your decrees.
[158] I have seen the disloyal and feel disgust
because they do not keep your word.
[159] Consider how I love your precepts;
Lord, give me life according to your faithful love.
[160] The entirety of your word is truth,
each of your righteous judgments endures forever.

Truth: The psalmist contrasts the great numbers of the wicked with the greatness of God's mercy. He emphasizes God's steadfast love as he pleads for God to give him life.

Thought: Do you ever feel like you are in the minority as a Christian? Does that make the expectation any less that we should be clothed with God's righteousness? Certainly not. Does that mean God's presence is harder to reach for His children? Certainly not. He's as close as the mention of His name. His love is steadfast. His Word is truth. His righteousness extends forever. Ask Him to fill you with His love today.

Tune: A pilgrim was I and a-wand'ring
In the cold night of sin I did roam
When Jesus the kind Shepherd found me
And now I am on my way home

Surely goodness and mercy shall follow me
All the days all the days of my life
Surely goodness and mercy shall follow me
All the days all the days of my life

Father, sometimes I feel like my witness doesn't make a difference in this world, because people are not giving You the glory that You deserve. However, Your mercy is sufficient to deliver all who would follow Your drawing to come to Your throne of grace.

Text: Psalm 119:161-164

¹⁶¹ Princes have persecuted me without cause,
but my heart fears only your word.
¹⁶² I rejoice over your promise
like one who finds vast treasure.
¹⁶³ I hate and abhor falsehood,
but I love your instruction.
¹⁶⁴ I praise you seven times a day
for your righteous judgments.

Truth: When warriors were victorious in battle, they were able to reap the "spoils", the things that were left behind by those that they defeated. This could be weapons, costly garments, money, jewelry, animals, or equipment. This made the victor rich and happy. The psalmist compares that to what is found in God's Word. It makes us rich and happy, and it is filled with treasure that God left for us to receive.

Thought: *"I rejoice over your promise"*, *"I love your instruction"*, and *"I praise you seven times a day for your righteous judgments",* all reflect back to the treasures found in God's Word. It is the only truly life-changing document ever created and it lives and breathes. It is sharp when it convicts. It is painful when it penetrates our heart. However, it is the balm that soothes our soul. Meditate on a verse in this passage or on another favorite passage today.

Tune: I have a song that Jesus gave me, it was sent from heav'n above
There never was a sweeter melody, 'Tis a melody of love

In my heart there rings a melody
There rings a melody with heaven's harmony
In my heart there rings a melody
There rings a melody of love

Lord, today I rejoice at Your Word! Your word is truth. Your word is love. Your word is life. Fill me with life from Your Word today.

Text: Psalm 119:165-168

165 Abundant peace belongs to those
who love your instruction;
nothing makes them stumble.
166 Lord, I hope for your salvation
and carry out your commands.
167 I obey your decrees
and love them greatly.
168 I obey your precepts and decrees,
for all my ways are before you.

Truth: The psalmist doesn't follow God's commandments out of reluctant obedience, nor does he feel like he is missing out on anything but turning His life over to God and following His Word. On the contrary, he loves God's Word, loves to follow His commands and knows that the great peace he has is because of God's Word within him.

Thought: Our lives are open books before God. The psalmist declared *"all my ways are before you"*. Regardless of your struggles, God loves you. Regardless of your strongholds, God loves you. He not only provides peace, but He IS peace. Once your soul is engaged, your habits and behaviors will follow suit. God is your peace in the midst of the storm, your refuge in time of trouble. Don't worry about trying to keep anything from Him, you can't do it. He knows it all – and loves you anyway!

Tune: Far away in the depths of my spirit tonight
Rolls a melody sweeter than psalm
In celestial-like strains it unceasingly falls
O'er my soul like an infinite calm

Peace, peace, wonderful peace, coming down from the Father above
Sweep over my spirit forever I pray, in fathomless billows of love

Holy God, there is nothing like Your wonderful peace! Reveal Your peace to me today, Holy God, for I am ready to surrender to You.

Text: Psalm 119:169-172

[169] Let my cry reach you, Lord;
give me understanding according to your word.
[170] Let my plea reach you;
rescue me according to your promise.
[171] My lips pour out praise,
for you teach me your statutes.
[172] My tongue sings about your promise,
for all your commands are righteous.

Truth: In each verse, the psalmist makes an appeal, followed by an affirmation. In his appeals, he asks that the Lord hear his cry and that the Lord deliver and teach him. He submits himself by praising the Lord in song. In his affirmation, he acknowledges that understanding comes from the Lord, as well as deliverance and teaching. All of these things can be trusted from the Lord because His commandments are right.

Thought: It is so easy for our prayers to become monologues, even a "grocery list" of things we are seeking to pull "off the shelves" of God's provision. Praising Him not only engages His ear, but puts us in a better mindset to pray according to His will. Singing of His truth helps implant His Word in our hearts. Why not spend a few minutes in prayer right now, beginning with praising Him and lifting up His Word? You might be surprised at what God reveals to you. Take a few moments to drink it in, maybe even jot it down. God has a plan for you TODAY.

Tune: Oh Lord You're beautiful
Your face is all I seek
And when Your eyes are on this child
Your grace abounds to me

Almighty Father, I open my ears and my heart. I wait for You to speak.

Text: Psalm 119:173-176

[173] May your hand be ready to help me,
for I have chosen your precepts.
[174] I long for your salvation, Lord,
and your instruction is my delight.
[175] Let me live, and I will praise you;
may your judgments help me.
[176] I wander like a lost sheep;
seek your servant,
for I do not forget your commands.

Truth: At the conclusion of this longest Psalm, this longest chapter in the Bible, it is still clear that the psalmist was in the midst of trouble at the time he composed this. His final statement serves as a reminder that the only path through the trials is by staying close to His Word, His commandments. Surrendering to God will not keep you from troubles, but it will keep you through them.

Thought*:* The agony that the psalmist expresses though this psalm is not unlike what many of us go through. As we go deeper in grace with the Lord, He reveals more that needs to be placed in His hand that needs to be lined up with His Word. This is why they call our life as a believer the "process of sanctification". We are all works in progress, seekers of holiness, and pictures of His grace. Let Him reveal the deeper things and do not be afraid to "go there".

Tune: And I'll praise You in this storm, and I will lift my hands
For You are who You are, no matter where I am
And ev'ry tear I've cried, You hold in Your hand
You never left my side
And though my heart is torn
I will praise You in this storm

Lord, I know that storms are temporary, even when they feel like they will last forever. Hold me close to You, shelter me, protect me today.

Text: Psalm 120

[1] In my distress I called to the Lord,
and he answered me.
[2] "Lord, rescue me from lying lips
and a deceitful tongue."
[3] What will he give you,
and what will he do to you,
you deceitful tongue?
[4] A warrior's sharp arrows
with burning charcoal!
[5] What misery that I have stayed in Meshech,
that I have lived among the tents of Kedar!
[6] I have dwelt too long with those who hate peace.
[7] I am for peace; but when I speak, they are for war.

Truth: The psalmist was being attacked with deceit and lies that were coming at him and causing pain like sharp arrows or being burned with hot coals. He was asking the Lord to deliver him, and he asked in such a way that he was expecting God to answer.

Thought: *"In my distress I called to the LORD, and he answered me."* Do you call to the Lord in your time of need with an expectant heart? I John 5:14 says, *"This is the confidence we have in approaching God: that if we ask anything according to his will, he hears us."* Focus your attention on God and not your circumstance..... that lets Him know you believe in Him and His ability to help you overcome whatever circumstance you face.

Tune: Oh I trust in Jesus
My great Deliverer; My strong Defender
The Son of God; I trust in Jesus
Blessed Redeemer; My Lord forever
The holy One (the holy One)

Lord Jesus, I come before you asking you to deliver me from my difficult situation. No matter the outcome, I know You will never leave me.

Text: Psalm 121

[1] I lift my eyes toward the mountains.
Where will my help come from?
[2] My help comes from the Lord,
the Maker of heaven and earth.
[3] He will not allow your foot to slip;
your Protector will not slumber.
[4] Indeed, the Protector of Israel
does not slumber or sleep.
[5] The Lord protects you;
the Lord is a shelter right by your side.
[6] The sun will not strike you by day
or the moon by night.
[7] The Lord will protect you from all harm; he will protect your life.
[8] The Lord will protect your coming and going both now and forever.

Truth: This powerful psalm exalts the Lord as our help, our keeper, always working, never sleeping, as well as being our protection. He is the Creator – He knows how to keep His creation. He is the sustainer – He knows how to keep His children. He never sleeps – He is always watching out for us. Nothing catches Him off-guard and His help is always perfect.

Thought: "I lift up my eyes" . . . when we think of exalting God we think upward. We raise our hands, we lift our eyes and we lift our praises. God is high and lifted up, we move upward with Him, and His ways are higher than ours. Lift up your eyes to the hills and seek your help.

Tune: I will lift up mine eyes to the hills from whence cometh my help
My help cometh from the Lord, the Lord, which made heaven and earth
He said, He will not suffer thy foot; thy foot to be moved
The Lord which keepeth thee, He will not slumber nor sleep

My help, my help, my help, all of my help cometh from the Lord

Father, You are my help and my keeper. Thank You for loving me.

Text: Psalm 122

[1] I rejoiced with those who said to me,
"Let us go to the house of the Lord."
[2] Our feet were standing
within your gates, Jerusalem—
[3] Jerusalem, built as a city should be,
solidly united,
[4] where the tribes, the Lord's tribes, go up
to give thanks to the name of the Lord.
[5] There, thrones for judgment are placed,
thrones of the house of David.
[6] Pray for the well-being of Jerusalem:
"May those who love you be secure;
[7] may there be peace within your walls,
security within your fortresses."
[8] Because of my brothers and friends,
I will say, "May peace be in you."
[9] Because of the house of the Lord our God, I will pursue your prosperity.

Truth: The psalm describes the glories of Jerusalem, where God is worshiped and where the dynasty of David rules, asking God to protect the city and its inhabitants.

Thought: When I was a child, sometimes I said "I HAVE to go to church, because my parents say so". Today I say "I GET to go to church", I'm glad when it is time to go to church. Worshiping God can happen alone or with a large group of people, but there is nothing like worshiping with the church family. It's God's house and HE has invited you in! Be glad!

Tune: I was glad when they said unto me
Let us go into Your house O Lord
No greater joy than to be in this place
To lift my voice and sing Your praise

Father, thank You for the privilege of worship in Your house!

Text: Psalm 123

[1] I lift my eyes to you,
the one enthroned in heaven.
[2] Like a servant's eyes on his master's hand,
like a servant girl's eyes on her mistress's hand,
so our eyes are on the Lord our God
until he shows us favor.
[3] Show us favor, Lord, show us favor,
for we've had more than enough contempt.
[4] We've had more than enough
scorn from the arrogant
and contempt from the proud.

Truth: This psalm uses analogies of servants to master, and maid to mistress. This suggests we are to be like the servant or maid and look upward to our Master and wait patiently for God's direction. Did you notice the phrase "Show us favor" is written twice? Favor was ultimately fulfilled through our Lord and Savior, Jesus Christ.

Thought: Look upward to God for every area of your life! That is a sign of total submission to God as Master over your life. We are to await God's will, with patience and trust. Total surrender.... Have you surrendered your life to God? In every area? Is He Master over your life?

Tune: You better give up, gotta stop running
It's the end of the line
It's time to surrender
Hands up
Turn it around
Fall to the ground
Are you gonna surrender

Father God, I surrender to You, I give You my life. You are my Master, who is full of grace and mercy. Thank you, Father, for all you have done for me.

Text: Psalm 124

[1] If the Lord had not been on our side—
let Israel say—
[2] If the Lord had not been on our side
when people attacked us,
[3] then they would have swallowed us alive
in their burning anger against us.
[4] Then the water would have engulfed us;
the torrent would have swept over us;
[5] the raging water would have swept over us.
[6] Blessed be the Lord,
who has not let us be ripped apart by their teeth.
[7] We have escaped like a bird from the hunter's net;
the net is torn, and we have escaped.
[8] Our help is in the name of the Lord,
the Maker of heaven and earth.

Truth: This is a thanksgiving hymn for the community, particularly for an occasion in which God's people have been under threat but have been delivered. These words are quite applicable in a wide variety of situations.

Thought: *"If the Lord had not been on our side"* . . . The psalmist is remembering some of the things that would likely have happened if The Lord had not been on their side. Israel would have been destroyed, or perhaps the flood would have ended everything. Think of where you would be *"If the Lord had not been on our side"*. You'd be lost, without hope, heading for a hopeless, painful eternity. *"Our help is in the name of the Lord"*!

Tune: If it had not been for the Lord on my side
Tell me where would I be
Where would I be

Father, if it had not been for Your name, Your love, Your grace, I'd be lost forever.

Songs for Life - Day 320 - November 16

Text: Psalm 125

[1] Those who trust in the Lord are like Mount Zion.
It cannot be shaken; it remains forever.
[2] The mountains surround Jerusalem
and the Lord surrounds his people, both now and forever.
[3] The scepter of the wicked will not remain
over the land allotted to the righteous,
so that the righteous will not apply their hands to injustice.
[4] Do what is good, Lord, to the good, to those whose hearts are upright.
[5] But as for those who turn aside to crooked ways,
the Lord will banish them with the evildoers.
Peace be with Israel.

Truth: The psalm begins by describing the secure position of those who trust in the Lord: they are like Mount Zion, which cannot be moved. The hills on which Jerusalem sits are a little lower than the hills around it, so that one can picture the surrounding hills as a wall. This serves as an image of the Lord's protection, as he surrounds his people like a high wall encircling the city.

Thought: There is a contrast here between those who trust in the Lord having a sure foundation and those who "turn aside to their crooked ways" being led astray. If you've ever been on an amusement park ride that got unpleasant, you probably had the feeling like it was never going to end. That is the truth for those who do not find their salvation in the Lord. Once God has saved you, NOTHING and NO ONE can take that away! You are on a sure foundation.

Tune: The Church's one foundation is Jesus Christ her Lord
She is His new creation, by water and the Word
From heav'n He came and sought her, to be His holy bride
With His own blood He bought her, and for her life He died

Father, You sent Your son as foundation of the church that You created.
May it always be that we seek Your face for wisdom in the church.

Text: Psalm 126

[1] When the Lord restored the fortunes of Zion,
we were like those who dream.
[2] Our mouths were filled with laughter then,
and our tongues with shouts of joy.
Then they said among the nations,
"The Lord has done great things for them."
[3] The Lord had done great things for us; we were joyful.
[4] Restore our fortunes, Lord,
like watercourses in the Negev.
[5] Those who sow in tears
will reap with shouts of joy.
[6] Though one goes along weeping, carrying the bag of seed,
he will surely come back with shouts of joy, carrying his sheaves.

Truth: The Israelites had been delivered and were happy and sharing what God had done for them. Then in verse 4, they are once again asking for God to restore them and see their repentance over their sins. They were seeking a harvest of God's joyful blessings.

Thought: Think about your journey. Good times.... Bad Times...Do you rejoice in the good? Do you rejoice in the bad? God does things in our lives to provide us with testimony to share with others how we overcame our difficult situations. James 1:2 says it like this: *"Consider it pure joy, my brothers and sisters, whenever you face trials of many kinds, because you know that the testing of your faith produces perseverance."* See joy in the journey my friends!

Tune: Holy Spirit You are welcome here,
Come flood this place and fill the atmosphere.
Your glory God is what our hearts long for,
To be overcome by Your presence, Lord.
The presence Lord

Father, help me to see joy in my journey, and how you are working.

Text: Psalm 127

[1] Unless the Lord builds a house, its builders labor over it in vain;
unless the Lord watches over a city, the watchman stays alert in vain.
[2] In vain you get up early and stay up late,
working hard to have enough food—
yes, he gives sleep to the one he loves.
[3] Sons are indeed a heritage from the Lord,
offspring, a reward.
[4] Like arrows in the hand of a warrior
are the sons born in one's youth.
[5] Happy is the man who has filled his quiver with them.
They will never be put to shame
when they speak with their enemies at the city gate.

Truth: The family and the home are wonderful illustrations of God's Kingdom and His relationship to us. God is Father and we are His children. We depend on Him to build a home for us, not only in this life but in the life to come. If your house is not on a sure foundation, it will surely fail. If Christ is the center of our lives, He can be the center of your family, the foundation on which He can build successful homes and families.

Thought: God has given us families to teach us about love, stewardship, and dependence on Him. He is the Watchman for us. He protects our families when we cannot see them. Is Christ the foundation of your home? Even if it didn't start out that way, Christ can re-build that foundation.

Tune: Jesus lover of my soul, Jesus I will never let You go
You've taken me from the miry clay, You've set my feet upon the rock
And now I know
I love You I need You
Though my world may fall, I'll never let You go
My Savior my closest Friend
I will worship You until the very end

Jesus, be my Foundation today. Without You, I am nothing.

Songs for Life - Day 323 - November 19

Text: Psalm 128

[1] How happy is everyone who fears the Lord,
who walks in his ways!
[2] You will surely eat
what your hands have worked for.
You will be happy,
and it will go well for you.
[3] Your wife will be like a fruitful vine
within your house,
your children, like young olive trees
around your table.
[4] In this very way
the man who fears the Lord
will be blessed.
[5] May the Lord bless you from Zion,
so that you will see the prosperity of Jerusalem
all the days of your life
[6] and will see your children's children!
Peace be with Israel.

Truth: The blessings of a man who is Godly include enjoying the fruit of their own labor, being happy, having spirits that are well, experiencing fruitful families, receiving the blessing of God, and peace.

Thought: If a man is sold out to God, his family is much more likely to follow suit than if he is not. The blessings on a home who is led by a Godly man are many. If you are a man, serve by leading a Godly life.

Tune: I have decided, I'm gonna live like a believer
Turn my back on the deceiver, I'm gonna live what I believe
I have decided, bein' good is just a fable
I just can't 'cause I'm not able
I'm gonna leave it to the Lord

Lord, I'm putting on the armor today and I'm choosing to serve You alone.

Text: Psalm 129

[1] Since my youth they have often attacked me—
let Israel say—
[2] Since my youth they have often attacked me,
but they have not prevailed against me.
[3] Plowmen plowed over my back; they made their furrows long.
[4] The Lord is righteous; he has cut the ropes of the wicked.
[5] Let all who hate Zion
be driven back in disgrace.
[6] Let them be like grass on the rooftops,
which withers before it grows up
[7] and can't even fill the hands of the reaper
or the arms of the one who binds sheaves.
[8] Then none who pass by will say,
"May the Lord's blessing be on you.
We bless you in the name of the Lord."

Truth: This is a community thanksgiving psalm acknowledging what God's people went through and how God sustained them during that time. Then it goes on to further ask God that all such enemies that hate God would always fail in their endeavors.

Thought: Verse 4 - *"The LORD is righteous."* He is Perfect Righteousness and we are not. We strive for practical righteousness. We have to make conscious efforts every day to choose to "put off" the things that are not of God, and to "put on" God's armor of light. (Romans 13:12) This will give us protection from the enemy and guard our hearts.

Tune: Righteousness, righteousness is what I long for
Righteousness is what I need
Righteousness, righteousness is what You want from me

Father God, I choose You and Your armor of light! Please guide my paths daily and take my heart and life and transform it to You.

Text: Psalm 130

¹ Out of the depths I call to you, Lord!

² Lord, listen to my voice; let your ears be attentive
to my cry for help.

³ Lord, if you kept an account of iniquities,
Lord, who could stand?

⁴ But with you there is forgiveness, so that you may be revered.

⁵ I wait for the Lord; I wait
and put my hope in his word.

⁶ I wait for the Lord
more than watchmen for the morning—
more than watchmen for the morning.

⁷ Israel, put your hope in the Lord.
For there is faithful love with the Lord,
and with him is redemption in abundance.

⁸ And he will redeem Israel from all its iniquities.

Truth: The psalmist begins by crying for help and pleading for God's mercy. He then asks for forgiveness by stating that no one could endure God's scrutiny for sins, but God forgives in order that He might be worshiped. The psalmist then describes his hope and anticipation of God's help in terms of night watchmen yearning for morning light.

Thought: If there was a running tally on your life, could you defend yourself against that? Certainly none of us could. *"But with you there is forgiveness"*. Focus on God's forgiveness today. We've been forgiven much, so we should forgive much as well.

Tune: So I'll cherish the old rugged cross
Till my trophies at last I lay down
I will cling to the old rugged cross
And exchange it some day for a crown

Father God, I can never thank You enough for allowing Your son to take my sins and bear them on the cross. I don't want to ever get over it.

Text: Psalm 131

[1] Lord, my heart is not proud;
my eyes are not haughty.
I do not get involved with things
too great or too wondrous for me.
[2] Instead, I have calmed and quieted my soul
like a weaned child with its mother;
my soul is like a weaned child.
[3] Israel, put your hope in the Lord,
both now and forever.

Truth: The psalmist is humbled before the Lord. Just as a child is content simply having his mother's presence, so the faithful worshiper is content with God's presence, even when there are many things he would like God to explain.

Thought: Picture an altar full of people kneeling at the end of a worship service. Is that a picture of weakness? Absolutely not, far from it. It is a God-honoring humility that brings people to their knees before God Almighty. Just as the psalmist isn't portraying arrogance or over-confidence, we must humble ourselves to hear His voice. God doesn't expect you to figure it out – He wants to increase your dependence on Him so His blessings can come more freely to and through you.

Tune: I've had many tears and sorrows
I've had questions for tomorrow
There've been times I didn't know right from wrong
But in ev'ry situation God gave blessed consolation
That my trials come to only make me strong

Through it all through it all
I've learned to trust in Jesus, I've learned to trust in God
Through it all through it all, I've learned to depend upon His word

Father God, teach me how to trust You more - every day, in every way.

Text: Psalm 132:1-10

[1] Lord, remember David
and all the hardships he endured,
[2] and how he swore an oath to the Lord,
making a vow to the Mighty One of Jacob:
[3] "I will not enter my house
or get into my bed,
[4] I will not allow my eyes to sleep
or my eyelids to slumber
[5] until I find a place for the Lord,
a dwelling for the Mighty One of Jacob."
[6] We heard of the ark in Ephrathah;
we found it in the fields of Jaar.
[7] Let us go to his dwelling place; let us worship at his footstool.
[8] Rise up, Lord, come to your resting place,
you and your powerful ark.
[9] May your priests be clothed with righteousness,
and may your faithful people shout for joy.
[10] For the sake of your servant David, do not reject your anointed one.

Truth: This prayer is David talking about the Ark of the Covenant and how it was moved around and housed in tents, while he lived in a nice permanent structure. David asked God to come and dwell there with the Ark, that the priests would be Godly men, and the people would worship.

Thought: *"At that moment the curtain of the temple was torn in two from top to bottom. The earth shook and the rocks split." -Matthew 27:51.* Now and forever we don't have to go to a "certain place" to talk to, to worship, or to feel God's mighty presence. Freely worship God wherever you are.

Tune: The ground began to shake; The stone was rolled away
His perfect love could not be overcome; Now death where is your sting?
Our resurrected King... has rendered you defeated!!

Father, Forever You reign over death and the enemy. I worship You!!

Text: Psalm 132:11-18

[11] The Lord swore an oath to David, a promise he will not abandon:
"I will set one of your offspring on your throne.
[12] If your sons keep my covenant
and my decrees that I will teach them,
their sons will also sit on your throne forever."
[13] For the Lord has chosen Zion;
he has desired it for his home:
[14] "This is my resting place forever;
I will make my home here because I have desired it.
[15] I will abundantly bless its food;
I will satisfy its needy with bread.
[16] I will clothe its priests with salvation,
and its faithful people will shout for joy.
[17] There I will make a horn grow for David;
I have prepared a lamp for my anointed one.
[18] I will clothe his enemies with shame,
but the crown he wears will be glorious."

Truth: The psalmist is retelling God's promises made to David. He reminds David that his sons need to keep God's commands to continue to sit on the throne, which would ultimately culminate with Jesus' coming. The Lord would continue to provide for His people and protect them.

Thought: Isn't it amazing that, even in the Old Testament, we see so many references to Christ's foretold coming? Just as God anointed David to be king, one would come through David's descendants who would be King of Kings, Lord of Lords, and would become our sacrificial lamb.

Tune: You plead my cause; You right my wrongs
You break my chains, You overcome; You gave Your life
To give me mine; You say that I am free (yeah)
(How can it be yeah); (How can it be) (yeah)

Jesus, You gave Your life, so that I could have mine, a love so amazing.

Text: Psalm 133

[1] How good and pleasant it is
when brothers live together in harmony!
[2] It is like fine oil on the head,
running down on the beard,
running down Aaron's beard
onto his robes.
[3] It is like the dew of Hermon
falling on the mountains of Zion.
For there the Lord has appointed the blessing—
life forevermore.

Truth: Acts Chapter 2 is a true picture of spiritual unity. The brothers and sisters shared meals together, worshiped together, prayed together, sat under the apostles' teaching together and shared their resources with one another. It was Koinonia – a true spiritual fellowship that only happens when people are worshiping in one accord.

Thought: There is no feeling like being unified, like being in peace with one another. Unity honors God, particularly in the body of Christ. Are there areas of your life where peace is not present? Are there relationships where there is tension? Ask God to show you what you are to do in response, pray for those who you have tension with, so you can live out verse 1.

Tune: Bind us together Lord
Bind us together with cords that cannot be broken
Bind us together Lord, bind us together Lord
Bind us together with love

There is only one God, there is only one King
There is only one body
That is why we can sing

Father, grant us true Koinonia – a unity of fellowship that glorifies You.

Text: Psalm 134

[1] Now bless the Lord,
all you servants of the Lord
who stand in the Lord's house at night!
[2] Lift up your hands in the holy place
and bless the Lord!
[3] May the Lord,
Maker of heaven and earth,
bless you from Zion.

Truth: The psalm is calling a group known as the "servants of the Lord" to bless the Lord. This is likely addressed to priests, Levites, or other called servants of the Lord. The worshiping congregation calls on them to lift up their hands to the holy place and bless the Lord.

Thought: Once we accept the call of God on our lives, the level of responsibility for our faith is raised. People follow the leaders, those who are "plugged in" to the work of the Lord. If the leaders lift their hands in the sanctuary, so will many in the congregation. If the leaders boldly bless and confess the Lord before men, so will many in the congregation. Where can you help set the tone in helping others exalt God today?

Tune: Bless the Lord, Oh my soul
And all that is within me
Bless His holy name

Bless the Lord, Oh my soul, and all that is within me
Bless His holy name

He has done great things, He has done great things
He has done great things
Bless His holy name

Father God, I bless Your name. Your name is wonderful, it is peace, it is majesty. Your name is high above the heavens. I glorify You today, God.

Text: Psalm 135:1-7

[1] Hallelujah!
Praise the name of the Lord.
Give praise, you servants of the Lord
[2] who stand in the house of the Lord,
in the courts of the house of our God.
[3] Praise the Lord, for the Lord is good;
sing praise to his name, for it is delightful.
[4] For the Lord has chosen Jacob for himself,
Israel as his treasured possession.
[5] For I know that the Lord is great;
our Lord is greater than all gods.
[6] The Lord does whatever he pleases in heaven and on earth,
in the seas and all the depths.
[7] He causes the clouds to rise from the ends of the earth.
He makes lightning for the rain and brings the wind from his storehouses.

Truth: The word "praise" is listed 4 times. It's in reference to praising the Lord. It's a command for us. Why? Because the Lord is good, He is great, He is above all gods, and ruler of Heaven and Earth!

Thought: *"For I know that the LORD is great,"* - Do you? Do you praise the Lord every day? Do you acknowledge His presence in your life? Do you share it with those around you? Do you BELIEVE it... or are you just going through the motions?

Tune: I don't wanna go through the motions
I don't wanna go one more day
Without Your all consuming passion inside of me
I don't wanna spend my whole life asking
What if I had given everything
Instead of going through the motions?

Heavenly Father, please fill me, and mold me and consume me from the inside out.

Text: Psalm 135:8-14

[8] He struck down the firstborn of Egypt,
both people and animals.
[9] He sent signs and wonders against you, Egypt,
against Pharaoh and all his officials.
[10] He struck down many nations
and slaughtered mighty kings:
[11] Sihon king of the Amorites,
Og king of Bashan,
and all the kings of Canaan.
[12] He gave their land as an inheritance,
an inheritance to his people Israel.
[13] Lord, your name endures forever,
your reputation, Lord,
through all generations.
[14] For the Lord will vindicate his people
and have compassion on his servants.

Truth: We see another reminder in these verses of how God saved His chosen Israelite people from the slavery of the Egyptians. Then we are reminded of the kings who were killed and how the Lord continued to care for His people by protecting them and giving them the Promised Land.

Thought: We serve such a great and mighty God, as verse 14 says: *"For the LORD will vindicate his people..."* He will have mercy and compassion on us, even when we don't deserve it. So even when (not if) we mess up... Seek God, ask forgiveness and Receive God's grace and mercy.

Tune: Seek ye first the kingdom of God
And His righteousness
And all these things shall be added unto you
Allelu, alleluia

Holy God, I know I mess up sometimes and don't follow Your directions. Please forgive me, and help me to seek You first, and Your righteousness.

Text: Psalm 135:15-21

[15] The idols of the nations are of silver and gold, made by human hands.
[16] They have mouths but cannot speak, eyes, but cannot see.
[17] They have ears but cannot hear;
indeed, there is no breath in their mouths.
[18] Those who make them are just like them,
as are all who trust in them.
[19] House of Israel, bless the Lord!
House of Aaron, bless the Lord!
[20] House of Levi, bless the Lord!
You who revere the Lord, bless the Lord!
[21] Blessed be the Lord from Zion;
he dwells in Jerusalem. Hallelujah!

Truth: Idols made by human hands are worthless, powerless and contain no eternal life. People who trust in idols or imaginary gods will fall down. The one true living God will stand superior to any imaginary idols.

Thought: Idol: an image or material object representing a deity to which religious worship is addressed. What "idol" do you worship? Is it a famous person, a thing, or activity? Spend time in prayer this week and evaluate yourself. Make the Lord - THE LORD of your life.

Tune: I've heard all the stories; I've seen all the signs
Witnessed all the glory; Tasted all that's fine
Nothing compares to the greatness of knowing You, Lord
Nothing compares to the greatness of knowing You, Lord
I see all the people; Wasting all their time
Building up their riches; For a life that's fine
I find myself just living for today; 'Cause I don't know what
Tomorrow's gonna bring; So no matter if I rise or fall
I'll never be alone, oh no

O Lord, Nothing compares to the greatness of knowing You... Please reveal to me any idols I need to remove and redirect my focus on You!

Text: Psalm 136:1-9

[1] Give thanks to the Lord, for he is good.
His faithful love endures forever.
[2] Give thanks to the God of gods.
His faithful love endures forever.
[3] Give thanks to the Lord of lords.
His faithful love endures forever.
[4] He alone does great wonders.
His faithful love endures forever.
[5] He made the heavens skillfully.
His faithful love endures forever.
[6] He spread the land on the waters.
His faithful love endures forever.
[7] He made the great lights:
His faithful love endures forever.
[8] the sun to rule by day,
His faithful love endures forever.
[9] the moon and stars to rule by night.
His faithful love endures forever.

Truth: This is a call God's people to give thanks to him: He is good, He is the God of gods, and He is the Lord of Lords. The psalm continues by giving thanks for the many "wonders" that the Lord did in creation.

Thought: Do you ever just consider how marvelous God's creation is? The beauty of a sunrise or sunset . . . the magnificence of the trees and flowers . . .the tranquility of the waters… the beauty of His creation.

Tune: Give thanks to the Lord, our God and King,
His love endures forever
For He is good He is above all things, His love endures forever
Sing praise sing praise
Forever God is faithful, Forever God is strong
Forever God is with us, Forever forever

Lord, Your steadfast love endures forever. With that, I can face anything.

Songs for Life – Day 335 - December 1

Text: Psalm 136:10-16

[10] He struck the firstborn of the Egyptians
His faithful love endures forever.
[11] and brought Israel out from among them
His faithful love endures forever.
[12] with a strong hand and outstretched arm.
His faithful love endures forever.
[13] He divided the Red Sea
His faithful love endures forever.
[14] and led Israel through,
His faithful love endures forever.
[15] but hurled Pharaoh and his army into the Red Sea.
His faithful love endures forever.
[16] He led his people in the wilderness.
His faithful love endures forever.

Truth: The psalmist recounts the period of history when God chose Moses to lead the Israelites out of bondage in Egypt. From the burning bush, to the plagues, to Passover, to the parting of the Red Sea, God pursued a love relationship with the Israelites. God never gives up.

Thought: Throughout Psalms, we see the love of God referred to as steadfast. If God brought about a burning bush, ten plagues, and destroyed an opposing army for the Israelites, He will continue to pursue a love relationship with you that is both real and personal.

Tune: I was sinking deep in sin, far from the peaceful shore,
Very deeply stained within, sinking to rise no more,
But the Master of the sea heard my despairing cry,
From the waters lifted me, now safe am I.
Love lifted me! Love lifted me!
When nothing else could help, Love lifted me!
Love lifted me! Love lifted me!
When nothing else could help, Love lifted me!

Father, show me the power of your steadfast love today. I need You.

Text: Psalm 136:17-26

[17] He struck down great kings
His faithful love endures forever.
[18] and slaughtered famous kings—
His faithful love endures forever.
[19] Sihon king of the Amorites
His faithful love endures forever.
[20] and Og king of Bashan—
His faithful love endures forever.
[21] and gave their land as an inheritance,
His faithful love endures forever.
[22] an inheritance to Israel his servant.
His faithful love endures forever.
[23] He remembered us in our humiliation
His faithful love endures forever.
[24] and rescued us from our foes.
His faithful love endures forever.
[25] He gives food to every creature.
His faithful love endures forever.
[26] Give thanks to the God of heaven!
His faithful love endures forever.

Truth: In vs. 23-25 of this passage we see a personal application of the steadfast love of the Lord. It is He who called sinful man to Himself, who rescued our soul from Hell and who nourishes us completely.

Thought: I Corinthians 13:4-5, *"[4] Love is patient and kind; love does not envy or boast; it is not arrogant [5] or rude. It does not insist on its own way; it is not irritable or resentful".* God is true love.

Tune: Over the mountains and the sea, Your river runs with love for me
And I will open up my heart and let the Healer set me free
I'm happy to be in the truth, and I will daily lift my hands
For I will always sing of when Your love came down yeah
I could sing of Your love forever, I could sing of Your love forever (repeat)

Heavenly Father, help me to speak and sing of Your love today.

Text: Psalm 137:1-9

1 By the rivers of Babylon—
there we sat down and wept when we remembered Zion.
2 There we hung up our lyres
on the poplar trees,
3 for our captors there asked us for songs,
and our tormentors, for rejoicing: "Sing us one of the songs of Zion."
4 How can we sing the Lord's song
on foreign soil?
5 If I forget you, Jerusalem, may my right hand forget its skill.
6 May my tongue stick to the roof of my mouth
if I do not remember you,
if I do not exalt Jerusalem as my greatest joy!
7 Remember, Lord, what the Edomites said that day at Jerusalem:
"Destroy it! Destroy it down to its foundations!"
8 Daughter Babylon, doomed to destruction,
happy is the one who pays you back what you have done to us.
9 Happy is he who takes your little ones
and dashes them against the rocks.

Truth: This psalm provides words by which the returned exiles can express their loyalty to Jerusalem and pray that God would pay out his just punishment on those who gloat over its destruction.

Thought: Here is both a promise to remain faithful as well as a submission to punishment (actually death) if that faithfulness is not kept by the psalmist. Wow! Can you make that kind of declaration of faithfulness today? May following in the footsteps of Christ be your primary focus.

Tune: I'd rather have Jesus than silver or gold
I'd rather be His than have riches untold
I'd rather have Jesus than houses or lands
I'd rather be led by His nail-pierced hand

Almighty God, You are all I need. Keep me from distraction today.

Songs for Life - Day 338 - December 4

Text: Psalm 138:1-8

[1] I will give you thanks with all my heart;
I will sing your praise before the heavenly beings.
[2] I will bow down toward your holy temple and give thanks to your name
for your constant love and truth.
You have exalted your name and your promise above everything else.
[3] On the day I called, you answered me;
you increased strength within me.
[4] All the kings on earth will give you thanks, Lord,
when they hear what you have promised.
[5] They will sing of the Lord's ways,
for the Lord's glory is great.
[6] Though the Lord is exalted, he takes note of the humble;
but he knows the haughty from a distance.
[7] If I walk into the thick of danger,
you will preserve my life
from the anger of my enemies.
You will extend your hand;
your right hand will save me.
[8] The Lord will fulfill his purpose for me.
Lord, your faithful love endures forever;
do not abandon the work of your hands.

Truth: The first line says it all. David is praising and thanking God.

Thought: David is mostly referring to physical enemies, but he was also plagued by internal enemies, just as we are today. We have access to the full armor of God, by the power of prayer.

Tune: I must tell Jesus; I must tell Jesus
I cannot bear; My burdens alone
I must tell Jesus; I must tell Jesus
Jesus can help me; Jesus alone

Lord, Thank You for giving us the accessibility to You, all day, every day.

Songs for Life - Day 339 - December 5

Text: Psalm 139:1-6

[1] Lord, you have searched me and known me.
[2] You know when I sit down and when I stand up;
you understand my thoughts from far away.
[3] You observe my travels and my rest;
you are aware of all my ways.
[4] Before a word is on my tongue,
you know all about it, Lord.
[5] You have encircled me;
you have placed your hand on me.
[6] This wondrous knowledge is beyond me.
It is lofty; I am unable to reach it.
    it is high; I cannot attain it.

Truth: The Lord knows all there is to know about you. He knows all of your activities, all of your words, even your inmost thoughts. The psalmist here is David, who is reflecting on the character of God. He is omniscient, meaning He is all-knowing. The reality is God knows all about us because He created us. He knows us better than we know ourselves.

Thought: The God who knows all about you is also the God who loves you passionately. He pursues you on a daily basis, ready to pour out His steadfast love, ready to give you new mercies, ready to fill you with His grace. He knows you intimately . . . and yet loves you anyway. That's true love! Nothing you can do will keep Him from loving you like crazy.

Tune: I once was fatherless, a stranger with no hope
Your kindness wakened me, wakened me from my sleep now
Your love it beckons deeply, a call to come and die
By grace now I will come, and take this life take Your life
Into marvelous light I'm running, out of darkness out of shame
Through the cross You are the truth, You are the life You are the way

Father, I'm so thankful that you know everything about me, and yet you love me with an everlasting love. I love You too!

Text: Psalm 139:7-12

[7] Where can I go to escape your Spirit?
Where can I flee from your presence?
[8] If I go up to heaven, you are there;
if I make my bed in Sheol, you are there.
[9] If I live at the eastern horizon
or settle at the western limits,
[10] even there your hand will lead me;
your right hand will hold on to me.
[11] If I say, "Surely the darkness will hide me,
and the light around me will be night"—
[12] even the darkness is not dark to you.
The night shines like the day;
darkness and light are alike to you.

Truth: The psalmist is reflecting here on the presence of the Lord. There is nowhere in the universe that God will not be present to lead and hold the believer, nowhere too dark for God to see him. Even if the psalmist tries to flee, God's hand will lead him and hold him. No matter if the psalmist were to ascend to Heaven or descend to Sheol, God is there.

Thought: Sometimes in those silences where we don't see God working, we can wonder if He is still there. The psalmist has made it clear that He IS with you, His presence is ever with His children. Did you just take a breath? That's God's presence. Did you wake up this morning with another opportunity to live? That's God's presence. You can speak to God at any moment and be confident that He is with you. Cry out to God in your loneliness. Cry out to God in your sadness. Cry out to God in your times of hurt. Cry out to God in your times of victory and celebration.

Tune: What a mighty God we serve, what a mighty God we serve
Angels bow before Him, Heaven and earth adore Him
What a mighty God we serve

Father, help me to experience Your presence today in a powerful way.

Songs for Life - Day 341 - December 7

Text: Psalm 139:13-18

[13] For it was you who created my inward parts;
you knit me together in my mother's womb.
[14] I will praise you
because I have been remarkably and wondrously made.
Your works are wondrous, and I know this very well.
[15] My bones were not hidden from you when I was made in secret,
when I was formed in the depths of the earth.
[16] Your eyes saw me when I was formless;
all my days were written in your book and planned
before a single one of them began.
[17] God, how precious your thoughts are to me; how vast their sum is!
[18] If I counted them,
they would outnumber the grains of sand;
when I wake up, I am still with you.

Truth: God's care for His child goes way before his physical birth. Even in your mother's womb, God was carefully putting you together. He created you in His image to be a reflection of His character. He formed your inward parts and knitted you together just as He designed.

Thought: *"I praise you, for I am remarkably and wondrously made"* (V14). Isn't the process of a child coming into the world a miracle? From egg to embryo to fetus to a precious baby, the fact that life can create life is totally in the hands of a loving God. God has set you apart for His purposes. What has God set you apart to do today?

Tune: No sweeter name than the Name of Jesus
No sweeter name have I ever known
No sweeter name than the Name of Jesus
No sweeter name than the Name of Jesus
No sweeter name have I ever known
No sweeter name than the Name of Jesus

Lord, I am fearfully and wonderfully made. Help me to reflect You today.

Text: Psalm 139:19-24

[19] God, if only you would kill the wicked—
you bloodthirsty men, stay away from me—
[20] who invoke you deceitfully.
Your enemies swear by you falsely.
[21] Lord, don't I hate those who hate you,
and detest those who rebel against you?
[22] I hate them with extreme hatred; I consider them my enemies.
[23] Search me, God, and know my heart; test me and know my concerns.
[24] See if there is any offensive way in me; lead me in the everlasting way.

Truth: The world has both those who delight in the Lord and those who oppose Him; those who embrace His presence, and those who deny His existence. When God displays his justice in the earth, if those who oppose Him will not repent, he will indeed slay them. The psalmist is submitting his heart and his thoughts to the Father, for he does not want to be found guilty of living as one who denies God.

Thought: Verse 23 and 24 can be recited as a prayer for any believer. Pray this prayer a few times and then wait and see what God reveals to you. Whatever sin He reveals to you, confess it and repent. Then you can experience the freedom and power of forgiveness.

Tune: The blood that Jesus shed for me, 'Way back on Calvary
The blood that gives me strength from day to day
It will never lose its pow'r
It reaches to the highest mountain, it flows to the lowest valley
The blood that gives me strength, from day to day
It will never lose its pow'r

*Search me, O God, and know my heart! Try me and know my thoughts!
See if there be any grievous way in me, and lead me in the way
everlasting!"*

Text: Psalm 140:1-8

1 Rescue me, Lord, from evil men.
Keep me safe from violent men
2 who plan evil in their hearts.
They stir up wars all day long.
3 They make their tongues as sharp as a snake's bite;
viper's venom is under their lips. Selah
4 Protect me, Lord, from the power of the wicked.
Keep me safe from violent men
who plan to make me stumble.
5 The proud hide a trap with ropes for me;
they spread a net along the path
and set snares for me. Selah
6 I say to the Lord, "You are my God."
Listen, Lord, to my cry for help.
7 Lord, my Lord, my strong Savior,
you shield my head on the day of battle.
8 Lord, do not grant the desires of the wicked;
do not let them achieve their goals.
Otherwise, they will become proud. Selah

Truth: Scripture promises us that life is a battle. Remember that when we give our lives to Christ, life's battle is no longer about flesh and blood, but it is a battle of spiritual warfare.

Thought: The Lord has not allowed us to go into life unprepared. Ephesians 6 assures us that we have been given the belt of truth, the breastplate of righteousness, feet ready with the gospel of peace, the shield of faith, the helmet of salvation and the sword of the Spirit. Are you ready for battle today? Put your armor on before you go any further.

Tune: A mighty fortress is our God, a sacred refuge is Your name
Your Kingdom is unshakable, and with You forever we will reign

Almighty Father, thank You for being my Rock, Fortress and Deliverer.

Text: Psalm 140:9-13

[9] When those who surround me rise up,
may the trouble their lips cause overwhelm them.
[10] Let hot coals fall on them.
Let them be thrown into the fire,
into the abyss, never again to rise.
[11] Do not let a slanderer stay in the land.
Let evil relentlessly hunt down a violent man.
[12] I know that the Lord upholds
the just cause of the poor,
justice for the needy.
[13] Surely the righteous will praise your name;
the upright will live in your presence.

Truth: The psalmist focuses on the speech of his opponents. He hopes their pattern of slanderous speech will entrap and ruin them. He also casts his confidence in terms of God's general help for the afflicted, who praise God when He helps them.

Thought: One of the most dangerous places we can be is when we seek to bring revenge on someone who has hurt us. Not only are we responding in an ungodly way, we are acting as God in someone else's life. The psalmist is praying for God to take care of the wicked, while also claiming protection and justice for those who are afflicted, those who call on His name. Taking God's work into our own hands only ends up hurting us further in the long run. Let God be God. He's quite experienced.

Tune: We have heard the joyful sound, Jesus saves, Jesus saves
Spread the tidings all around, Jesus saves, Jesus saves
Bear the news to every land, climb the mountains cross the waves
Onward 'tis our Lord's command
Jesus saves Jesus saves

Lord, you know my afflictions and you know my heart. I ask you to give me the grace to release my anxiety and allow You to fight for me.

<u>Songs for Life - Day 345 - December 11</u>

Text: Psalm 141:1-4

[1] Lord, I call on you; hurry to help me.
Listen to my voice when I call on you.
[2] May my prayer be set before you as incense,
the raising of my hands as the evening offering.
[3] Lord, set up a guard for my mouth;
keep watch at the door of my lips.
[4] Do not let my heart turn to any evil thing
or perform wicked acts
with men who commit sin.
Do not let me feast on their delicacies.

Truth: This prayer is asking God for protection, not from enemies, but from himself. He asks God to keep guard over his words and to control his heart and to help him avoid temptations.

Thought: Do you ask God to help you guard your words or actions? Do you try to avoid evil deeds or unwholesome talk? It's easy to slip into a gossip conversation. Social media really can bring on slanderous remarks about people. So, let that be a prayer for you today......... ask God to guard your words and actions. You are not alone.

Tune: I'm lost without You, I'll never doubt You
Your grace is beyond compare
And though when it rains, it pours, You know all I have is Yours
You smile when you hear my prayer
You rescued me and I believe
That God is love and He is all I need
From this day forth for all eternity
I'll never wander on my own
For I am Yours until you call me home
I close my eyes and I can hear You say
You're not alone! You're not alone!

Jesus, Thank You for not leaving me all alone - for always being with me.

Songs for Life - Day 346 - December 12

Text: Psalm 141:5-10

[5] Let the righteous one strike me—
it is an act of faithful love;
let him rebuke me—
it is oil for my head; let me not refuse it.
Even now my prayer is against the evil acts of the wicked.
[6] When their rulers will be thrown off the sides of a cliff,
the people will listen to my words, for they are pleasing.
[7] As when one plows and breaks up the soil, turning up rocks,
so our bones have been scattered
at the mouth of Sheol.
[8] But my eyes look to you, Lord, my Lord.
I seek refuge in you; do not let me die.
[9] Protect me from the trap they have set for me,
and from the snares of evildoers.
[10] Let the wicked fall into their own nets,
while I pass by safely.

Truth: This prayer continues from yesterday's passage where the psalmist is asking God for discernment and protection, and to keep his eyes focused on God and safely away from sinful behaviors.

Thought: In Matthew 14:28-31, Peter goes out to walk on the water toward Jesus. He did fine as long as he focused on Jesus, but began to sink when he took his focus off Jesus. That is the same for us. When we look at our circumstances, we take our focus off God and begin to sink.

Tune: Love like I'm not scared, give when it's not fair
Live life for another, take time for a brother
Fight for the weak ones, speak out for freedom
Find faith in the battle, stand tall but above it all
Fix my eyes on You, on You

Father, please fix my eyes only on You, and not my circumstances.

Text: Psalm 142:1-7

[1] I cry aloud to the Lord; I plead aloud to the Lord for mercy.

[2] I pour out my complaint before him;
I reveal my trouble to him.

[3] Although my spirit is weak within me, you know my way.
Along this path I travel they have hidden a trap for me.

[4] Look to the right and see: no one stands up for me;
there is no refuge for me; no one cares about me.

[5] I cry to you, Lord;
I say, "You are my shelter, my portion in the land of the living."

[6] Listen to my cry, for I am very weak.
Rescue me from those who pursue me,
for they are too strong for me.

[7] Free me from prison so that I can praise your name.
The righteous will gather around me
because you deal generously with me.

Truth: This is a psalm expressing earnest prayer in the face of imminent danger.

Thought: Why can the psalmist so confidently cry out to the Lord in his distress? Because He knows that is where his mercy, his clear path and his refuge is. God wants to reach out to you in your despair and turn your tragedy into triumph, your mess into bless.

Tune: Great is Your faithfulness O God
You wrestle with the sinner's restless heart
You lead us by still waters into mercy
And nothing can keep us apart
So remember Your people, remember Your children
Remember Your promise O God
Your grace is enough, Your grace is enough
Your grace is enough for me

Father, hear my cry, pour out Your mercy, make my path straight today.

Text: Psalm 143:1-6

[1] Lord, hear my prayer.
In your faithfulness listen to my plea,
and in your righteousness answer me.
[2] Do not bring your servant into judgment,
for no one alive is righteous in your sight.
[3] For the enemy has pursued me, crushing me to the ground,
making me live in darkness like those long dead.
[4] My spirit is weak within me; my heart is overcome with dismay.
[5] I remember the days of old; I meditate on all you have done;
I reflect on the work of your hands.
[6] I spread out my hands to you; I am like parched land before you. Selah

Truth: The psalmist seems to be at the end of his strength, but that doesn't mean he's giving up. Instead, if he can remember the days of old, thirsting for God as his source of energy.

Thought: When you ask a question, do you typically ask someone who you think might know the answer, or someone who you know has no clue about it? Of course, you ask the person who you think might have some insight into whatever you are seeking answers to. The psalmist is going to the Source for mercy and righteousness. Reach out to Jesus for water for your soul, for answers to your questions.

Tune: Like the woman at the well I was seeking
For things that could not satisfy
And then I heard my Savior speaking
Draw from my well that never shall run dry

Fill my cup Lord, I lift it up Lord, come and quench this thirsting of my soul
Bread of heaven feed me till I want no more
Fill my cup fill it up and make me whole

Fill my cup, Lord. I lift it up Lord. Come and quench this thirsting of my soul.

Text: Psalm 143:7-12

[7] Answer me quickly, Lord; my spirit fails.
Don't hide your face from me,
or I will be like those going down to the Pit.
[8] Let me experience your faithful love in the morning, for I trust in you.
Reveal to me the way I should go because I appeal to you.
[9] Rescue me from my enemies, Lord;
I come to you for protection.
[10] Teach me to do your will, for you are my God.
May your gracious Spirit lead me on level ground.
[11] For your name's sake, Lord, let me live.
In your righteousness deliver me from trouble,
[12] and in your faithful love destroy my enemies.
Wipe out all those who attack me, for I am your servant.

Truth: The psalmist wants to hear in the morning of God's steadfast love – whatever time of day he prays, he looks for reassurance soon! The specific relief may take longer, but the reminder of God's steadfast love enables him to endure.

Thought: When something is described as difficult, it sometimes is said that it is "like going uphill both directions." Following in the will of God doesn't always promise that there will be no barriers along the way, but on level ground you won't wear yourself out unnecessarily by spending all of your energy going uphill.

Tune: I know He rescued my soul, His blood has covered my sin
I believe I believe
My shame He's taken away, my pain is healed in His name
I believe I believe
I'll raise a banner, 'Cause my Lord has conquered the grave
My Redeemer lives, My Redeemer lives,
My Redeemer lives, My Redeemer lives

Lord, I ask you today to lead me on level ground. Teach me and lead me.

Songs for Life - Day 350 - December 16

Text: Psalm 144:1-5

¹ Blessed be the Lord, my rock who trains my hands for battle
and my fingers for warfare.
² He is my faithful love and my fortress, my stronghold and my deliverer.
He is my shield, and I take refuge in him;
he subdues my people under me.
³ Lord, what is a human that you care for him,
a son of man that you think of him?
⁴ A human is like a breath; his days are like a passing shadow.
⁵ Lord, part your heavens and come down.
Touch the mountains, and they will smoke.

Truth: David's foundation, or rock, was God; who is solid and unshakeable. God had equipped David for war and he found 6 benefits that God provided in verse 2: faithful love, fortress, stronghold, deliverer, shield and refuge.

Thought: Look at those benefits again. Faithful love, fortress, stronghold, deliverer, shield and refuge. Notice that most of them have the possessive word, "my", before them. God is personal - for you and me. What can you say...God is my _____?

Tune: Draw me close to You never let me go
I lay it all down again
To hear You say that I'm Your friend
You are my desire no one else will do
'Cause nothing else could take Your place
To feel the warmth of Your embrace
Help me find the way bring me back to You

You're all I want; You're all I've ever needed
You're all I want; Help me know You are near

Father God... You are ALL I need. You are my everything! Fill me with Your love and grace, Oh, how I need You today!

Songs for Life - Day 351 - December 17

Text: Psalm 144:6-11

[6] Flash your lightning and scatter the foe;
shoot your arrows and rout them.
[7] Reach down from on high;
rescue me from deep water, and set me free from the grasp of foreigners
[8] whose mouths speak lies,
whose right hands are deceptive.
[9] God, I will sing a new song to you;
I will play on a ten-stringed harp for you—
[10] the one who gives victory to kings, who frees his servant David
from the deadly sword.
[11] Set me free and rescue me from foreigners
whose mouths speak lies, whose right hands are deceptive.

Truth: David is addressing God and asking that God would rescue him from people who would shake his hand and then dishonor him behind his back. David would then sing God a new song, to acknowledge God's presence and provision of protection.

Thought: We have all known someone who is nice to our face and then degrades us in front of others and behind our backs. David was fighting the same thing as well and asks God to rescue him. Proverbs 26:23 - *"Like the glaze covering an earthen vessel are fervent lips with an evil heart."* Guard your words and people will see that we are Christians by our love and our fruit. As Matthew 7:16 says, *"You will recognize them by their fruits."*

Tune: We are one in the Spirit, we are one in the Lord
We are one in the Spirit, we are one in the Lord
And we pray that all unity may one day be restored
And they'll know we are Christians by our love, by our love
They will know we are Christians by our love

Heavenly Father, Please help me to guard my words about others and allow me to be one in the Spirit with you.

Text: Psalm 144:12-15

[12] Then our sons will be like plants nurtured in their youth,
our daughters, like corner pillars that are carved in the palace style.
[13] Our storehouses will be full, supplying all kinds of produce;
our flocks will increase by thousands
and tens of thousands in our open fields.
[14] Our cattle will be well fed.
There will be no breach in the walls,
no going into captivity,
and no cry of lament in our public squares.
[15] Happy are the people with such blessings.
Happy are the people whose God is the Lord.

Truth: This last part of the psalm is asking for healthy children; strong sons and beautiful daughters and for their farms to be productive and their livestock to flourish. They wanted peace, not turmoil to characterize their land. This closes with blessing on the people and God.

Thought: This psalm prayer is not unlike any of the many prayers we have all prayed at one time or another. We've all asked God to protect our families and our jobs, so we could provide. The best part is the last 2 verses, and this is how *The Message* says it, "*How blessed the people who have all this! How blessed the people who have God for God!*"

Tune: You are the Maker, you tell the sun when to rise
I'm just a house on a hill
But You make me brighter than all the stars in the sky
Keep me from growing down
'Cause in Your perfection, I'm just a reflection
So pull me closer to You
I catch like a fire and I'll hold You higher
'Cause You put the light in me

Father God: We are blessed that we have You for our God, and that You put Your light in our life and made us a way to be with You for eternity.

Text: Psalm 145:1-7

[1] I exalt you, my God the King, and bless your name forever and ever.

[2] I will bless you every day;
I will praise your name forever and ever.

[3] The Lord is great and is highly praised; his greatness is unsearchable.

[4] One generation will declare your works to the next
and will proclaim your mighty acts.

[5] I will speak of your splendor and glorious majesty
and your wondrous works.

[6] They will proclaim the power of your awe-inspiring acts,
and I will declare your greatness.

[7] They will give a testimony of your great goodness
and will joyfully sing of your righteousness.

Truth: Every generation needs to know the goodness and mighty acts of the Lord. In the Old Testament day, they had to largely depend on word of mouth to even pass on the knowledge of Scriptures. If we don't share the goodness and mighty acts of the Lord with our current generation and the generations coming behind us, where will be the personal testimony of "satisfied customers" to reach future generations?

Thought: Too often we depend on other people to teach our children and grandchildren the things they should know, whether that be school teachers, preachers, Sunday School teachers, etc. We all have both a privilege and a responsibility to share the works of the Lord with those we have influence over. There is no greater power in a word but that it comes from the mouth of one who has experienced it. YOU have a witness that is important!

Tune: Men of faith rise up and sing, of the great and glorious King
You are strong when you feel weak, in your brokenness complete
Shout to the north and the south, sing to the east and the west
Jesus is Savior to all, Lord of heaven and earth

Lord, empower me to share Your goodness with those around me. Today.

Songs for Life - Day 354 - December 20

Text: Psalm 145:8-13

[8] The Lord is gracious and compassionate,
slow to anger and great in faithful love.
[9] The Lord is good to everyone;
his compassion rests on all he has made.
[10] All you have made will thank you, Lord;
the faithful will bless you.
[11] They will speak of the glory of your kingdom
and will declare your might,
[12] informing all people of your mighty acts
and of the glorious splendor of your kingdom.
[13] Your kingdom is an everlasting kingdom; your rule is for all generations.
The Lord is faithful in all his words and gracious in all his actions.

Truth: The psalmist paints a clear picture here of the character of God. He is gracious, merciful, slow to anger, and abounding in love. He is good to all, and to all that He has made He shows his mercy. In return, everything that He has made shall give Him thanks, and share His works with others.

Thought: Sometimes when we are thinking about the fact that we need to share the goodness of God with others, we think "what would I say???" The psalmist lays it out for us here – all we have to do is talk about the Lord. Have you experienced His grace? His mercy? Just talk about who He is and what He's done, that's all!

Tune: Celebrate Jesus celebrate
Celebrate Jesus celebrate
Celebrate Jesus celebrate
Celebrate Jesus celebrate
He is risen He is risen, and He lives forevermore
He is risen He is risen,
Come on and celebrate, the resurrection of our Lord

Jesus, You have done more than enough for me to give me things to share about You. Help me to tell others about You today.

Text: Psalm 145:14-21

[14] The Lord helps all who fall;
he raises up all who are oppressed.
[15] All eyes look to you,
and you give them their food at the proper time.
[16] You open your hand
and satisfy the desire of every living thing.
[17] The Lord is righteous in all his ways
and faithful in all his acts.
[18] The Lord is near all who call out to him,
all who call out to him with integrity.
[19] He fulfills the desires of those who fear him;
he hears their cry for help and saves them.
[20] The Lord guards all those who love him,
but he destroys all the wicked.
[21] My mouth will declare the Lord's praise;
let every living thing bless his holy name forever and ever.

Truth: The Lord is kind to all of His creatures. He is our Sustainer, our Provider, He is kind, He is near, He hears our cry for salvation, and He is our Preserver.

Thought: *"My mouth will declare the Lord's praise; let every living thing bless his holy name forever and ever."* Is that your confession today? Who will speak the praise of the Lord? All flesh – that includes you. We are to bless his holy name forever and ever. His blessings never stop, so neither should our praise.

Tune: Living He loved me dying He saved me
Buried He carried my sins far away
Rising He justified freely forever
One day He's coming, O glorious day

Father, You were so gracious and kind to me to send Your Son to be my sacrificial lamb. You would have done that if I were the only one in need.

Text: Psalm 146:1-4

[1] Hallelujah!
My soul, praise the Lord.
[2] I will praise the Lord all my life;
I will sing to my God as long as I live.
[3] Do not trust in nobles,
in a son of man, who cannot save.
[4] When his breath leaves him, he returns to the ground;
on that day his plans die.

Truth: The whole congregation receives the invitation to Praise the Lord. Each person then applies it to himself, declaring that he will praise the Lord as long as he lives. In contrast, we are not to put our trust in earthly men, in princes, in whom there is no salvation. Trust Jesus, He saves!

Thought: Sometimes, when you don't know what to pray, it's best just to let the Word of God pray it for you. Verse 1-2 can be worded as a prayer that you can recite over and over again.

Tune: Hark the herald angels sing, Glory to the newborn King
Peace on earth and mercy mild, God and sinners reconciled
Joyful all ye nations rise, Join the triumph of the skies
With th'angelic hosts proclaim, Christ is born in Bethlehem
Hark the herald angels sing, Glory to the newborn King

Hail the heav'n-born Prince of Peace, Hail the Sun of Righteousness
Light and life to all He brings, Ris'n with healing in His wings
Mild He lays His glory by, Born that man no more may die
Born to raise the sons of earth, Born to give them second birth
Hark the herald angels sing, Glory to the newborn King

Lord, I will praise You as long as I have breath to breathe.

Text: Psalm 146:5-10

[5] Happy is the one whose help is the God of Jacob,
whose hope is in the Lord his God,
[6] the Maker of heaven and earth, the sea and everything in them.
He remains faithful forever,
[7] executing justice for the exploited and giving food to the hungry.
The Lord frees prisoners.
[8] The Lord opens the eyes of the blind.
The Lord raises up those who are oppressed.
The Lord loves the righteous.
[9] The Lord protects resident aliens
and helps the fatherless and the widow,
but he frustrates the ways of the wicked.
[10] The Lord reigns forever;
Zion, your God reigns for all generations. Hallelujah!

Truth: Yahweh, the God of Jacob, is the very one who made heaven and earth, the sea, and all that is in them. His power is unlimited, and he has the character that keeps faith forever. In verses 7-9, the psalmist gives hope to all who are weak.

Thought: This time of year there are many who are saddened by Christmas rather than filled with joy. They either are sidelined by circumstances or they are failing to acknowledge that this celebration is about the One who came to fulfill what this passage describes. He sets prisoners free, opens blind eyes, and lifts up the fallen. Ask God to lay someone on your heart today who may be discouraged and lift them up.

Tune: Joy to the world the Lord is come, let earth receive her King
Let ev'ry heart prepare Him room
And heav'n and nature sing, And heav'n and nature sing
And heav'n and heav'n and nature sing

Heavenly Father, direct my heart today that I may be a blessing to someone who may not realize the joy that is Christmas.

Text: Psalm 147:1-6
147 Praise the LORD!
[1] Hallelujah!
How good it is to sing to our God, for praise is pleasant and lovely.
[2] The Lord rebuilds Jerusalem;
he gathers Israel's exiled people.
[3] He heals the brokenhearted
and bandages their wounds.
[4] He counts the number of the stars;
he gives names to all of them.
[5] Our Lord is great, vast in power;
his understanding is infinite.
[6] The Lord helps the oppressed
but brings the wicked to the ground.

Truth: These verses focus on praising God for all His care over the Israelites and rebuilding the temple. They were showing loyalty to God and putting their trust in God topunish the wicked.

Thought: *"How good it is to sing to our God."* Today is Christmas Eve and 'it is good' to remember our Savior's birth. 'It is good' to spend time with your loved ones reading the Christmas story. 'It is good' to gather with believers and worship Christ our Savior. 'It is good' - for HE is good.

Tune: O holy night the stars are brightly shining
It is the night of our dear Savior's birth
Long lay the world in sin and error pining
Till He appeared and the soul felt its worth
A thrill of hope, the weary world rejoices
For yonder breaks a new glorious morn
Fall on your knees, O hear the angels' voices
O night divine, O night when Christ was born
O night divine, O night.....O night divine.

Father God, Thank you for sending us Your son to be our Savior.

Text: Psalm 147:7-11

[7] Sing to the Lord with thanksgiving;
play the lyre to our God,
[8] who covers the sky with clouds,
prepares rain for the earth,
and causes grass to grow on the hills.
[9] He provides the animals with their food,
and the young ravens, what they cry for.
[10] He is not impressed by the strength of a horse;
he does not value the power of a warrior.
[11] The Lord values those who fear him,
those who put their hope in his faithful love.

Truth: "Sing to the LORD with thanksgiving." Who gives us rain and feeds the animals? These verses remind us that God does these things. These are God's provisions. But what pleases the LORD are those who have put their trust in Him and have God as Lord of their lives.

Thought*: "For God so loved the world that he gave his one and only Son, that whoever believes in him shall not perish but have eternal life." -John 3:16*...God gave us the ultimate Christmas gift. Merry Christmas!

Tune: Alleluia O how the angels sang
Alleluia how it rang
And the sky was bright with a holy light
'Twas the birthday of a King

In the little village of Bethlehem
There lay a Child one day
And the sky was bright with a holy light
O'er the place where Jesus lay

Jesus, Savior, King...I worship You for who You are today.

Text: Psalm 147:12-15

[12] Exalt the Lord, Jerusalem;
praise your God, Zion!
[13] For he strengthens the bars of your city gates
and blesses your children within you.
[14] He endows your territory with prosperity;
he satisfies you with the finest wheat.
[15] He sends his command throughout the earth;
his word runs swiftly.

Truth: The psalmist is reminding them once again to praise God for He was the one that provided the security and prosperity for His people by rebuilding the Jerusalem walls. God provided peace and the best bread for them. God also sent His promises to earth.

Thought: "Exalt the LORD" - It's a command...not a suggestion. We have so many things to praise the Lord for each day. As we are in the Christmas season, reflect on praising God for His Son, Jesus, who was born to a woman named Mary, and lived His sinless life to ultimately die for our eternal salvation.

Tune: Oh Mary did you know
That your baby boy is Lord of all creation
Mary did you know
That your baby boy will one day rule the nations
Did you know
That your baby boy
Is heaven's perfect Lamb
And the sleeping Child you're holding
Is the great I Am
Oh Mary

Father God, Thank You for all the blessings You have given us. Thank You for sending us Your Son. I give You all the praise and glory, for great things You have done.

Text: Psalm 147:16-20

¹⁶ He spreads snow like wool;
he scatters frost like ashes;
¹⁷ he throws his hailstones like crumbs.
Who can withstand his cold?
¹⁸ He sends his word and melts them;
he unleashes his winds, and the water flows.
¹⁹ He declares his word to Jacob,
his statutes and judgments to Israel.
²⁰ He has not done this for every nation;
they do not know his judgments.
Hallelujah!

Truth: God can speak and the wind, waters and other environmental elements will obey. God spoke His words to Jacob and to Israel, who were His covenantal people, to declare His ways and laws.

Thought: God spoke the world into existence. God still speaks to us today (as taught in *Experiencing God)* by the Holy Spirit through the Bible, prayer, circumstances and the church to reveal Himself, His purposes and His ways! Listen and let God speak to you today.

Tune: Breath of heaven, hold me together
Be forever near me, Breath of heaven
Breath of heaven, lighten my darkness
Pour over me your holiness
For you are holy, Breath of heaven
Do you wonder as you watch my face
If a wiser one should have had my place
But I offer all I am
For the mercy of your plan
Help me be strong; Help me be; Help me

Heavenly Father, I listen for You words today. Please pour Your holiness over me, for You are Holy.

<u>Songs for Life - Day 362 - December 28</u>

Text: Psalm 148:1-8

¹ Hallelujah!
Praise the Lord from the heavens; praise him in the heights.
² Praise him, all his angels;
praise him, all his heavenly armies.
³ Praise him, sun and moon;
praise him, all you shining stars.
⁴ Praise him, highest heavens, and you waters above the heavens.
⁵ Let them praise the name of the Lord,
for he commanded, and they were created.
⁶ He set them in position forever and ever;
he gave an order that will never pass away.
⁷ Praise the Lord from the earth, all sea monsters and ocean depths,
⁸ lightning and hail, snow and cloud,
stormy wind that executes his command,

Truth: This hymn of praise calls on all of God's creatures to join in praising him: from the heavenly hosts all the way to all mankind.

Thought: Praising the Lord is different from thanking Him. When we praise Him, we focus on who He is and His character. When we thank Him, we are acknowledging something He has done in our lives. Give Him praise today! Tell Him how good He is! Focus on who He is!

Tune: You are holy (You are holy), You are mighty (You are mighty)
You are worthy (You are worthy), Worthy of praise (worthy of praise)
I will follow (I will follow), I will listen (I will listen)
I will love You (I will love You), All of my days (all of my days)
I will sing to and worship, the King who is worthy
And I will love and adore Him, and I will bow down before Him
And I will sing to and worship, the King who is worthy
And I will love and adore Him, and I will bow down before Him
You're my Prince of Peace, and I will live my life for You

Holy God, You are worthy! You are awesome! You are mighty!

Text: Psalm 148:9-14

[9] mountains and all hills,
fruit trees and all cedars,
[10] wild animals and all cattle,
creatures that crawl and flying birds,
[11] kings of the earth and all peoples,
princes and all judges of the earth,
[12] young men as well as young women,
old and young together.
[13] Let them praise the name of the Lord, for his name alone is exalted.
His majesty covers heaven and earth.
[14] He has raised up a horn for his people,
resulting in praise to all his faithful ones,
to the Israelites, the people close to him. Hallelujah!

Truth: God is so good that even creation, which does not have a physical voice, praises Him. Scripture tells us that if we do not praise Him, the rocks will cry out and give Him praise. Don't let any rock steal your praise!

Thought: As you ponder the beginning of a new year, it is often a time of reflection. We think back on the good things and the things we wish had been different. As you get ready to launch into a new year, it will only be a good year if the Holy Spirit is in control of your life. So, put on your praise today and get your heart in tune with His and let Him guide your path. He will not lead you astray.

Tune: I've heard a thousand stories, of what they think You're like
But I've heard the tender whisper, of love in the dead of night
You tell me that You're pleased, and that I'm never alone
You're a good good Father, it's who You are
It's who You are, it's who You are
And I'm loved by You, it's who I am, it's who I am, it's who I am

Lord, You are indeed a good, good Father. I want my voice to be filled with Your praise today, coming from the depths of my heart. Praise You!

Text: Psalm 149:1-9

[1] Hallelujah!
Sing to the Lord a new song, his praise in the assembly of the faithful.
[2] Let Israel celebrate its Maker;
let the children of Zion rejoice in their King.
[3] Let them praise his name with dancing
and make music to him with tambourine and lyre.
[4] For the Lord takes pleasure in his people;
he adorns the humble with salvation.
[5] Let the faithful celebrate in triumphal glory;
let them shout for joy on their beds.
[6] Let the exaltation of God be in their mouths
and a double-edged sword in their hands,
[7] inflicting vengeance on the nations
and punishment on the peoples,
[8] binding their kings with chains
and their dignitaries with iron shackles,
[9] carrying out the judgment decreed against them.
This honor is for all his faithful people.
Hallelujah!

Truth: This hymn of praise calls to mind the expectation that the faithful will one day be God's agents of judgment through the world.

Thought: The psalmist not only is urging individuals to praise Him, but also that the entire congregation will join in. What is the best way to get the entire assembly lifting their voices in praise? It starts with you!

Tune: It's Your breath in our lungs, so we pour out our praise
We pour out our praise, it's Your breath in our lungs
So we pour out our praise to You only
And all the earth will shout Your praise,
Our hearts will cry these bones will sing, Great are You Lord

Lord, let all that I am and all that You have given me praise You!

Songs for Life - Day 365 - December 31

Text: Psalm 150:1-6

[1] Hallelujah! Praise God in his sanctuary. Praise him in his mighty expanse.
[2] Praise him for his powerful acts; praise him for his abundant greatness.
[3] Praise him with trumpet blast; praise him with harp and lyre.
[4] Praise him with tambourine and dance; praise him with strings and flute.
[5] Praise him with resounding cymbals; praise him with clashing cymbals.
[6] Let everything that breathes praise the Lord.Hallelujah!

HE IS

In Genesis He's the breath of life
In Exodus, the Passover Lamb
In Leviticus, He's our High Priest
Numbers, the Fire by night
Deuteronomy, He's Moses voice
In Joshua, He is Salvation's choice
Judges, Lawgiver
In Ruth, the Kinsman Redeemer
I & II Samuel, our trusted Prophet
In Kings & Chronicles, He's sovereign
Ezra, true & faithful Scribe
Nehemiah, He's the Rebuilder of
        broken walls & lives
In Esther, He is Mordicai's courage
In Job, the Timeless Redeemer
In Psalms He is our Morning Song
In Proverbs, Wisdom's Cry
Ecclesiastes, the Time & Season
In the Song of Solomon, He is the
        lover's Dream
In Isaiah He's the Prince of Peace
Jeremiah, the Weeping Prophet
Lamentations, the Cry for Israel
Ezekiel, He's the Call from sin
Daniel, the Stranger in the fire
In Hosea He is forever faithful
In Joel, He's the Spirit's power
In Amos, the arms that carry us
In Obadiah, He's the Lord our Savior
In Jonah, He's the Great Missionary
In Micah, the promise of peace
In Nahum He is our Strength & our Shield

In Habakkuk & Zephaniah He is
        pleading for revival
In Haggai He restores a lost heritage
In Zechariah, Our Fountain
In Malachi He is the Son of Righteousness,
        rising, healing in His wings
In Matthew Mark Luke & John He is God,
        Man, Messiah
In the Book of Acts He is, the Fire from
        Heaven
In Romans He is the Grace of God
In Corinthians the Power of Love
In Galatians He is Freedom from the
        curse of sin
Ephesians, our Glorious Treasure
Philippians, The Servants Heart
In Colossians, He is the Godhead Trinity
Thessalonians our Coming King
Timothy, Titus, Philemon He's Our
        Mediator & Our Faithful Pastor
In Hebrews the Everlasting Courage
In James, the One who heals the sick
In I & II Peter He's our Shepherd
In John & in Jude , He's the Lover
        coming for His bride
In the Revelation, He is the King of Kings
        and Lord of Lords!

Lord, I want to begin the new year with
praising You as my King of Kings!
Lyrics for the song "He Is" by Triumphant Quartet.

Made in USA - Kendallville, IN
72242_9781726879033
09.06.2024 1925